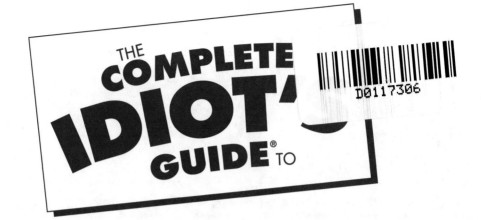

THE
**COMPLETE**
**IDIOT'S** GUIDE® TO

# Understanding Iraq

*by Joseph Tragert*

**ALPHA**

A Pearson Education Company

International Standard Book Number: 0-02-864398-4
Library of Congress Catalog Card Number: 2002108507

05   04   03      8   7   6   5   4   3   2   1

Interpretation of the printing code: The rightmost number of the first series of numbers is the year of the book's printing; the rightmost number of the second series of numbers is the number of the book's printing. For example, a printing code of 03-1 shows that the first printing occurred in 2003.

*Printed in the United States of America*

Note: This publication contains the opinions and ideas of its author. It is intended to provide helpful and informative material on the subject matter covered. It is sold with the understanding that the author and publisher are not engaged in rendering professional services in the book. If the reader requires personal assistance or advice, a competent professional should be consulted.

The author and publisher specifically disclaim any responsibility for any liability, loss, or risk, personal or otherwise, which is incurred as a consequence, directly or indirectly, of the use and application of any of the contents of this book.

For marketing and publicity, please call: 317-581-3722

The publisher offers discounts on this book when ordered in quantity for bulk purchases and special sales.

For sales within the United States, please contact: Corporate and Government Sales, 1-800-382-3419 or corpsales@pearsontechgroup.com

Outside the United States, please contact: International Sales, 317-581-3793 or international@pearsontechgroup.com

**Publisher:** *Marie Butler-Knight*
**Product Manager:** *Phil Kitchel*
**Managing Editor:** *Jennifer Chisholm*
**Acquisitions Editor:** *Gary Goldstein*
**Development Editor:** *Jennifer Moore*
**Production Editor:** *Billy Fields*
**Copy Editor:** *Cari Luna*
**Illustrator:** *Chris Eliopoulos*
**Cover/Book Designer:** *Trina Wurst*
**Indexer:** *Lisa Wilson*
**Layout/Proofreading:** *Angela Calvert, Mary Hunt, Kimberly Tucker*

# Contents at a Glance

# Contents

# Foreword

Iraq first seized the attention of most Americans in August 1990, when Iraqi troops poured over the border of the tiny neighboring Emirate of Kuwait and Iraqi dictator Saddam Hussein declared the country his nineteenth province. Overnight, the United States unexpectedly became involved in a massive ground war in the Middle East. By the following spring, United States and Allied forces had swept to unprecedented victory on the battlefield and liberated Kuwait. Yet, for reasons still controversial and misunderstood, Desert Storm was an unfinished victory. Saddam Hussein retained control of Iraq, and today he remains a threat to his neighbors, and to the United States.

Iraq is located literally in the middle of the Middle East, a region that has increasingly dominated United States national security concerns. Iraq continues to be a major petroleum exporter, despite United Nations-mandated sanctions. Saddam Hussein still seeks to obtain weapons of mass destruction, and his regime continues its assault on basic human rights and dignities, against Kurds, Shiites, or any citizens brave enough to voice dissent. Meanwhile, U.S. pilots flying under UN authority engage Iraqi ground targets on a weekly if not daily basis, and U.S. Navy vessels steadfastly enforce trade restrictions designed to prevent Saddam's rearmament. Yet, as the Iraqi regime grows more bellicose, U.S. war planners continually update and revise contingency plans with a view toward responding to or preempting Saddam's aggressive moves. Iraq may soon become the newest theater in America's War on Terror.

Iraq has been an historical crossroads of conflict. The Persians conquered this land, as did Alexander the Great, and later the Mongol hordes. The town of Tikrit is the birthplace of Saladin, the vanquisher of the Crusaders, and inspiration for Saddam, who also calls Tikrit home. In recent decades, Iraq was the setting for European Imperial competition, and the devastating decade-long war with Iran.

Yet, there is an Iraq beyond the brutish totalitarian regime one sees portrayed in the news, a face beyond the smiling mustachioed petty dictator. This is a land and a people whose story stretches to the dawn of civilization. Iraq traces its lineage to ancient Mesopotamia, to Babylon and King Hammurabi the Lawgiver. For much of its history, this has been a region of prosperity and culture, of riches and legends. Baghdad is the setting of the *Tales of the Arabian Nights*, and the home of Sinbad the Sailor. Iraq is a nation of many peoples—Arab, Kurd, and Turkoman, among others—and the birthplace of the Shiite Islamic sect. It is a country of seacoast and mountains, of fertile river plains and desolate wasteland. These are the complexities that concerned Americans should understand about Iraq, and this book contains the essential information on America's most imposing national security threat. In the post-Saddam future, however it arrives, the United States may be called upon to shift from war fighting to nation building. Iraq may one-day make the transition to a friendly state, perhaps even a democratic ally of the United States, and resume its path to a prosperous and peaceful future.

—James S. Robbins, Ph.D.

**Dr. James S. Robbins** is a national security analyst and contributing editor for *National Review Online*. He hold a Ph.D. from the Fletcher School of Law and Diplomacy.

# Introduction

In recent years, Iraq in general, and Saddam Hussein in particular, have become dark icons in American popular culture. But if you're interested in learning about the troubled history that gave rise to the nightly news sound bites about Iraq (or, for that matter, the hilariously over-the-top *South Park* references to Saddam), you won't find much in the way of user-friendly fare in your local library or bookstore. This book is intended to remedy that situation. It offers a painless introduction to a country that has been a recurrent "hot spot" in world history for many centuries. Iraq retains that status today, of course, but its story would remain darkly fascinating even if this were not the case.

## What You'll Learn in This Book

This book is divided into five parts that will help you learn more about the modern nation of Iraq and its ancient precursor states. Iraqis are deeply conscious of their long past, just as most Westerners are unaware of it.

**Part 1, "The Basics,"** gives you the fundamentals about modern Iraq. You'll find out why it has become such an important player in world affairs, get a sense of Iraq's ancient roots, and get a snapshot of the modern nation.

**Part 2, "From Babylon to Baghdad,"** lets you in on Iraq's early history ... which happens to coincide with that of human civilization. You'll also find out about the remarkable series of empires that have risen and fallen in this region.

**Part 3, "The Rise of Saddam,"** offers an answer to the question, "What made Saddam Hussein's reign possible?" The answer involves at least a century of global conflict, superpower diplomacy, ancient rivalry, and modern geopolitics. (There are some disagreements about oil along the way, too.)

**Part 4, "The Gulf War,"** tells you all about the origins, the key events, and the aftermath of Iraq's conflict with the U.S.-led coalition. Here you'll find out how and why the coalition formed, how the war unfolded, and how Saddam lost the war ... but won the peace.

**Part 5, "Victory from Defeat,"** explains what Saddam Hussein has been up to since the Gulf War, and why he continues to worry Western policymakers.

At the end of the book, you'll find a number of helpful appendixes.

## Extras

As you make your way through the book, you'll notice little nuggets of information distributed throughout the text. They are meant to help you gain an immediate understanding of some aspect of the topic under discussion. Here's how you can recognize them:

**Oil Spill Ahead**

These boxes will alert you to common misconceptions and potential problem areas.

**Desert Diction**

Here you'll find concise summaries of key terms that may not be familiar to you.

**Iraq Fact**

These boxes answer important questions about Iraq.

**Increase Your Iraq IQ**

Background details or supporting information that can accelerate and streamline the learning process. Breeze in and out of these boxes—we think you'll be fascinated by what you find.

## Acknowledgments

Grateful thanks go out to my wife, Bernadine Tragert; my father, Henry Tragert (builder of Baghdad power plants); my development editor, Jennifer Moore; my agent, Gene Brissie; Gary Goldstein; David Toropov; and Judith Burros.

## Trademarks

All terms mentioned in this book that are known to be or are suspected of being trademarks or service marks have been appropriately capitalized. Alpha Books and Pearson Education, Inc., cannot attest to the accuracy of this information. Use of a term in this book should not be regarded as affecting the validity of any trademark or service mark.

# Part 1

# The Basics

Sure, you know that Iraq is located smack-dab in the middle of the Middle East and that Saddam Hussein is the president of this oil-producing nation, but do you know how many people he rules over, how big his army is, and how long Iraq has been, well, Iraq?

"Just the facts, Ma'am" could be the motto for the chapters in this part of the book—you'll find out everything you need to make sense of this most complicated of countries.

# Why Iraq Matters

## In This Chapter

◆ The Israelis take action

◆ Recent run-ins with Iraq

◆ Saddam's mysterious staying power

◆ The big question about Iraq

The year is 1981. A nuclear power plant is nearing completion.

In and of itself, this fact isn't particularly remarkable. Many countries have nuclear power plants … but this one is different. This state-owned and state-operated plant is located in Iraq, near the capital city of Baghdad. And the state of Israel isn't at all happy about it.

Two factors combine to make this plant disturbing to Israeli politicians, diplomats, and military planners. First, Iraq is a member of *OPEC*. That means it can easily construct a conventional oil-burning, steam-generating power plant, thus taking advantage of its own massive petroleum reserves.

**Desert Diction**

OPEC stands for the Organization of Petroleum Exporting Countries. The 11 member countries are Algeria, Libya, Nigeria, Indonesia, Iran, Iraq, Kuwait, Qatar, Saudi Arabia, the United Arab Emirates, and Venezuela. OPEC countries exert a measure of control over world oil prices by producing more or less oil.

Why, the Israelis wonder, is the Iraqi leadership opting to create a more expensive nuclear plant?

Second, Iraq is led by Saddam Hussein, whose hostility toward Israel is a) a matter of Iraqi national policy and b) a central feature of Iraq's ongoing effort to inspire an international *pan-Arab movement* to be led by (you guessed it) Saddam Hussein.

The Israelis conclude that the purpose of the plant is to develop material for nuclear weapons—weapons they assume to be meant for deployment against Israel. They respond by engaging in an aerial bombardment of the plant on June 7, 1981. The attack levels the plant.

**Desert Diction**

The **Pan-Arab movement** advocates Arab unity today. Pan-Arabism states that all Arabs should be unified into one state (like the early days of Islam), and that all Arabs have a duty to support the freedom of Arab peoples (notably, Palestinians). The modern Pan-Arab movement was promoted by Nasser of Egypt in the 1950s and 1960s, but Iraq and Egypt vied for control of the movement during that time. The movement achieved a zenith when Egypt, Syria, and Yemen formed the United Arab Republic, and Iraq and Jordan formed a rival Arab Union. Both political experiments failed after just a few years, and no formal political union has been achieved since. The Arab League of 21 Arab-majority states and Palestine continues the Pan-Arab concept, though in watered-down form, and attempts at unification were all but abandoned.

# The Iraqi Threat

Since the bombing of the nuclear plant, Iraq has started two wars, concluding the first (against Iran) in a bloody standoff, and being soundly trounced in the other (the Gulf War).

Eventually, an oil-burning power plant was built by General Electric in the nuclear plant's former location. (The plant was destroyed by U.S. bombers during the Gulf War, many of them powered by General Electric engines!) An intriguing sequence of questions arises about the post-1981 world. Suppose the Israelis hadn't destroyed that nuclear facility … and suppose further that the Israelis were correct in their assessment that the plant's purpose was to produce weapons-grade uranium.

Would the outcomes of the Iran-Iraq War or the Gulf War have been any different? Would other conflicts have come about? How would they have concluded?

# Who Is Saddam?

Today, it's impossible to understand Iraq without understanding Saddam Hussein. And that, unfortunately, is a very tricky business. Here's a brief timeline that will help put his rule in context:

Saddam Hussein was born in Auja, near the city of Tikrit in the vicinity of Baghdad, in 1937, to a middle-class Iraqi family. He joined the Ba'th (Arab Socialist Resurrection) Party in 1956. He participated in the two Ba'thist coups of July 17 and July 30, 1968. After the second coup (which resulted in the Ba'thists taking power in Iraq), Saddam was responsible for internal security. In that role, he became very well-known inside Iraq.

Hussein took power on July 16, 1979, when he forced out Ahmed Hassan al-Bakr as chairman of the Revolutionary Command Council (the group that makes the real day-to-day decisions in the country), as president of Iraq, and as chairman of the Regional Command of the Ba'th Party. After his ouster, Saddam put al-Bakr under house arrest, and purged the former leader's inner circle.

Prior to assuming these titles, Saddam had steadily been assuming more and more authority within the Revolutionary Command Council; the final takeover in 1979, when al-Bakr was placed under arrest, was simply the culmination of his growing power within Iraq.

Shortly after Saddam formally assumed control of state and party structures, an attempted coup was claimed; several members of the Revolutionary Command Council were executed for their alleged role in the plot. Whether there actually was a plot or not is still not clear, but the allegations that there was one provided Saddam with a good excuse for clearing out al-Bakr followers and other factions—and bringing in his own supporters.

**Oil Spill Ahead**

The Ba'th Arab Socialist Resurrection Party doesn't practice socialism the same way that socialism is practiced in Europe. Like "traditional" socialism, the Ba'th platform believes in land reforms, trade unions, public ownership of natural resources, and worker-managed companies; however, in practice the Ba'th Party suppresses free association and independent trade unions, and state control of resources and factories is dominated from the top.

Since then, Saddam has made a habit of tightening his grip on power in Iraq by murdering potential rivals (including his own son-in-law), and by ordering lethal attacks on possible insurgent groups within Iraq, such as the Shiites and the Kurds. (You'll learn more about Saddam and his rise to power and the Kurds and Shiites in Chapter 3.)

# Iraq Yesterday, Iraq Today

Thus far, the story of Iraq under Saddam has been one of violence, chaos, and uncertainty. Today, Iraq matters because Saddam's actions (and imagined future actions) cause concern, fear, and outrage among his neighbors and in the West.

It's easy to forget how important the question of "how to handle Iraq" has become. In the remainder of this chapter, you'll get a brief overview of Saddam's actions over the last two-plus decades, and you'll see why dealing with him and anticipating his actions have become central concerns of U.S. foreign policy.

# Saddam and the West: A Timeline

There's a lot to say about what happened in Iraq before 1981 (and I'll say them later on in the book). For the purposes of this chapter, though, I want you to have an overview of recent events, so you can see how these events have shaped the current tense relationship between Iraq and the West.

## Prelude: The Iran-Iraq War

In the early 1980s, Iraq was considered an ally of the United States against Iran. The United States had just gotten out from under the Iranian hostage crisis and had no diplomatic relations with Iran. Iraq had recently begun a war against Iran (the Iran-Iraq War from 1980 to 1988), in an apparent dispute over territory along the *Shatt-al-Arab* waterway.

**Desert Diction**

The **Shatt-al-Arab** is a name for the waterway at the confluence of the Tigris and Euphrates rivers, where they join to flow into the Persian Gulf. The region is marshy, with several islands dotting the mouth of the waterway.

The Shatt-al-Arab is the main shipping channel for food and supplies from the Gulf to the city of Basra. Until the start of the war, the two countries bordered a portion of the main shipping channel. Controlling the islands on *both* sides of the channel would provide more security in shipping to the country in charge of those islands.

---

| Increase Your Iraq IQ |
| --- |

About 90 percent of the Muslim world, calling themselves Sunnis, believed the caliphs were the successors to the Prophet, and leader and protector of the united community of believers. However, the remaining 10 percent of Muslims—the Shiite sect—rejected the authority of the caliphs. The Shiites argued that the true successors of Mohammed, and thus the true leaders of Islam, are his cousin, Ali and his descendents. While other groups have splintered from the main group of Muslims (the so-called Sunnis), the Shiite group is the largest sect to have survived to the modern time. The Sunnis consider themselves the true "keepers of the faith," while the Shiites consider themselves to be the same. The Ayatollah Khomeni was a Shiite Muslim, like the vast majority of Iranian Muslims, and more than 50 percent of Iraqi Muslims. However, Saddam Hussein and his followers are Sunni Muslims. You can read more on the Sunni-Shiite differences in Chapter 3, but suffice it to say, Saddam was only too happy to remove a Shiite leader from Iraq, given the preponderance of Shiites in his own country.

---

The islands originally belonged to Iraq, but they were seized by Iran in 1971. At this time, Iraq protested but did nothing. Finally, in 1981, Saddam used the Iranian occupation of the islands as a pretext for picking a fight with Iran.

Saddam appears to have assumed that the Iranians were weakened and distracted by their recent revolution, which overthrew the Shah (the ruler of Iran) and established an Islamic republic. Relations between the Shah and Saddam had never been warm, but the relationship between Saddam and the Ayatollah Khomeini (the Shah's replacement) was even colder. In fact, Saddam had expelled the Ayatollah from Iraq in the 1970s, at the request of the Shah.

The United States provided tentative support for Iraq in this dispute, on the theory that Iraq was the lesser of the two evils, and in the hope that Iraq could topple the Ayatollah.

The war, however, didn't go well for Iraq. The Iranians put up a strong fight, and the war settled into a grinding battle of attrition, where neither side was gaining much of an advantage. The battles were costly, and eventually both sides were ready to quit. Finally, after years of indescribably bloody conflict, the fighting ended in a standoff in 1988, with no change in the borders or shared control of the Shatt-al-Arab. Both sides rested and reloaded.

# 1987–1990: Iraq Turns Its Attention to Kuwait

Saddam soon began planning a new conflict with Iraq's tiny, oil-rich neighbor Kuwait. From Saddam's perspective, a new and provocative campaign had certain advantages:

- Invasion offered the potential to enrich Iraq and improve its strategic position in the Middle East.

- Military victories would help legitimize Saddam's authority within Iraq, which was diminished after the Iranian stalemate.

- New military conflicts would provide an excuse for shortages of consumer goods within Iraq.

- New military conflicts would provide cover for counter-insurgency work inside Iraq.

Thus, during this period, Iraq became increasingly belligerent against its (militarily weak) neighbor, Kuwait, and even began to behave in a way that alienated other members of the OPEC cartel.

## 1990: Iraq Invades Kuwait

The other shoe finally dropped on August 2, 1990, when Iraq invaded Kuwait. The United Nations (UN) Security Council Resolution 660 demanded complete withdrawal, but Saddam refused to leave. The United States led a diplomatic initiative at the United Nations to get international support for a coalition to get Iraq out of Kuwait. This initiative resulted in UN Security Council Resolution 661, passed on August 6, 1990, which imposed economic sanctions on Iraq.

Saddam responded by formally annexing Kuwait on August 8.

## 1991: Operation Desert Storm

By January of the next year, President George H. Bush's administration had completed the task of assembling a coalition of Western and Arab states to get Saddam out of Kuwait. Military action started when the coalition forces began bombing Iraq on January 16, 1991. The ground attack began on February 24 and ended three days later, with a total Iraqi military collapse and Kuwait liberated.

However, UN forces did not invade Baghdad, and didn't remove Saddam from power. The only goal of the coalition had been the liberation of Kuwait. To many policy makers' disapproval, the removal of Saddam was not on the agenda.

## 1991: Cease-Fire and Sanctions

The United Nations and Iraq, negotiated a cease-fire that took effect on March 3, 1991. The Bush administration fully expected Saddam's government to collapse due to the spectacular failure of his military, but he managed to hang on. In fact, by April of that same year, Iraqi forces were soon up to their old tricks, brutally suppressing Shiite insurgents in southern Iraq, and Kurdish rebels in the North. In response, the United Nations established no-fly zones in northern and southern Iraq to provide havens for the Kurds in the north, and the Shiites in the south. U.S. and British aircraft patrol the no-fly zones and do not allow Iraqi military flights in those areas.

At the time of the cease-fire, the United Nations placed stiff sanctions on Iraq, forbidding them to export oil without UN approval. Oil is the only major export product of Iraq, and thus selling it is the only way the country can make money and buy arms. The sanctions were seen as a good way to control how much money Iraq could bring in. The cease-fire also included measures for UN weapons inspectors to monitor Iraqi facilities that may make biological, chemical, or nuclear weapons.

According to the agreements of the cease-fire, UN weapons inspectors were supposed to be able to see any facility, anywhere in Iraq, that they suspected could be used for weapons production. However, as history has taught us again and again, agreements seem to be made to be broken.

## 1995–2000: Conflicts over Sanctions and Inspections

Recent years have seen dramatic setbacks in the U.S. effort to impose sanctions and deter weapons-development activity in Iraq.

### Sanctions

Enforcing the sanctions turned into a public relations and logistical nightmare for the United States and its allies. First, it has been reported that hundreds of thousands, and possibly as many as 1 million, Iraqi citizens (mostly children) have died due to UN-imposed and U.S.-enforced sanctions. Whatever the number, and whatever the direct cause, the Iraqi people didn't get needed medicine and died in large numbers as a result.

The sanctions became difficult for U.S. allies in Europe and the Gulf to support. Iraq counted on increasing international discomfort with the effects of the sanctions on Iraqi civilians, to bring about an easing of the restrictions. On April 14, 1996, UN Security Council Resolution 986 allowed for the partial resumption of Iraq's oil exports to buy food and medicine. Iraq argued over the conditions of the program, and didn't accept the terms until May 1996. The first shipments started in December 1996. By 2000, international air travel was resumed.

Also in 2000, Iraq attempted to have oil buyers put a $.50/barrel payment into a separate account, not controlled by the United Nations; Iraq could use this money to buy whatever it wanted, rather than medicine or food for its people. The United Nations rejected this attempt, but the episode illustrates the degree to which the original sanctions have eroded. In 2001, rail traffic was resumed with Turkey, and Iraqi trade has steadily returned to pre-sanction levels.

## Inspections

The weapons inspection program has been a notable foreign-policy failure for the United States and its allies.

The initial goal of the program was to take away Iraq's ability to make weapons of mass destruction. This goal has not been accomplished. The George W. Bush administration has stated that it suspects there are weapons facilities in Iraq. Iraq has taken advantage of loopholes in the inspections agreement that stipulated that the weapons inspectors could not inspect any "Presidential Palaces." Saddam simply designated hundreds of facilities as "Presidential Palaces," and refused to allow the inspectors in to see them.

The only real enforcement mechanism available to the United Nations when Saddam didn't comply was more bombing. Over time, this drastic military response became increasingly difficult for the Arab states, and many of the Western allies, to support. Bombing seemed an unreasonable response to Iraqi stubbornness. Also, it is difficult to determine if the bombings have done the job.

**Iraq Fact**

Since the close of the Gulf War, the Bush Sr., Clinton, and Bush Jr. administrations have maintained a steady pace of bombing, cruise missile, and air-ground missile attacks on Iraq. These raids have concentrated on destroying Iraqi air defense installations. The difficulty of maintaining the international coalition against Iraq is underscored by international distaste for the continued bombing campaigns, and even some support for Saddam as the "victim" of U.S. aggression.

On October 31, 1998, Iraq ended all forms of cooperation with the UN Special Commission to Oversee the Destruction of Iraq's Weapons of Mass Destruction (UNSCOM) and threw out the weapons inspectors. The United Nations did virtually nothing in response.

On December 16, the United States and Britain initiated "Operation Desert Fox." The bombing campaign was supposed to destroy Iraq's nuclear, chemical, and biological weapons capabilities, but the affects of the attacks are not clear. Since the original

UNSCOM inspection set up was not working, the United Nations replaced it with the United Nations Monitoring, Verification and Inspection Commission (UNMOVIC). Iraq has rejected this commission as well.

Finally, in February 2001, the United States and Britain attacked Iraqi air defense systems in order to ensure the continued safe patrolling of the no-fly zones. However, the attacks were criticized by the Arab states in the region, and by Western European allies, showing how far the support for inspections has fallen.

## 2002 and Beyond: What's Next?

During the Cold War, the big question was what to do about the Soviets, but in the post–Cold War era, it is what to do about *rogue states*. The George W. Bush administration has singled out three countries in particular as the so-called "Axis of Evil": Iran, Iraq, and North Korea. The United States and the West in general have had a very tough time dealing with these rogue countries. In fact, the Bush administration has alienated its European allies with the "Axis" analogy, and by lumping the three nations together. Some European countries enjoy better relations with Iran or Iraq than the United States, and don't wish to have their relationships stigmatized with the "Axis of Evil" label.

In the wake of the Gulf War, Iraq has steadily, and effectively, managed to wriggle out from under the sanctions and inspections, despite the fact that the goals of the sanctions and inspections have not been achieved. In fact, the inspectors say Iraq is in fact making weapons of mass destruction.

The second Bush administration is focusing its efforts in Iraq toward creating a more effective method for inspections and sanctions, in order to maintain some kind of control over Saddam.

**Desert Diction**

**Rogue states** are states that don't work with the rest of the world, and are probable exporters of terrorism. Isolation, imposed or self-created, is a hallmark of a rogue state. Rogue states typically also threaten their neighbors with destruction.

# An International Hot Spot

Today, Iraq is a focal point of an ongoing and escalating global controversy. This controversy has three main elements:

♦ **Human rights.** Iraqi laws are, to Western sensibilities, incomprehensibly harsh. Many laws call for death or dismemberment for crimes like theft, currency speculation, and military desertion. Furthermore, Saddam has persistently attacked the Shiites and Kurds within his own country, even using chemical weapons against them. These continued human rights abuses call for some kind of response.

> **CAUTION**
>
> **Oil Spill Ahead**
>
> The images of dead Iraqi children, suffering from lack of food and medicine, will continue to fuel a global PR disaster that is likely to haunt U.S. foreign policy for years to come. Iraq has managed to turn public perception in much of the world totally against the sanctions, and by association, the weapons inspections.

- **Ongoing uncertainty about Saddam's intentions.** This is the guy who has started two wars, used chemical weapons on his own people, killed his son-in-law, and tried to assassinate former President Bush. This is not a person who can be relied on to behave rationally.

- **Sanctions.** The current sanctions program has failed. The sanctions themselves are divisive, with most U.S. allies and Arab states objecting to them. Unrest in the Islamic world over U.S. policy toward Iraq has been particularly intense, and the sanctions themselves have become unenforceable without escalation to total military response.

# The Big Question

One big question looms for U.S. policy-makers: "What do we do about Saddam?"

It is a recurrent question, and one that is unlikely to go away. Any answer is likely to be both loud and unpopular in certain quarters of the world.

## The Least You Need to Know

- Iraq is vital to U.S. interests due to its strategic location in the oil-rich Persian Gulf region.

- Iraq is an ongoing focal point for U.S. policy-makers, and an ongoing PR disaster for the U.S. administrations enforcing the UN sanctions.

- Saddam Hussein, the leader of Iraq, is demonstrably hostile to the United States and its allies.

- Iraq is an even greater threat to the U.S. national interests as a potential exporter of terrorism, than as a direct military threat to U.S. allies in the Gulf.

- The future actions of Iraqi leadership, Iraqi foreign policy, and the continuance of UN sanctions, have never been more uncertain.

# Chapter 2

# Just the FAQs: Common Questions About Iraq

## In This Chapter

- Where Iraq is
- Making sense of Saddam
- Shiites vs. Sunnis
- Common misperceptions

Now that you know why Iraq matters so much to stability in the Middle East and, consequently, the world more generally, you probably have a lot of other questions about this "rogue state." In this chapter, we'll tackle some frequently asked questions about Iraq's geography, military strength, religion, and, of course, its leader.

Let's start with a very basic question.

### Oil Spill Ahead

The Middle East is fraught with instability that seems to constantly threaten to blossom into full-fledged war. Iraqi internal instability or weakness would certainly draw in neighboring countries, and instability or weakness in neighboring countries would tempt Iraq to intervene to its advantage. We have seen this happen twice in the past 20 years.

# Where Is Iraq?

Iraq is smack dab in the middle of the Middle East. It is in the center of a perpetual "hot spot" in world affairs. It's located in the heart of the oil-rich Persian Gulf region. The country sits astride the Tigris and Euphrates Rivers, in the ancient region of Mesopotamia. Iraq borders Kuwait, Saudi Arabia, Iran, Turkey, Jordan, and Syria, and has an outlet to the Persian Gulf. Most of the world's oil comes from this region. The United States and the West need this oil to keep flowing. If Iraq invades its neighbors, they would have an unacceptable control over prices at U.S. gas pumps. If the region erupts into warfare, deliveries would be interrupted, driving up fuel costs.

*The Middle East.*

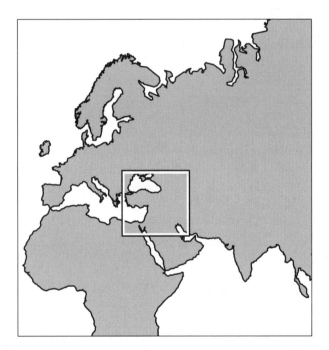

# How Big Is the Iraqi Army?

Iraq's army is about one million men, the largest in the Middle East, when reserves are included. The core of the army is the Republican Guard. The Republican Guard are personally loyal to Saddam and are the best trained and equipped soldiers in the Iraqi army. The remainder of the Iraqi army is made up of conscripts, who are less well trained and equipped.

Compared to its neighbors, Iraq's land army is quite formidable. However, the neighboring Iranian army is a potent threat to Iraq, as are the Turkish army and airforce. The Kuwaiti and Saudi military are not the equal of Iraq in terms of manpower. In fact, there has been a large U.S. military presence in Saudi Arabia, since the start of Operation Desert Shield, that shores up the Saudi and Kuwaiti military.

The Iraqi air force and navy are practically nonexistent. Almost all Iraqi aircraft were destroyed or disabled in the Gulf War, and Iraq has been unable to buy many more since then. However, it has been able to pay the Russians to repair some of its MiG fighter jets. The Iraqi navy consists of a few small coastal patrol boats.

> **Increase Your Iraq IQ**
>
> Many Muslims object to the non-Muslim American soldiers being based in Saudi Arabia, the country in which Mecca and Medina—the two holiest cities in Islam—are located.

# Who Are the Kurds?

The Kurdish people occupy a region known as Kurdistan. Kurdistan is divided between Turkey, Iraq, Iran, Sryia, and Armenia. The Kurds are a minority in each of those countries, and have controls placed upon them that are not placed on the majority populations in those countries. The Kurdish people aren't Arab; rather, they are of Indo-European descent. Most Kurds are Sunni Muslims.

The name of the Kurds is attributed to a name for Babylonian palace guards in 600 B.C.E., the "Kardakas." These guards came from the ethnic group that later become known as the Kurds. The high point for the Kurd people came around 1150 C.E., and paralleled the rise of King Saladin. Saladin was himself a Kurd, and gained fame in the West during the Third Crusade.

Saladin's armies defeated Richard the Lion-Hearted and reinstated Muslim control over Jerusalem. Saladin was credited with showing extraordinary mercy toward the defeated Crusaders in Jerusalem. Rather then slaughter them (as earlier Crusaders had done to the Muslim inhabitants of Jerusalem when they took power), Saladin spared their lives. Saladin's Ayyubid Empire also defeated the Shiite (Fatimid) rule in Egypt and Syria in 1171. The Ayyubids continued to rule these regions until 1250, when they gave way to the Mamluks.

As the Ayyubid Empire receded, the relative power of the Kurds receded with it. Over the next centuries, the Kurds were not an integral part of the ruling groups that controlled the region where Kurdistan is located. As a result, the Kurds did not gain political independence.

By the end of World War II, Kurdistan (the region where the Kurds live) was divided among Turkey, Iraq, and Iran, and no provisions were made to accommodate Kurd autonomy. The Kurds have rebelled against these governments to varying degrees of violence ever since.

*Kurdish lands.*

*(Source: University of Texas Library Online Perry-Castañeda Library Map Collection)*

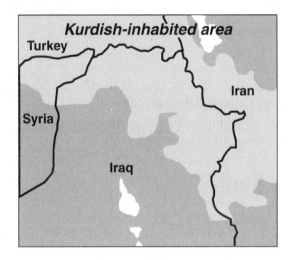

The Iraqi regime has consistently suppressed the Kurds and waged conventional and even chemical war against them. The Kurds could be a significant ally for the West in a struggle against the current Iraqi regime. However, it is doubtful they will ever be given autonomy, due to the fact Turkey (a NATO member) and Iran would not tolerate an independent Kurd state on their borders, for fear that the Kurds in their own countries would want to break away and join them.

The best the Kurds can hope for is more rights and autonomy under a new Iraqi government. The Kurds have enjoyed greater defacto autonomy under the protection of the United Nations, and the no-fly zone over their territory. If the United Nations (and U.S. aircraft) were to leave, you can bet that Saddam Hussein's government would immediately step up its campaigns against the Kurds.

# Who Are the Shiites and the Sunni?

The two dominant Islamic groups in Iraq are the Shiite Muslims and the Sunni Muslims. About 90 percent of all Muslims today are Sunni. Fewer than 10 percent of all Muslims are Shiites. The Sunnis are the minority within Iraq (about 32 percent), but the majority in most of the remainder of the Muslim nations.

Although the controversies of the ninth and tenth centuries did have something to do with the coalescence of Sunni and Shiite theological positions, it is better understood as a result of early political controversies over succession to the Prophet.

Those who became the Sunnis in the ninth and tenth centuries held that preservation of the unity of the community and avoidance of difference, even at the expense of acquiescing to the less-than-morally-pure rule of a given *caliph*, was of primary importance. They tolerated a wide range of difference of opinion. The Ulama, men of religion, became the authorities on proper practice.

Several groups have splintered off the main Sunni body of Islam, but most have not survived the death of their first leader. The Shiite sect, or Shia, is the only major Islamic sect that has persisted in the face of overwhelming Sunni predominance.

The Shiites first broke away from the rest of Islam after a series of political and military disputes over the caliphate in the seventh century. The Shiites insisted that the Prophet's authority as imam, or leader of the community, was transmitted in his lineage through Ali. There remain two major branches of Shiism: the Twelvers in Iran, Iraq, and elsewhere, who await the return of the twelfth imam, and the Ismailis, who have a living imam (the Agha Khan).

The differences in philosophy can be seen in Iran (Shiite controlled) where Ayatollahs, who are clerical figures, run the state, versus Iraq (Sunni controlled) where a secular government (Hussein and the Ba'th Party) run the state.

**Iraq Fact** _____

The Shiites are a majority within Iraq (about 65 percent) and are the vast majority in Iran. Iraq and Iran are the only two Muslim countries in which the Shiites constitute the majority of the population.

**Desert Diction** _____

The **caliph** was the spiritual leader in Islam who claimed succession and authority from Mohammed. Over time, the power of the caliphs was diminished, and they were relegated to a purely spiritual role by the end of eleventh century.

The Iraqi regime military has waged a counter-insurgency campaign against rebel groups in the Shiite-dominated southern part of Iraq. This program has ranged from military and possibly chemical weapons attacks on Shiite rebels, to more long-term methods to disrupt the Shiite livelihood. For example, currently the Iraqi government is engaged in a canal building program in the Shatt-al-Arab region that has drawn off much of the back water that formed the marshes in southern Iraq. These marshes have nurtured a significant portion of the Shiites in Iraq and their way of life. This canal project has disrupted a traditional Shiite power base. As the marshes have drained, the Shiites have been forced to leave the area due to the increased salt content of the water, which makes it useless for agriculture and drinking.

> **Increase Your Iraq IQ**
>
> Saddam Hussein and the leaders of his regime are Sunnis. The Iraqi army is controlled by the Sunnis.

The Shiite majority could become a major factor in toppling the Saddam regime from within, if his power base begins to fracture. However, the opposition leadership within the Shiite population has been systematically decimated by Saddam Hussein's counter-insurgent campaigns, and their economic base severely weakened, so that the chances of a spontaneous Shiite uprising (without U.S. military support) are slim.

# Who Will Take Over If Saddam Is Overthrown?

This is the $64,000 question. The George W. Bush administration has made it clear that they are committed to changing the regime in Baghdad. However, it is not clear who would be a better choice.

## Not the Kurds

The Kurds are against Saddam, but they would not be able to run the country of Iraq. They are a minority in Iraq, and the Shiites and Sunnis both would never accept a Kurd-run Iraq. Also, as noted previously, there is no way Turkey and Iran would tolerate an independent Kurd state on their borders.

## Maybe the Shiites

The Shiites in the southern part of Iraq are a possibility, particularly because they are the majority population of the country. The main Shiite political group in Iraq is called the Iraqi National Congress. They are outlawed, but members also live outside of Iraqi borders. Of course, the Sunnis in the middle of the country wouldn't welcome a Shiite regime. If the Shiites were to take over, there would be bloodshed between the two groups. Furthermore, the Sunni-dominated Arab countries in the Gulf region would not want to see a powerful Shiite state in their midst.

## Qsay Can You See?

The last possibility is that Saddam is removed, but his Sunni followers retain power. This would be as close to a status quo as there can be, while still changing the leadership. So far, it looks like Saddam is grooming his son, Qsay, to take over. He is an unknown, but is considered to be a chip off the old block. Or perhaps a general or a member of the Revolutionary Command Council (RCC) who is more reasonable than Saddam could step in.

**Iraq Fact** _____

The real decision-making authority in Iraq is the Revolutionary Command Council (RCC). They are the supreme executive, legislative, and judicial power in the country. The RCC consists of 8 to 10 members, and is directed by a chairman, currently Saddam Hussein. The chairman of the RCC is also the president of Iraq, the supreme commander of the military, and general secretary of the Ba'th Party, and the prime minister. The Revolutionary Command Council was formed after the July 30, 1968, coup, when the Ba'th Party finally assumed complete control over the country. This group makes all major internal and foreign policy decisions affecting Iraq, and takes its marching orders from Saddam. A decision from the RCC is considered the law of the land. Most major decisions are made by Saddam Hussein alone, or in consultation with a small number of advisors on the committee. The RCC represents authority to the Iraqi people. When a major decision is publicized, it is attributed to the RCC and the Ba'th Party leadership, to reinforce the authority of the choice.

The short answer is: We don't yet know who would take over if Saddam were ousted.

# What Else Do I Need to Know?

It's easy to assume that the Iraqi people are all carbon copies of their leader, particularly since most people in the West know very little about the country and its culture, and most of the time the media only focuses on Saddam and his military. But don't make the mistake of thinking all Iraqis think alike! Here are some common misconceptions:

## Saddam Doesn't Represent All the Iraqi People

Saddam Hussein is a leader of the Ba'th Socialist Revolutionary Party, but most Iraqis are not party members. Saddam is a Sunni Muslim, whereas most of the Iraqi people are Shiites, and a significant minority are Kurds. Saddam was not freely elected, and in fact, oversees a brutal dictatorship within Iraq.

The Iraqi people have never had a democratic state, and they certainly didn't pick Saddam as their leader. He was picked for them by the Ba'th Party leadership. That party came to power against a monarchy that was picked for them by the British, and the British supplanted the Ottomans, who invaded like countless others before. All that history will be reviewed in the scope of this book, but the key point here is that Saddam Hussein is not a popularly elected leader, governing by the will of the Iraqi people.

## Arab Islam Doesn't Represent All Islam

Islam is a religion, just like Judaism or Christianity or Buddhism. It is practiced by millions of people across the world. Saddam does not represent all of Islam, any more than the Arabs represent all of Islam. There are vast numbers of non-Arab Muslims, in places like western China, Central Asia, Indonesia, Iran, and Turkey. These people are not Arab, yet they are Muslim.

## Iraqi Arabs Don't Represent All Arabs

The Arab world is vast, complex, and culturally rich. About 250 million Arabs live in an area stretching from Northern Africa, across Egypt into the Persian Gulf region.

**Oil Spill Ahead**

Any statements about the Iraqis should not be extended to include all Arabs or Muslims.

The history of the Arab world, and its relationship to the West—from the Crusades to its relationship with Israel—goes far beyond the story of Iraq.

Not all Iraqis are Arab or Kurd. Iraq includes a number of other minorities, including Turkmans, Nestorian Christians, and Persian-speaking groups, none of whom are Arabs.

---

**Increase Your Iraq IQ**

Arabs are people living in North Africa and the Middle East, from western Morocco to Oman, and from Turkey in the north to Yemen and Sudan in the south. Two hundred-fifty million Arabs live in this area, about four million live in Europe, and two million in the Americas. The Arabic heartland is a region called "Hijaz" (now western Saudi Arabia).

Ethnically, Arabs are mostly dark haired with brown eyes, and medium light skin. But some Arabs are black, and others are blond. These differences are regional, and a result of the intermixing and absorption of populations. The number of ethnically pure Arabs is down to a single digit percentage. More than 95 percent of all Arabs are Muslims, while fewer than 5 percent are Christians. An estimated 55 percent live in urban areas and 45 percent live in rural areas. Today, less than 1 percent live as nomads, and of these many are nomads only in the dry season.

---

## Terrorists Come from Many Cultures

The escalating conflict between terrorist movements and the civilized nations is taking a new shape. This book will examine Iraq's role as a possible exporter of terrorism. However, this is not to say that all Iraqis, Muslims, or Arabs are terrorists … far from it. This book will examine terrorism that is created by Saddam Hussein and his followers, who happen to be Arab and Muslim. Before assuming that all terrorists are Arab Muslim fanatics, one should consider that some of the most persistent terrorists are Irish and Catholic, and work their trade in Belfast, not Baghdad.

## The Least You Need to Know

- Iraq is located in the heart of the Middle East and is bordered by six countries.

- Iraq has the most potent army in the Middle East.

- Saddam Hussein is not a popularly elected leader and doesn't necessarily have the support of the majority of the Iraqi people.

- Not all Iraqis are alike, and they differ culturally, ethnically, and religiously from many of their neighbors.

# 3

# Babylon to Baghdad: Iraq in 2,000 Words or Fewer

## In This Chapter

- ◆ Iraq's relationship to ancient culture and civilization
- ◆ The introduction of Islam by the Arabs
- ◆ Iraq under British rule
- ◆ Saddam Hussein takes control

Think of this chapter as your "cheat sheet" on Iraqi history. It takes you on a whirlwind tour of Iraqi history from its ancient roots as the "cradle of civilization" to its current status as a "rogue state" in the eyes of many world leaders. We'll only touch on the most important events in Iraq's history in this chapter, because they will be covered more thoroughly in later chapters.

## Iraq Is as Old as It Gets

Iraq's beginnings are as old as civilization itself. Iraq is truly a "cradle of civilization." Some of the first known cities and urban cultures emerged in the Tigris and Euphrates region, known as *Mesopotamia,* around 5,000 years ago. The other "cradles" of civilization include the Nile River region and Indus River region.

Archeological evidence shows that cities were thriving in Mesopotamia by 3000 B.C.E.

The first people who lived in Mesopotamia were called the Sumerians (see Chapter 5). The Sumerians are credited with inventing the wheel, the plow, and legal codes. Most important, the Sumerians developed the earliest forms of writing, called cuneiform, which was created by pressing a reed end into wet clay that, once dry, became tablets.

## On the Record

The cuneiform records confirm the development of the centralized monarchies, bureaucracies, and social hierarchies that enabled the creation of urban centers. The Sumerians also introduced the concept that the state, rather than the victim or the members of his family, is responsible for exacting revenge on behalf of the victim when a crime is committed. This is a central notion of modern civilization; by assuming this responsibility, the state legitimizes its role, and ensures more cooperation among increasingly crowded cities.

The earliest urban centers in what is now Iraq included Uruk, Ur, and Babylon. These cities were the stage for a number of biblical and historical figures (see Chapter 5).

# A Prize Worth Fighting For

The ancient history of the area we now know as Iraq shows a series of empires that emerge, dominate, and are replaced by a new wave of invasion and dominance.

The reasons for this pattern are simple: The fertile land of Mesopotamia was a place worth controlling and enriching oneself from. The water, the irrigation system, the fertile river valleys, and the sophisticated cities were plums to be plucked. Starting with the Akkadians, who seized the region from the Sumerians, several groups invaded Mesopotamia between 2500 B.C.E. and 600 C.E. Most of them adopted the cultures and innovations of the Sumerians, with some improvements from their own cultural backgrounds. Each of these groups gave way to succeeding waves of invaders.

Finally, in the last centuries before Christ, the Greeks and Persians invaded Mesopotamia. These invaders were different in that they did not invade Mesopotamia as their final stop. These invaders moved through the region, on to other places. The Persians moved west to attack Greece, the Greeks moved East to attack the Persians and beyond. These last invasions by the Greeks and Persians signaled an end to the central role Mesopotamia played in ancient history. Simply put, there were bigger plums to pluck elsewhere.

# Iraq Flowered Under Islam

The next defining phase in Iraqi history occurred in the seventh century C.E. At this time, the Arabs wrestled Mesopotamia away from the Persians, and introduced Islam to the region. These two pillars—Arab and Islam—define Iraqi culture today. In the following centuries, Baghdad flourished as a cultural, intellectual, and technical center of the world. Baghdad was a new capital, built after 750 by the newly victorious Abbasid (Arab) caliphs, who replaced the Umayyad (non-Arab) caliphs.

Baghdad had universities, and even a teaching hospital. There were mathematicians, scientists, and teachers throughout the region, and it was a crossroads between Persia, Central Asia, India and the Far East, and the Mediterranean cultures. The Arabs introduced several Far Eastern concepts to the West, including modern numerals, the concept of zero, and algebra. Muslim rule eventually spanned from northern Africa to Asia Minor to Persia, and Baghdad was its major center. In fact, around 1000 C.E., Baghdad was second only in size to Constantinople in terms of population and stature.

---

**Increase Your Iraq IQ**

Mohammed is the founder of Islam. He was born in Saudi Arabia. Orphaned early in life, he was adopted by an uncle, married, and became a prosperous merchant. At the age of 40, he was called to preach by a vision in a cave north of Mecca. His subsequent teachings, believed to be based upon divine inspiration, are recorded in the Qur'an. Mohammed fled from his enemies to the city of Yathrib (now called Medina, meaning City of the Prophet), in 622 C.E. and remained there for the rest of his life. The Islamic calendar starts in 622 C.E., for this is when Islam is considered to have begun. Mohammed died on June 8, 632 C.E. By the time of his death, converts to Islam were fanning out all over the Middle East, and over the next centuries, Islam swept across Northern Africa, into Spain, as far north as France, through the Middle East and into Central Asia. Successor empires to Mohammed's original one in Medina gradually shifted their center to Baghdad, in the center of what is now Iraq. Baghdad became the heart of a thriving Arab Muslim empire until the thirteenth century.

As Islam matured, schisms in its hierarchy appeared, and outlying regions and sects carved away power and prestige from the center in Baghdad. Gradually, Baghdad lost some of its influence, but it was still an important place in the Islamic empire, and thus the world.

# Iraq Becomes a Cultural Backwater

Baghdad's status as a cultural and political center was not to last, however. Things changed when the Mongol Hordes swept through, destroying everything in their path. The Khans leveled cities, murdered the existing power elites who had resisted them, and pillaged what was left. Baghdad and the region around it fell to the invaders, and a period of decline followed. Baghdad now was on the periphery of a much larger Mongol empire until 1334, when the last Mongol Khan died. After his death, the central Mongol authority waned. Eventually, the Ottomans emerged; in the process of building their own empire, they began to push into the region. The Ottomans fought for control of the region with the Persians until 1623, when the Ottomans finally asserted their full control.

**Iraq Fact**

The **Hashemite kings** came from a prominent Arabian family. The Hashemites were a princely Meccan family of sharifs who claim to be descendents of the Prophet. The Hashemites controlled the Holy Cities of Mecca and Medina under Ottoman rule.

They didn't rebuild the area to any major degree, however. In fact, they allowed the region to remain a backwater.

The Ottomans eventually gave way to the British Empire after World War I (1914–1918). The British saw the Iraqi region as a bridge to their holdings in India, and occupied the region to keep the Germans out. The British set up regional power players to help control each region of their empire, and Iraq was no different. By 1920, the British set up a *Hashemite king* (a monarch who was not from the region) to rule over Iraq.

# From Pro-Western to Anti-Western

The creation of modern Iraq after World War I wasn't accomplished by an indigenous uprising, or the emergence of a regional power, or by matching political boundaries to ethnic or physical boundaries. Instead, the lines in the sand were designated in British boardrooms.

As if an artificial country with an artificial king wasn't enough, the country the British created wasn't a homogenous grouping of people. The modern Iraq included a substantial minority of Kurds in the north, which has been a consistent source of tension in the country. The country also thrust together a Shiite Muslim majority in the south, and a Sunni Muslim minority in the center.

A major tenet of the newly independent, but still pro-British, Iraqi government was an expansion-oriented foreign policy that focused on annexing Kuwait, and (after World War II) an anti-Israel policy.

# It's Ba'th Time

The Hashemite kings weren't popular with the Iraqi people. Insurgent groups came together in Iraq to fight the Hashemite monarchs. These insurgents were part of a wave of anti-monarch revolutions that began in Egypt in 1952. One of these groups was the Arab Ba'th Socialist Party, which included Saddam Hussein in its ranks. The Hashemites were overthrown by a group of army officers lead by Abdul Karim Kassem in 1958. Over the next decade, a series of coups continued to destabilize the republican leadership. Finally, in 1963, the Ba'th Party overthrew the Republic leadership, but soon after lost power to rival groups. The Ba'th Party finally took power for good in 1968. The Ba'th-led Republic was a *republic* only in name; the Ba'th created a dictatorship.

The new regime continued to try to influence events in the Gulf. The Iraqi military continued to participate in the wars against Israel, and to promote the Pan-Arab movement.

Fostered by Gamal abdel Nasser, the modern Pan-Arab movement had its heyday in the early 1950s and 1960s, but has gradually fallen out of favor. The Pan-Arab movement was born also out of the reaction to the creation of Israel, with its strong Western support. Ever in competition with Egypt for leadership of the Arab world, Iraq tried to assume the mantle of leadership over the movement. It was not until Egypt alienated other Arab states by signing the Camp David Peace Accords that Iraq was able to seize some of the initiative from Egypt.

**Desert Diction**

A **republic** is a type of governmental structure where the head of state is not a monarch or hereditary ruler. In a republic, there is a central government that has authority over a collection of states. The United States is a republic, as is Mexico, and France. Most people think of a republic as a place where citizens have the right to vote, and select their representatives to the central government.

---

**Increase Your Iraq IQ**

Gamal abdel Nasser was the charismatic leader of the newly independent Egypt from 1956 to 1970. Nasser attempted to extend his vision by creating the United Arab Republic, which would encompass all Arab states in the Middle East. This did not work, but Nasser remained a powerful influence in Arab politics and policy. Nasser is best remembered for the Aswan High Dam that he championed, and for restoring Arab pride after long periods of foreign dominance in Egypt.

---

# Saddam Sees a Vacuum

Undeterred, Saddam took advantage of the loss of prestige for Egypt after Nasser's successor, Anwar Sadat, signed the Camp David Accord peace agreement with Israel.

**Oil Spill Ahead**

Some people say the dire suffering of the Iraqi civilians due to UN sanctions is entirely Saddam Hussein's fault because he started the war. Others argue that the civilian suffering is due solely to the sanctions and the West's insistence on keeping them in place. Regardless of which perspective is more accurate, Saddam Hussein's role as an opportunist and dictatorial ruler is hard to dispute.

Iraq stepped up its push for leadership in the Arab community, and Saddam sought to improve his standing in the region.

Saddam continued the pattern of frustrated foreign adventures pursued by Iraqi leaders with two conflicts we've already examined, the Iran-Iraq War and the Gulf War. In each war, Saddam's attempt to take territory by force (the Shatt-al-Arab from Iran, and the entire nation of Kuwait) was defeated. In each case, Iraq lost prestige in the international Arab community on the narrow question of Saddam's expansionism; eventually, however, Arab sympathy for Iraq's difficulties in the post–Gulf War era grew, as did Arab antagonism toward U.S. policy. This sympathy should not, however, be mistaken for broad Arab support for Saddam Hussein's regime.

# Where Saddam Stands Today

As a result of his own failed foreign policy, and the reactions of the West to his plans, Saddam Hussein has steadily crystallized his anti-West position, and is basically an outcast among the other Middle East leaders.

Today, Hussein is trying desperately to minimize the strength and unity of the countries trying to contain him—and making the most of Arab resentment toward the United States for the sufferings of the Iraqi people.

## The Least You Need to Know

◆ Iraq is as old as it gets.

◆ Iraq has been invaded, conquered, and reconquered over the centuries.

◆ Baghdad was once was the center of a great Muslim empire.

◆ The British created Iraq, and forced different peoples together to make one country.

◆ Iraq has struggled unsuccessfully to assume the leadership position among the Arab nations.

# Chapter 4

# By the Numbers: Iraq Today

## In This Chapter

- ◆ Iraq's size and population
- ◆ How Iraq is governed
- ◆ About the Iraqi people
- ◆ What Iraq produces

Remember those old social studies textbooks that were chock-full of information like the population of Bangladesh, the size of Mexico, and the climate of Australia—all of which you had to memorize for a test? Without proper context, such statistics are quite meaningless. However, now that you know why Iraq is important to world affairs, where it is located, and a little bit about its people and culture, Iraq by the numbers should help to round out your understanding of this most important of countries.

I promise: There *won't* be a quiz at the end of the chapter.

## The Lay of the Land

**Size:** Iraq is 169,235 square miles (437,072 square kilometers), It's smaller than Iran, and slightly larger than Syria. Iraq is much larger than Kuwait.

*Map of Iraq.*

*(Source: University of Texas Library Online Perry-Castañeda Library Map Collection)*

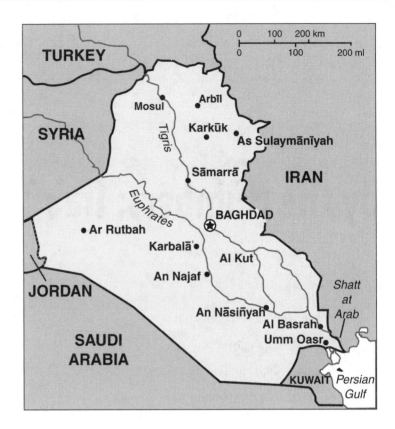

**Climate:** Iraq temperatures swing substantially between summer and winter. The mountain region in the north has cold winters with occasional heavy snows. It would be tough to play hockey in Iraq (sand hockey, anyone?), but it does get cold. The mean January temperature in Mosul, the chief city in the north, is 44°F; the mean July temperature there is 90—F. Farther south, away from the mountains, it gets much hotter. The mean January temperature in Baghdad, which lies in the central lowland part of the country, is 50°F; for July it is 95°F.

**Oil Spill Ahead**

Dress light and bring along a fan if you find yourself summering in Iraq. Temperatures as high as 123°F have been recorded.

From October to May, 12 to 22 inches of precipitation fall in the mountainous north, but in the central region, in the south and near the Persian Gulf there is only six inches for the whole year. The desert in the west gets little or no precipitation.

**Terrain:** The desert lands are mostly plains, with marshes along its border with Iran in the south, and mountains along the Iran and Turkey borders in the north. The highest point in Iraq is Haji Ibrahim at 11,834 feet, or 3,600 meters, near the border with Iran. The vast majority of the landscape is a grayish sandy plain that eventually merges into the Syrian Desert. The Tigris and Euphrates Rivers have created a broad plain, with a fertile area between and on both sides of the rivers, and in the irrigated areas. The extreme southeastern portion of Iraq is a low-lying, marshy area adjacent to the Persian Gulf, and along the Shatt-al-Arab.

**Natural resources:** Iraq's biggest natural resource by far is oil, then natural gas and sulfur. The country has large concentrations of phosphates, too. Otherwise, there isn't much else there in terms of natural resources. There are small deposits of salt, coal, gypsum, and sulfur.

**Land use:** About 12 percent of Iraqi territory is farmable. A series of flood control and irrigation dams on the Tigris and Euphrates Rivers feed an irrigation system and maintain a more even flow through the seasons. The rest of the land (79 percent) is mostly desert, and is not much suited for agriculture or other human activity. The land is mainly used as pasture for sheep and goats.

> **Increase Your Iraq IQ**
>
> Iraq's coastline along the gulf is only 19 miles long. Its only port on the gulf, Umm Qasr, is small and located on shallow water, so big tankers cannot use it. Iraq's other port is further inland at Basra, on the Shatt-al-Arab waterway. There are larger offshore oil loading facilities for tankers—or there were, prior to their getting bombed during the Gulf War.

# People and Places

**Principal cities:** Baghdad is the capital and largest city of Iraq. Other major cities include Basra, Iraq's port on the Shatt-al-Arab, and Mosul, a primary oil nexus in the northern part of the country. Most of the people are concentrated in the urban centers.

**Population:** Iraq has 23,331,985 people (July 2001 est.). By comparison, the United States has about 280 million people. In 2001, Iraq had a population growth rate of 2.84 percent.

**Life expectancy:** Males: 66 years, Females: 68 years. Forty percent of the population is younger than 14, showing the high birth rate in the country. Health standards have declined significantly after the end of the Gulf War, and imposition of UN sanctions that have limited imports of food and medicine to the Iraq.

**Ethnic groups:** Most of the population is Arab. Arabs are 80 percent of the total in Iraq. The Kurds are 15 percent of the population; and other ethnic groups including Turkoman and Assyrian make up the remaining 5 percent.

# The Word on the Street (and in the Mosque)

**Language:** Arabic is the official language of Iraq and is spoken by the majority of the population. The Kurds speak Kurdish. Armenian and Assyrian are spoken in some rural areas in the north and west.

**Religions:** The official religion of Iraq is Islam. Muslims make up 97 percent of the population. (Shiites are 65 percent and Sunnis are 32 percent of the total.) The remaining 3 percent of the population represents a scattering of other religions. These include a few Christian Nestorians, Jacobite Christians, and offshoots of these two sects, respectively known as Chaldean and Syrian Catholics. In addition, smaller religious groups include the Yazidis, who live in the hill country north of Mosul, and a Gnostic sect known as the Mandaean Baptists living in Baghdad. The Yazidis are a syncretic sect, which combines the beliefs of different religions. A small community of Jews lives in Baghdad.

# Politics: The Lowdown

**Government divisions:** Iraq is nominally a republic, with 18 provinces. Baghdad is the capital. The three provinces in the Kurdish area are called the Kurdish autonomous region. The other 15 provinces are run by a governor appointed by the Revolutionary Command Council (RCC). Towns and cities are run by councils headed by mayors. The Kurdish autonomous region, established in 1970, has an elected 50-member legislature. However, infighting among Kurdish factions has paralyzed this legislature. In 1998 two rival Kurdish parties signed an agreement, brokered by the United States, which provided for a transitional power-sharing arrangement. However, the agreement has not been implemented, and each of the two parties governs its own slice of Kurdish territory.

**Iraq Fact**

Iraq dates its independence from October 3, 1932, when the League of Nations mandate freeing it from British administration was issued. Prior to the British administration, Iraq didn't exist as a political entity called "Iraq," but was a part of the Ottoman Empire, and several empires before that.

**Government structure:** Iraq follows a republic style of government with executive, legislative, and judicial branches. The Constitution of Iraq, adopted when the Ba'th Party took power in 1968, created the RCC with supreme executive power. The RCC is a group of about 10 members. This group is led by the chairman of the RCC (Saddam Hussein). The chairman of the RCC also is the president of the Republic (Saddam Hussein). The RCC also appoints a council of ministers, who are led by the prime minister (Saddam Hussein).

The legislative branch consists of a National Assembly, which is elected by the Iraqi people. It is made up of 250 members elected to four-year terms. The legislature's main task is to ratify or reject legislation proposed by the RCC. In practice, the National Assembly is a big rubber stamp.

The judiciary system consists of civil courts, criminal courts, and religious courts. The president appoints all judges. Iraq's highest court is the Court of Cassation. It has 12 to 15 judges. At least three judges must hear a case. In cases where the offense is punishable by death, five judges are required.

In criminal cases, a complaint of a crime is investigated by a magistrate, who decides if the matter is a "major offense" or a "lesser offense." Lesser offenses are tried in a penal court, which usually consists of one judge. Major offenses are tried in a great court, which usually consists of three judges. Criminal courts and religious courts are located wherever there are civil courts. Religious courts try personal cases, such as divorce cases. There are Sunni, Shiite, and Christian religious courts.

**Leadership:** Saddam Hussein wields absolute power. He is president, prime minister, and chairman of the Revolutionary Command Council. The rest of the governmental leadership are Sunnis who are part of Saddam's inner circle. There are no Kurds or Shiites in the inner circle.

> **CAUTION** **Oil Spill Ahead**
>
> In general, the Iraqi criminal code is extremely strict. There are several crimes that result in the death penalty, and dismemberment is a routine punishment.

The leadership of the Kurds and the Shiites are split among several factions. There is no clear single leader among the Kurds or Shiites who can rally the full support of either group in a movement against the Sunni-controlled government.

Outside of Iraq, the London-based Iraqi National Congress has offered itself as an alternative civilian leadership for Iraq. However, the Bush administration and members of Congress have openly expressed doubt over the group's competence, and ability to represent the Iraqi people, given their distance from the country, physically and socially.

**Political parties:** The only legal political organization in Iraq is the Arab Ba'th Socialist Party, which bases its policies on pan-Arab and socialist principles. Other (illegal) parties in Iraq include the Iraqi Communist Party (ICP), the Kurdistan Democratic Party (KDP), and the Patriotic Union of Kurdistan (PUK). The two main Shiite opposition parties are the Da'wa Islamic Party and the Supreme Assembly of the Islamic Revolution in Iraq (SAIRI). There is no single alternative party that represents a majority of the Iraqi people.

# Money, Money

**Economy:** Iraq's economy is dominated by the oil sector, and the country is a member of OPEC. Iraq has about 10 percent of the world's proven reserves of petroleum, and oil provides about 95 percent of Iraqi foreign exchange earnings. Other Iraqi products include dates, wool, and hides and skins.

---

### Increase Your Iraq IQ

Since the UN sanctions were imposed, Iraq has been unable to export the same amount of oil it used to, and thus cannot import the materials it once did. The United Nations has gradually been lifting the limits to how much Iraq can export in one month. However, because of the bombings, and the sanctions, Iraqi oil production hasn't reached its monthly export limits. The economy has shrunk significantly since 1990, when the Gulf War ended and the UN sanctions began.

---

**Currency:** The official currency is called the "dinar" (ID). One dinar equals 20 "dirham" or 1,000 "fil," the Iraqi coins. The official exchange rate in 1999 was about 1 ID to 3 US$. In reality, the black market rate is very different. The dinar is worth much, much less relative to the dollar. In 1999, the black market exchange rate was 1,200 ID to 1 US$.

**GDP:** Iraq's Gross Domestic Product (GDP) was approximately $57 billion in 2000. The GDP of the United States, by comparison, was greater than $8 trillion in 2000.

**Industries:** Most Iraqi industry revolves around petroleum and its peripheral industries. Iraq also has chemicals, textiles, construction materials, cigarettes, and food processing operations, based upon imports of raw materials for those industries. Iraq privatized all major national industries. Most are governed by a specific ministry that oversees the management of each enterprise in that sector.

**Military:** Iraq has an army of about 1 million men, including reservists. It has a small air force. The Iraqi navy has only about 2,000 members. Iraq has artillery, tanks, and anti-aircraft weapons of both U.S. and Russian manufacture. Consistent bombing raids by the United States and British air forces have destroyed much of Iraq's military capacity. The Iraqi military probably has biological and chemical weapons, and is almost certainly working on developing nuclear weapons. As a result, Iraq must be regarded as a formidable power in the region.

## The Least You Need to Know

◆ Iraq is a major oil-producing country, in the middle of the major oil-producing region of the world.

◆ Iraq is a dictatorship, despite its republic trappings.

◆ Iraq is a complex combination of peoples (Arabs and Kurds) and religious sects (Sunni and Shiite).

◆ Iraq's military has been seriously weakened by U.S. and UK attacks, but is still formidable.

# Part 2

# From Babylon to Baghdad

The area comprising modern-day Iraq has been continuously populated since the dawn of human civilization. But like its desert sands, the region's population and rulers have undergone a remarkable number of shifts.

In the following chapters we'll trace the series of empires that have risen and fallen in this region and find out about a few of their major contributions—if you call the wheel and writing major, that is—to the world. We'll take a look at the lasting impact of one of the empires—the Arabs—and how Western powers were responsible for the creation of the modern state of Iraq.

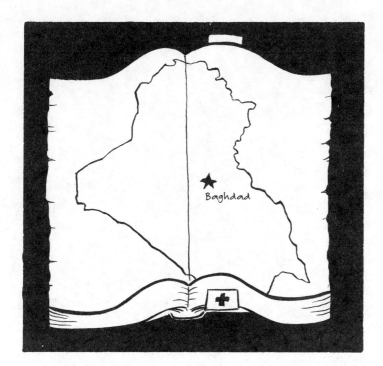

# Chapter 5

# Who Put the "Ur" in "Urban"?

## In This Chapter

- ◆ Ancient urban civilization in the area we now know as Iraq
- ◆ The importance of two rivers
- ◆ The emergence of the building blocks of future empires

The story of Iraq begins with two rivers—the Tigris and Euphrates. From the bounty of these two rivers we can attribute the earliest writing, the development of the wheel, and many other features of modern civilization that we still rely on. And it all took place where Iraq is today.

## Who Was First?

Urban civilization emerged in Mesopotamia over 5,000 years ago. Some of the earliest known cities, including Ur, Lagash, and Uruk, emerged in what is now Iraq.

Archaeologists and other scholars continue to debate exactly where the earliest urban civilization emerged. Most scholars believe urban life appeared at Jericho, hundreds of miles to the west, even earlier than in Mesopotamia. It is impossible to deny, though, that the civilization that came out of what is now Iraq is among the oldest, and was certainly more influential, than any that came before.

What happened in Mesopotamia had a huge influence on Western culture, science, and history.

---

### Increase Your Iraq IQ

Archaeologists digging on the site of Jericho in the 1950s, hoping to find evidence of the walls whose collapse was related in the Bible in Joshua 6:20, soon realized that there were walls older than the ones assumed to have been built in biblical times. (Warning: The dating of such finds, and the assignment of biblical episodes to known periods of history remains a highly controversial matter.) They found evidence of a 20-foot-high wall that was built in 8000 B.C.E. These walls were built 5,000 years before the first temples in Mesopotamia, or even the Pyramids of Egypt! These walls were found some 50 feet below the modern surface. A wall's existence signifies that people had the time and excess resources to gather together, organize themselves, and assemble the resources and intelligence to construct sophisticated architecture. As for the famous biblical walls that tumbled down, no evidence has yet been found.

---

### Desert Diction

**Nomads** are people who don't live permanently in one place. They tend to move from place to place, generally in a specific pattern. That pattern could be governed by the seasons or by the availability of food. Nomads typically have herds of animals that travel with them, providing food on the hoof.

# Settle Down!

Indications of permanent settlements in Mesopotamia appear around 5000 B.C.E. Before that, the people of the region tended to be more *nomadic*, or lived in less permanent structures.

The first permanent settlement in the region that can be confirmed appears at a place called Jarmo. At Jarmo, there is evidence of domesticated animals and plants, as well as permanent structures. It's estimated that as many as 150 people lived in the village of Jarmo. There were permanent mud-walled houses, and the inhabitants grew wheat, barley, and lentils, and had domesticated animals.

## Stuff to Drink, Stuff to Eat

What led ancient nomads to settle down and build Jarmo and settlements like it? The struggle for water and food. Simply put, the region between the Tigris and Euphrates Rivers was a good place to find both.

Remember that this region is basically desert. And yet these two rivers, and the silt that they deposited along their banks, made it possible for people to survive and grow food year after year in this otherwise forbidding environment. The two rivers flow almost parallel from mountains in the northern parts of Mesopotamia to their mouth, at the head of the Persian Gulf, and the region between them is a great place to grow food.

These early settlements set in motion a series of cultural advances that leaves us face to face with some enterprising, expansionist folks known as the Sumerians.

**Iraq Fact**

The Tigris is east of the Euphrates, closer to Iran. The rivers join before they reached the Gulf, into a single river called the Shatt-al-Arab.

---

### Increase Your Iraq IQ

Before they were tamed by irrigation and flood control dams, the Tigris and Euphrates meandered across the Mesopotamian plains. They would sometimes flood and sometimes run very low; the water level fluctuated because rainfall is scarce in the region. A heavy rain (or winter snow) would mean flood. An extended dry spell would mean the river levels would drop.

In ancient times, canals were dug from the Tigris over to the Euphrates, which is lower than the Tigris. These small waterways provided irrigation in the plain between the rivers. (Today, a series of dams and irrigation canals control the rivers' flow and maximize water for irrigation.)

# The Sumerians Get the Ball Rolling

The ancient Sumerians are credited with inventing, among other things, the wheel, the plow, and cuneiform writing. These three inventions enabled transportation, increased agricultural yields, and commerce—cornerstones to the success of ancient urban centers.

## Getting Acquainted

While little is known about the Sumerian origins, a great deal is known about their accomplishments. Among other things, the Sumerians invented cuneiform writing, and wrote their words on clay tablets.

Archaeologists have found hundreds of clay tablets in the region bearing cuneiform writing. The presence of these tablets indicates that knowledge was being transferred to other people and being saved in writing. This allowed the early inhabitants to build (literally) on the intellects and memories of other people, to codify laws, and to establish a permanent record of their oral traditions.

Many of the oldest surviving cuneiform tablets detail commercial transactions and property listings among the ancient Sumerians. These transactions seem mundane, but they are invaluable to showing us daily life in Mesopotamia.

The regularly flood-renewed fertile land, with abundant water, enabled the Sumerians to grow surplus crops, and therefore sustain larger populations. The unpredictability of the rivers also prompted the Sumerians to band together to create irrigation and buildings on a communal scale.

**Desert Diction**

**Pantheism** refers to belief in a group of gods where each represents a specific human action, or emotion, or a physical element, such as one for the sun, one for the moon. **Anthropomor-phism** is the belief that gods take human form, have human emotions, and act in many ways like humans.

Like the Greeks who followed them, the Sumerian religions were pantheistic and their gods were *anthropomorphic*. The Sumerians developed unique cults and religious beliefs in their various city-states, but they shared the *pantheistic* and anthropomorphic characteristics.

The concentration of peoples into permanent, ever developing centers led to cultural and technological innovation that could not occur among the nomadic tribes that populated the regions surrounding Mesopotamia. Settlement and permanence promoted the cultural and economic growth of the region, and attracted the attention of other cultures and traders. The rivers themselves were natural trade routes, enabling the cities that sprouted beside them to trade their surplus commodities with other regions. Even the predecessors to the silk road passed though Mesopotamia, opening the riches of the Orient to these urban populations. The central position of Mesopotamian cities resulted in trade with other emerging civilizations in the Mediterranean and North Africa, as well as the Far East. This trade brought further riches to the region, and prompted further innovations in technology.

---

### Increase Your Iraq IQ

People have been trading across the world for centuries. Overland trade routes from ancient China and India to the ancient Mesopotamia and on to ancient Egypt and Phoenicia were established almost as early as the first cities emerged. The earliest people were mostly nomads, so it is easy to see how they would wander into one another and compare goodies. Over time, this developed into more sophisticated trade. Along with trade came trade routes. The more modern silk road was simply the descendent of a series of ancient routes that wound their way from various parts of China and India, across various parts of Central Asia, through various cities in Mesopotamia, and on to the Mediterranean. Marco Polo certainly wasn't the first to go to China from the West, but he was the first to get lasting credit for it.

---

# Lawyers, Guns, and Money: The Early Ruling Class

Along with the food surpluses and trade came wealth, and, ultimately, spare time for those who didn't have to work every waking hour for their survival. As a result, these cities were able to further improve their positions through the development of new technologies, and even leisure pursuits. Temples and city walls were among the results of this surplus.

## From Family to King

The ancient people who lived in this area gradually evolved from a process of clan and patriarchal decision-making to appointing a king who ruled them. How did this happen?

The food surpluses meant that a ruling class and its bureaucracy and army could be supported by the work of other people. These institutions, and the power elites who ran them,

**Iraq Fact**

The oldest wheel yet discovered by archaeologists was found in Mesopotamia (present-day Iraq). It is thought to be more than 5,500 years old.

gradually solidified their authority by making themselves kings and establishing administrators in the place of tribal elders. The kings further entrenched themselves by claiming that they were divine relations of the gods of the day.

The evolution of the divinely justified king, supported by a bureaucracy and propped up by an army, who ruled over an increasingly complex social and economic structure, accompanies the development of the pre-Sumerian city-states in Mesopotamia. The king enriched a priest-class bureaucracy and military class, so that they would support him and remain loyal to him. They benefited by not having to work every day in the dirt to survive.

## A Question with Modern Implications Arises

Why would people allow themselves to be ruled by a king in that way? In other words—why did people collectivize and submit to central power? And for that matter, why do they still do so?

**Iraq Fact**

The city-states that rose in Mesopotamia in the 4000–2500 B.C.E period weren't a cohesive empire. It wasn't until 2750 B.C.E that the first Sumerian dynasty of Ur was able to consolidate political hold on the major cities in southern Mesopotamia. This was the first empire in the region, where the central authority (based in Ur) was able to control the surrounding city-states.

The simple answer was, and is, survival.

In the case of the ancient region of Mesopotamia, it was a tough and dangerous place. Water and food were often hard to come by if you decided to go it alone, but there was some guarantee of access to both within the storehouses and reservoirs of the cities. Then, too, there was the ever-present problem of marauding bandits and tribal warfare.

Much like in feudal Europe, people accepted the king because the king promised protection during dangerous times. Along with their king, people in one city-state would regard people in another city-state as potential enemies, to be conquered and plundered, before they decided to conquer and plunder first.

While not exactly patriotism or tribal fealty, the individual's association of membership to a state (instead of a tribe) marked the beginnings of more modern concepts of citizenship. This notion eventually took hold during the Sumerian era, and enabled the Sumerians to come together and create a unified identity that paralleled—or even surpassed—one's immediate family circle.

This is the occasionally bloody, not always graceful dance of civilization. And as far as we can tell, it first played out in the place we now call Iraq.

**Iraq Fact**

Some highlights in Mesopotamian pre-history.

◆ 5000 B.C.E.: First settlements at Jarmo.

◆ 4700 B.C.E.: Hassunah period—pottery-making emerges. The ability to make pottery is considered a requirement for urban living.

◆ 4400 B.C.E.: Halaf period—metal-working emerges. Like pottery, a requirement for urbanization.

◆ 3900 B.C.E.: Ubaid period—first temple and complex buildings appear. The ability to build temples means surplus materials, food, and time, all by-products of increasing efficiencies and urbanization.

◆ 3600 B.C.E.: Warka period—first written characters appear. The ability to record information, to pass along, and add to it, is a foundation of modern civilization.

◆ 2900 B.C.E.: Sumerians appear. These people use all the innovations that came before them, and create a sophisticated urban civilization.

## The Least You Need to Know

◆ Mesopotamia is where it all began. The earliest known settlements appeared more than 7,000 years ago.

◆ The key elements of civilization—pottery, iron working, architecture, and writing—all evolved in Mesopotamia.

◆ The Tigris and Euphrates Rivers are the central elements of Mesopotamia. Without them, civilization would not exist in that region.

◆ The societies that emerged evolved from tribal settlements to sophisticated city-states, ruled by divine-kings, not tribal elders.

◆ Ancient Mesopotamia was linked to the Orient and African regions through trade even way back then.

# Biblicalities

## In This Chapter

- ◆ Mesopotamia's role in the Bible
- ◆ An ancient Sumerian epic influences the Bible
- ◆ What the Hebrews were doing in Mesopotamia
- ◆ How Zoroastrianism may have influenced Christianity

Believe it or not, when you walk into a church or synagogue, you are, in a way, walking into a Sumerian temple (or at least *through* one to get to your pew or bench). That's because historical Mesopotamia (the precursor to the modern Iraq) greatly contributed to Western Judeo-Christian beliefs. In this chapter, you will learn how ancient Sumerian legends found their way into contemporary Hebrew culture, and thus into the Bible we know today.

## It All Starts in Mesopotamia

The Hebrew scriptures, and thus the Judeo-Christian creation story, began in the region we today identify as Iraq.

In case you missed it, the biblical Creation story is described in Genesis 1–3. God created light, heaven, earth, plants, sun, moon, stars, animals, birds, and finally, man. God named the first man Adam. Then God made woman from Adam's rib, and, called her Eve. God placed Adam and Eve in the Garden of Eden, and told them to eat the fruit of any tree they wanted, *except* the Tree of Knowledge. All went well until a serpent convinced Eve to eat the fruit from the Tree of Knowledge (he told her that it would allow her to be like God). Eve ate the fruit, and gave some to Adam, who also ate it. At this point, Adam and Eve gained knowledge, and realized they were stark naked. They covered themselves with leaves. Then God came to them in the Garden, and when he realized that they had eaten the fruit of the Tree of Knowledge, he cast them out of the Garden of Eden for going against him. From these beginnings, the remainder of the Bible tells of humanity's path back to God's grace through a covenant with God, and, for Christians, through the coming of Jesus.

In the Book of Genesis, the first humans emerged in Mesopotamia. The Garden of Eden, some scholars believe, was located near modern Mughair in the southern part of ancient Mesopotamia, in the ancient Tigris and Euphrates delta region, though the actual site hasn't been confirmed. To the ancient Hebrews, humanity itself was regarded as having arisen in Mesopotamia.

## A Word About the Holy Words

The Hebrew Scriptures are divisible into three parts: the *Law* or *Torah*, which is the first five books of the Christian Bible's Old Testament; the *Prophets* (books detailing the actions of the prophets); and the *Hagiographia* or *the Twelve* (Ecclesiastes, Ruth, Song of Solomon, Psalms, Proverbs, Job, Ruth, Nehemiah, Esther, Daniel, Ezra, and Chronicles). The Christian scriptures add a "New Testament" describing the life of Christ and the apostles to the existing Jewish scriptures, and so Christians refer to the Jewish scriptures (*Law, Prophets, Hagiographia*) as the Old Testament. The Bible is a collection of Old and New Testaments. This chapter focuses on stories found in the Hebrew Scriptures, and thus in the "Old Testament" of the Christian Bible. However, in recognition of the fact that these stories were written before Christ, I am going to refer to them as the Hebrew Scriptures rather than the Old Testament.

## Why Mesopotamia?

Why did the Hebrews designate Mesopotamia as the starting point for everything? And why does this region figure so prominently in the stories of the Hebrew struggles throughout the ages?

The importance of Mesopotamia in the Bible really isn't surprising when we take two things into account:

- ◆ The Hebrews were held captive in Mesopotamia (that is, in Babylon), and so it is no surprise that their scriptures would include stories that came from there.

- ◆ The Mesopotamians invented writing, and recorded many ancient legends and lessons on their clay tablets. The Hebrews came into contact with this trove of surviving writing, and certainly read some of what they saw.

# Overlapping Stories

Some key stories of the Hebrew Scriptures may have been copied from ancient Mesopotamian legends. Many of these legends are found in a Sumerian legend called the "Epic of Gilgamesh."

# The Epic of Gilgamesh (in Brief)

The "Epic of Gilgamesh" is a collection of legends of the ancient Sumerian king, Gilgamesh. Around 2600 B.C.E., Gilgamesh was king of Uruk (known as Erech in the Hebrew Scriptures). The story recounts the exploits of Gilgamesh, who was semi-divine—part god, part human—but a brutal ruler. The people under Gilgamesh's rule ask Anu, chief deity of Uruk, to help them deal with Gilgamesh. Anu creates Enkidu, a subhuman wild man to counter the super human Gilgamesh. Enkidu is gradually humanized by shepherds, and then enters the city, where Gilgamesh is presiding over a wedding. Gilgamesh, the lout, is about to claim the right to sleep with the bride on her wedding night. Enkidu is outraged, and bars the way to the wedding chamber. In the manner of many epics and legends, Gilgamesh and Enkidu fight for days.

Enkidu finally concedes to Gilgamesh, and the two become friends. They go out to cut down all the cedars in the forest in what we would now identify as southern Iran to make a gate for Uruk, but before doing so they must defeat Humbaba, the monster who guards the forest. With a god's help, they are able to succeed against Humbaba and proceed to make the gate.

When they get back to Uruk, Gilgamesh and Enkidu battle and kill the Bull of Heaven, and ultimately the gods take revenge by causing Enkidu to die. Upon his friend's death, Gilgamesh goes out from Uruk, and meets Utnapishtim, who is immortal. Utnapishtim tells Gilgamesh of how he survived a great flood by making a boat, riding out the storm, and coming to rest on a mountain. After Utnapishtim shares the secret to immortality, a sly and devious serpent steals Gilgamesh's immortality from him. Finally, Gilgamesh returns to Uruk, where the epic ends.

Any of that sound familiar?

## More on the Gilgamesh Connection

At least two incidents in the "Epic of Gilgamesh" echo events told in the Hebrew Scriptures:

♦ **The serpent and the loss of immortality.** A nasty serpent in both stories is responsible for stealing immortality from its victims.

♦ **An old man and a great flood.** The Bible tells of Noah (who at the time was 800 years old) building an ark to survive a great flood imposed on the land by God. At the end of the flood, his ark ends up on Mount Ararat (and even old Noah himself was from the city of Fara, in Mesopotamia). The "Epic of Gilgamesh" recounts Gilgamesh's encounter with a wise old man, Utnapishtim, who had survived a devastating flood by building an ark and eventually landing on a mountain.

Scholars believe the "Epic of Gilgamesh" precedes the composition of the Hebrew Scriptures, and the fact that both the "Epic of Gilgamesh," and the Hebrew Scriptures share the same story indicates the influence Mesopotamian culture had on the Hebrews and their culture.

# References to Mesopotamia in the Hebrew Scriptures

The Hebrew Scriptures repeatedly mention Mesopotamian people and places. However, most of the Mesopotamian cities referenced in the Old Testament are not given high marks by the Hebrew authors. This isn't surprising, given that the Hebrews were taken as captives to Babylon in 586 B.C.E.

What kinds of conclusions did the authors of the Hebrew Scriptures come to about the area we now know as Iraq?

## The Babylon Blues

Babylon is described in the Hebrew Scriptures as a place of sadness, as seen in II Chronicles, Lamentations, Jeremiah, and Ezekiel. King Nebuchadnezzar, a Babylonian king, captured Judea (the homeland of half of the Jewish nation), and destroyed their capital city of Jerusalem, including the Temple of Solomon, the center of Jewish religious expression. He also exiled most of the prominent Hebrews to Babylon. The Hebrews attributed their defeat and exile to their own wickedness—and not to a clash of cultures and resources in which the stronger side won. Regardless of the causes of the defeat, the Hebrews' conflict with Babylon was not exactly regarded as a high point of Hebrew history.

During this time of exile, the Hebrews were exposed to the collection of stories and legends of ancient Sumeria that had survived on clay tablets for all to read (who could read). The more prominent, and literate, Hebrews certainly had the opportunity to read many of these stories, and these were probably the same class who eventually composed what we know today as the Hebrew Scriptures.

So then what happens? (From the Hebrew point of view, that is.)

## Nineveh as Backdrop for Jonah

Jonah, a Hebrew, is commanded by God to go to Nineveh (the place of the great library) and preach about the city's coming doom, because of the wickedness of its inhabitants. Jonah eventually gets there, by way of sea cruise in a whale's belly.

Jonah beseeches God to ruin Nineveh. However, God, in the end, decides not to destroy Nineveh. God reasons that there are over 120,000 people living there, and it wouldn't be an equitable response to their sins to destroy them all, no matter how grieved Jonah is (see Jonah 4:11).

## Abraham Leaves the Area to Start a New Race

The Hebrew patriarch Abraham was first called Abram. He was from Ur, in (you guessed it) Mesopotamia.

Abram is commanded by God to go forth and found a nation. As Abraham, he goes forth to Canaan, an ancient region that is located in Israel. If you think about Abraham as the patriarch of a nomadic tribe (which is exactly what the Hebrews were at this time), it is easy to understand his travels to Canaan and then to Egypt. However, it's important to put those travels in the right context. Abraham *left* bad old Mesopotamia in order to come to a new place and start over.

## The Tower of Babel: Symbol of Wickedness

The Tower of Babel is described in the Bible as a sign of the depth that the Babylonian people had sunk to at the time. In God's eyes, according to the Bible, they were forsaking God for the sake of multiple illegitimate deities. To make matters worse, they were even building a structure (the Tower of Babel) for one of those false gods.

The Hebrews, of course, viewed the pantheistic (multi-god) religions of the Babylonians as heresy. The Tower of Babel was probably one of the tallest structures ever built at the time. The Hebrews took this height to be a symbol of man building a tower to reach to heaven. The ultimate structural failure of the Tower was taken by the Hebrews as a vindication for their faith in the one God, Yahweh.

# Thus Spake Zarathustra

Zoroaster (Zarathustra) is credited with creating the briefly powerful religion that bore his name: Zoroastrianism. The Persians introduced the religion of Zoroastrianism to Mesopotamia. Rather than an examination of man's struggle with himself, Zoroastrians saw the world as a fundamental struggle between good and evil. Zoroastrians believed in the final victory of the ultimate good god, Ahurah Mazdah. The Zoroastrian Persians, who conquered Babylon while the Hebrews were captive there, were more tolerant of other religions and other gods. When they met the Hebrews, and learned about their God, they included Yahweh, the Hebrew God, into their pantheon. The Zoroastrians believed that Yahweh was a "good" god, whose power would only further their goal of battling evil and support Ahurah Mazdah in the struggle. The Persians eventually allowed the Hebrews to return to Jerusalem and rebuild the Temple of Solomon. The Books of Ezra and Nehemiah narrate this portion of Hebrew history.

While the Hebrews didn't embrace the fundamental good versus evil philosophies of the Zoroastrians, they probably brought these ideas with them in some form when they came back to Jerusalem.

It's possible that the first Christians may have taken the fundamentals of both Judaism and Zoroastrianism with them when they launched Christianity. (This is, however, an extremely controversial point—one where scholars have not yet reached agreement.) If this were true, ancient Mesopotamia's role in the development of both Judaism *and* Christianity would be critically important.

---

### Increase Your Iraq IQ

Look how much of the Bible takes place in (what we would now call) Iraq:

- Adam and Eve live in the Garden of Eden, now connected with southern Mesopotamia.
- Noah is from Fara.
- Job is from the area around Uz.
- Abram is from Ur. He becomes Abraham, father of the Hebrew nation; God commands him to lead his people from Mesopotamia to Canaan.
- Assyrians, from Nineveh, conquer the northern Hebrew kingdom of Israel.
- The Chaldeans, from Babylon, conquer the southern Hebrew kingdom of Judah, and exile the Hebrews to Babylon.
- The Tower of Babel is built by Nebuchadnezzar near Babylon.
- Jonah is commanded by God to preach in Nineveh. He travels there via a whale's belly.

---

The moral: Whether you realized it at the time or not, you were reading about the region we today identify as Iraq when you read or heard some of the most famous stories from the ancient Hebrew Scriptures.

## The Least You Need to Know

- The Hebrews were exiled in Babylon and were exposed to Mesopotamian culture while they were there.

- Mesopotamian culture survived on clay tablets, and the Hebrews who wrote the Scriptures learned about that culture and probably borrowed from it.

- Many key figures in the Hebrew Scriptures came from Mesopotamia, including Adam and Eve, Noah, Job, and Abraham.

- The "Epic of Gilgamesh" and other Sumerian legends contain legends that correspond to key Bible stories and probably were the inspiration for them.

- Persians introduced Zoroastrian concepts of good and evil to the Hebrews during the exile in Babylon. The Hebrews took these concepts with them when returning to Jerusalem; the concepts may have had an influence on the development of Christianity.

# The Cultural Chain: Empires in Iraq

## In This Chapter

◆ Rotating empires

◆ Sumerian culture endures

◆ Marching through Mesopotamia

Viewed from the distance of history, it seems as though the ancient world consisted of successive waves of invasions and counter-invasions. And the wealthier the region—in terms of agricultural resources, storehouses of food, and/or a thriving trade economy—the more likely jealous neighbors and vandals were to invade.

In this chapter, we will look at Mesopotamia as a place where the emerging Sumerian city-states' great wealth became the prized target of one invader after another. As we shall see, in most cases, the prize captured them.

The invaders often abandoned their own culture in favor of the one they found there. We shall also see how the larger movements of world events eventually led to the decline of Mesopotamia as the central prize.

# Loosely Connected

The city-states that rose in Mesopotamia in the 4000–2500 B.C.E. period were not a cohesive empire. These states generally worshipped different gods, and maneuvered with alliances to maintain their own independence, or to exert dominance over their neighbors.

It wasn't until 2750 B.C.E. that the first Sumerian dynasty of Ur was able to consolidate political hold on the major cities in southern Mesopotamia. This was the first empire in the region, where the central authority (based in Ur) was able to control the surrounding city-states.

## Sumerian Technical Innovations

Sumerian civilization is credited with many inventions, some of which we've already discussed. Many people even claim the Sumerians invented time!

It is true that the Sumerians developed a mathematical system based upon 60, which is still the basis for hours and minutes and seconds. They came up with new irrigation methods, and architectural techniques. They used double-entry accounting methods, and even had early forms of banks. Deposits of grain, cattle, metals, and tools were accepted at palaces and temples that emerged in the ancient cities. The priests that ran these temples would meticulously record the deposits, and make the appropriate payments on behalf of the account holder. We know this because of the durability of their writing.

> **Increase Your Iraq IQ**
>
> The Sumerians:
>
> ◆ **Ruled:** 3000 B.C.E. to 2000 B.C.E.
>
> ◆ **Religion:** Pantheistic (several gods)
>
> ◆ **Key cities:** Uruk, Ur, Lagash, Eridu
>
> ◆ **Claim to fame:** "Epic of Gilgamesh," ziggurats, wheel, plow, cuneiform

The Sumerians also developed a calendar system of 12 lunar months. Over time, they realized that the lunar year was significantly shorter than the solar year, so they added a "leap month" every third year to get things back on target.

The Sumerians were almost constantly at war with each other and outside groups. The struggles for control of water and arable land were almost constant, and the Sumerian city-states under the Ur dynasty slowly succumbed to outside invaders.

# Meet the New Boss ...

Around 2340 B.C.E., the Akkadians swept up from the Arabian peninsula, and subdued the Ur dynasty. The Akkadians were a Semitic people and spoke a language that is related to Hebrew and Arabic. They founded a capital city at Akkad, later called Babylon.

The Akkadians adopted the best of what the Sumerians had to offer in the ways of government, societal structures, religion and law, and abandoned much of their own culture when they gained control of the Sumerian territories around Ur.

Sargon I started the era of Akkadian rule that lasted for about two centuries. The Akkadians were the first to unite the region of Mesopotamia under one ruling system. The Sumerian city-states had operated as a loose confederation, but the Akkadians centralized their control.

Rather than destroy the Sumerian cities, the Akkadians instead occupied them as a prize of conquest. In this spirit, the Akkadians allowed the various Sumerian city-states to recover from the conquest. The Akkadians eventually succumbed when the Sumerians in the city of Ur revolted in 2125 B.C.E., and the other Sumerian city-states followed suit.

**Iraq Fact**

This method of copying the best of what the Mesopo-tamian city-states had to offer became a common practice for most of the conquerors of the region over then next few thousand years.

---

**Increase Your Iraq IQ**

The Akkadians:

- **Ruled:** 2300–2100 B.C.E.
- **Race:** A Semitic people, related to the Arabs and Hebrews, not ethnically or lin-guistically linked to Sumerians
- **Key figure:** Sargon I
- **Claim to fame:** First empire to dominate the region of what is now Iraq under a single regime

---

# The Sumerians Come Back, But Not for Long

The demise of the Akkadians led to the reemergence of a Sumerian dynasty of Ur founded by Ur-Nammu. But this reemergence of Sumerian dominance was short-lived. The Sumerians were again overwhelmed by another migration of Semitic peoples, known as the Amorites, who consolidated their hold on southern Meso-potamia around 1900 B.C.E. They founded a capital at Akkad, in the center of Mesopotamia.

# An Eye for an Eye

The Amorites centralized their empire on the city of Babylon, which was founded near the old city of Akkad. The Amorite capital is known as Old Babylon, and the Amorite Empire (1900–1600 B.C.E.) is known as the Old Babylon period. The Amorites claimed their rulers were descended from gods, and that the central state had more power over people's lives than their own city-states did.

### Iraq Fact

The Amorites instituted far-reaching taxation and involuntary conscription to finance and maintain their new empire. This increasing centralization of power led to a new set of laws that defined crimes against the state, rather than against other individuals. The state also took a more active role in punishing criminals.

---

### Increase Your Iraq IQ

The Amorites:

◆ **Ruled:** 1900–1600 B.C.E.

◆ **Capitol:** Babylon

◆ **Race:** Semitic people, related to Hebrews and Arabs

◆ **Claim to fame:** Hammurabi Code, writing down the "Epic of Gilgamesh" (a collection of Sumerian legends)

The Amorites enacted a body of law, called *lex talionis*, or law of retribution. Punishments matched the nature of the infraction, creating the principle of "an eye for an eye, a tooth for a tooth, an arm for an arm, a life for a life." About this time, an Old Babylonian king, Hammurabi, set these laws down in writing. This written body of law is known as the Code of Hammurabi; it reflects the key tenets of Amorite and Sumerian law.

The Code is made up of some 282 individual laws. Many deal with the conduct of, and treatment of, slaves and one even decrees death for "bad behavior in a bar." Basically, the Amorites took the Sumerian law, and made it more severe, and more state-oriented, to serve their needs.

The main concepts of the Code are:

◆ **Administration:** Law is retribution that is administered by a centralized authority, not by individuals acting on their own or their clan's behalf.

◆ **Writing:** Law is written; and has a higher authority than individuals. Oral or cultural traditions are not written, and are subject to individual interpretation. The written law is permanent and supercedes the life of any one individual.

◆ **Retribution:** Law is basically a method of exacting revenge. By using law to exact revenge, society avoids personal vendettas and an increasing cycle of retribution for a given crime.

# The Hittites Take Over

Despite their centralization of power and authority, and conscript armies, the Amorites were unable to withstand the constant pressures of the Hittites, who swept away the Amorites around 1600 B.C.E. Like the conquerors before them, the Hittites adopted much of the cultural and societal elements of the region. The Hittite Empire eventually stretched from Mesopotamia, to Syria and Palestine. The Hittites spent a great deal of energy and resources battling with the Egyptians, who regarded them as savages.

Remember that the Amorites had adopted the Sumerian culture as their own, so the Hittites encountered a Sumerian culture when they encountered the Amorites.

The Hittites own empire covered a huge region, and they traded and fought with the Greeks, Egyptians, and other Mediterranean cultures. The Hittites never had the same grip on their territories that the Amorites had, and their legal system was much less punitive than Hammurabi's. The death penalty only applied to a relatively small number of crimes.

The Hittites also freely accepted the gods they encountered and even included them in their own religion. The other side of this looser authority was the increasingly loose grip that was maintained over the Mesopotamian city-states. Hittite control over these cities fluctuated, and eventually the Hittites gave way to an invasion of the Kassites, around 1100 B.C.E.

**Iraq Fact**

The Hittites are responsible for exporting Sumerian customs and innovations (that they encountered when they got to Mesopotamia) to other parts of the Ancient World.

| Increase Your Iraq IQ |
| --- |

The Hittites:

◆ **Ruled:** 1600–1100 B.C.E.

◆ **Origins:** Indo-European, fleeing from Asian invasions of their territory

◆ **Claim to fame:** Spread Sumerian culture throughout the Ancient World

# Enter the Kassites

The Kassites came into Mesopotamia from Asia. Like the Hittites, they were fleeing from invaders that displaced them from their original lands. The Kassites stormed into the central part of Mesopotamia, around Babylon (the city founded by the Amorites). They renamed Babylon Karanduniash, and built a new capitol city called Durkurigalzu. Rather than try to assimilate with the local (Sumerian) culture, the Kassites attempted to assert their own culture in Mesopotamia. However, the Kassites never controlled more than the central area around Babylon, and after a few centuries, they were swept away by a new wave of invaders, the Assyrians, who seized Babylon in 1200 B.C.E.

> **Increase Your Iraq IQ**
>
> The Kassites:
>
> ◆ **Ruled:** 1500–1200 B.C.E.
> ◆ **Origins:** Indo-European
> ◆ **Key facts:** Ruled central Mesopotamia, Hittites controlled the rest

# The Military Men Step In

The Assyrians pushed both the Kassites and Hittites aside, starting in 1200 B.C.E. and finally subdued the last Hittite strongholds around 700 B.C.E. The Assyrians gradually built an empire that included Syria, Armenia, Palestine, and Mesopotamia.

Unlike the conquerors before them, the Assyrians adopted a policy of forcible migration of the peoples they conquered. This included the peoples of the city-states in Mesopotamia, including Babylon. The Assyrian king Sargon II also forced the migration of the Hebrews from their northern kingdom of Israel, marking the first Jewish *diaspora*.

However, the Assyrians also tolerated the religious beliefs of the peoples they conquered. (The Assyrians allowed the Hebrews to maintain their religion, even when their lands were taken.) And in the case of the Babylonians, even feared the native gods. True story: The Assyrians razed Babylon and then, fearing the wrath of Babylonian god, Marduk, started rebuilding it again.

The Assyrians set up their capital at a new city, called Nineveh. Rather than destroy the Sumerian culture they conquered, they attempted to preserve it. The last great Assyrian king, Ashurbanipal, assembled a

**Desert Diction**

**Diaspora** is a term that means a scattering of people from a central place. As we see here, the Assyrians used the dispersal technique to eliminate organized resistance from conquered peoples. Many cultural groups have suffered diaspora, some never to survive it. The ancient Hebrews suffered a number of diaspora, including ones forced by the Assyrians, the Chaldeans, and the Romans.

huge library of Sumerian writings at Nineveh. The 30,000 tablets that survive are thus both an invaluable record of Sumerian culture and a testament to that culture's ability to win the respect of incoming conquerors like the Assyrians.

---

### Increase Your Iraq IQ

The Assyrians:

◆ **Ruled:** 1200–612 B.C.E.

◆ **Origin:** Semitic, from the northern parts of Mesopo-tamia

◆ **Key figures:** Sargon II, conqueror of Israel; Ashurbani-pal, creator of library at Nineveh

◆ **Claim to fame:** Development of latitude and longitude, 360 degree partition of circle, medical science, iron swords, body armor, and the battering ram

---

The Assyrians were a highly militaristic society, with the largest army in the region at the time. They developed a number of innovative weapons, and their technological advancements were significant. Despite their military and technical achievements, the Assyrians eventually succumbed to a revolt led by the city-state of Babylon, which culminated in the fall of Nineveh in 612 B.C.E.

# Babylon on the Ascent

The emergence of the Babylonian city-state heralded the start of the Neo-Babylonian, or Chaldean, period. King Nebuchadnezzar II expanded and improved Babylon (remember, the Assyrians had wrecked the place, then started to rebuild it), and conquered the southern Hebrew kingdom of Judah. They destroyed the Temple of Solomon, and deported the Jews to Babylon.

Babylon itself flourished under the Chaldean period. Nebuchadnezzar built the famous Hanging Gardens of Babylon (one of the Wonders of the Ancient World). He also built the Tower of Babel as a temple to the Babylonian god, Marduk. However, the Chaldean empire collapsed in less than a century.

**CAUTION**

**Oil Spill Ahead**

The location of the Hanging Gardens isn't certain. In fact, their existence at all is uncertain. The Babylonian records of the time do not mention the Gardens, though later Greek writings describe them in great detail. If they did exist, the Gardens did not actually "hang" but were supported on huge terraces. Supposedly, Nebuchadnezzar built the Gardens for his wife.

---

**Increase Your Iraq IQ**

The Chaldeans:

◆ **Ruled:** 612–539 B.C.E.

◆ **Origins:** Babylonian area

◆ **Key figures:** Nebuchadnezzar II

◆ **Claims to fame:** Conquest of Judea, deportation of Hebrews to Babylon, Hanging Gardens of Babylon, Tower of Babel

---

The constant attacks from the recently displaced Assyrians drained the empire. Finally, the Chaldeans succumbed to the Persians rather than yield to the ceaseless Assyrians, who had again conquered their city. The Chaldeans decided that the Persians would make a better master than the Assyrians—and they supported the Persians against the Assyrians as the Persians crossed into Mesopotamia from the East.

# The Persians—and Alexander the Great—Pass Through

In 539 B.C.E., the Persians conquered Babylon. The conquest of Mesopotamia by the Persians signaled the end of Mesopotamia as a central focus on world cultural evolution. The Persians were bent on world domination, not just control of Mesopotamia; the Greeks who in turn conquered the Persians were, in essence, marching through Mesopotamia on their way to Persia and beyond. The great Sumerian city-states became a sideshow, from that point forward, on the stage of world history.

**Desert Diction**

Satrapies are administrative regions within ancient Persian Empire. A satrap was the title of the ruler of that regional division. The Persians were able to maintain control of their far-flung empire by giving the satrap relative autonomy in his region (or "satrapy").

Cyrus the Great, from Persia, took control of the whole region by 500 B.C.E. Cyrus extended the Persian Empire from India to Macedon and Mesopotamia.

Cyrus was a devotee of the new religion of Zoroastrianism, which, as noted in Chapter 6, saw the world as an epic struggle between good and evil, light and dark. When Cyrus conquered Babylon, he freed the Jews, and encouraged them to rebuild the Temple of Solomon and worship Yahweh. (Cyrus saw the Hebrew god, Yahweh, as a "good" god.)

The Persians set up *satrapies*, or administrative regions, to rule their lands, including the territories of

Mesopotamia. Thus the region became just another department in their empire. Several of the city-states led revolts against the Persian satrapy during this time, and Persian grip on the city-states fluctuated from tight control, to loose control, to no control. Eventually, Persian authority over Mesopotamian city-states was reconsolidated by Darius the Great, in his push to extend the Persian Empire.

The Persians pushed on to Greece, were stopped there, and then came under attack themselves by the Macedonians under Alexander the Great. Steadily, Alexander pushed the Persians out of Asia Minor and Mesopotamia. Alexander crossed the Euphrates in 331 B.C.E., and entered Babylon in 330 B.C.E. Alexander continued on through Persia, Central Asia, and even into India before turning back. On his way back through Mesopotamia, when heading home, Alexander stopped off in Babylon. He fell ill, and eventually died in Babylon in 323 B.C.E.

After Alexander's death, his followers divided the empire. One of Alexander's military commanders, Seleucus, was given control of Mesopotamia, Syria, and Persia, creating the Seleucid dynasty. This empire was governed from Antioch in Syria and a new city, called Seleucia, in Mesopotamia. Seleucia and the other new power-center cities in Mesopotamia were founded by Greek and Macedonian colonists and soldiers. These colonists chose to create new cultural centers, rather than move into the Mesopotamian cities like Babylon or Nineveh.

The Seleucid Empire eventually lost control of Mesopotamia to the Parthians, who invaded from what is now Iran, around 170 B.C.E. The Parthians ruled Mesopotamia from a new city that they founded and called Ctesiphon. Ctesiphon was across the Tigris from Seleucia. This marked a physical as well as symbolic shift of power from Greek to Persian control.

---

### Increase Your Iraq IQ

The Persians and the Greeks:

◆ **Ruled:** Persians—539–331 B.C.E., Greeks/Macedonians—331–170 B.C.E.

◆ **Key figures:** Cyrus the Great, Darius the Great, Alexander the Great, Seleucus

◆ **Key events:** Cyrus liberates the Jews from Babylon, Alexander dies in Babylon, Seleucids shift power from ancient Semitic cities to new Hellenistic ones

---

# The Parthians and Sassanians Pass Through, Too

The Parthians were able to withstand Roman attacks, including a bold defeat of Crassus in 53 B.C.E. at Haran in northern Mesopotamia. The Parthians eventually gave way to the Sassanians—who, like the Parthians, also emerged from within the region we would identify as modern Iran.

The Sassanians ruled Mesopotamia from 224 C.E. to 637 C.E. Like the Parthians before them, the Sassanians resisted Roman and later Byzantine attacks on their territories, and maintained their own control over Mesopotamia. But the region still wallowed in relative obscurity during this time, as the great movements of history took place outside its borders.

---

### Increase Your Iraq IQ

The Parthians and the Sassanians:

- **Ruled:** Parthians—170–224 C.E., Sassanians—224–637 C.E.
- **Origins:** Persia
- **Key figures:** Mithradates I; Parthian; who defeated the Romans; Ardashir I, founded the Sassanian Empire

---

# The End of Ancient Mesopotamia

The Sassanid period is a fitting place to mark the end of ancient Mesopotamian history.

After the Sassanians came the Arabs, and with them a new religion called Islam. The dual impact of Arab culture and Islamic theology ultimately would define Mesopotamian (and eventually Iraqi) culture in a way that no previous invader could.

## The Least You Need to Know

- The Sumerians started it all, and laid the groundwork for civilizations that came after.
- The succeeding waves of invaders tended to adopt the Sumerian culture and religions, and discard their own.
- Each invader left a mark, and made their own contributions to the Sumerian foundations.
- Ultimately, Mesopotamia was not the place to be, and invaders began to move through the region in order to conquer other places.

# Chapter 8

# The Arab Empire and the Coming of Islam

## In This Chapter

◆ The Arab conquest and the Golden Age of Baghdad

◆ The Mongol invasions and decline of the region

◆ A series of petty dictatorships carry the day

As you learned in the last chapter, Mesopotamia was peopled by many different groups, including Sumerians, Assyrians, and Sassanians. It was only in the seventh century C.E.—thousands of years after Mesopotamian civilization first began—that Arabs began to dominate the area and introduced Islam. However, these late arrivals managed to hang on to their land and bring about dramatic changes to the area.

## The Beginning of an Era

In 638 C.E., the Sassanians fell before an Arab Muslim invasion, marking the beginning of Arab dominance of Mesopotamia and the introduction of

Islam to the region. This invasion, while it seemed like so many of the others that came before, was different in that it brought two elements to Mesopotamia that have survived to become dominant elements in modern Iraq:

**Oil Spill Ahead**

Don't confuse the words "Arab" and "Muslim." The first refers to a culture; the second refers to a religion. There are many Muslims who are not Arabs. The Muslims in Iran, Malaysia, the Philippines, Central Asia, Pakistan, China, and Turkey are not Arab.

- **The invaders were Arabs,** who gradually came to dominate the region and remain the vast majority in Iraq to this day.

- **The invaders were Muslims,** bringing Islam to the region and eventually wiping out the pantheistic (many-gods) and anthropomorphic (imposing human qualities on divine beings) religions that they found there. Islam is still the dominant religion in Iraq.

### Increase Your Iraq IQ

The word "Arab" describes the people whose culture and language derive from the Arabian peninsula, an area that borders present-day Iraq. The word "Muslim" describes an adherent of the global religion known as Islam, which traces its origin to the prophet Mohammed (570?–632). Arab groups have predominated for centuries in the region we know today as the Middle East, but not all Middle Eastern Muslims are Arabs. Modern-day Iran, most notably, is an Islamic country, but its culture descends from the Persian Empire, not from Arabia, and the language that dominates in Iran is known as Farsi, not Arabic.

# Mohammed's New Faith

To understand the Arab conquest of Mesopotamia, you have to understand a little bit about Islam, one of the world's great faiths and the youngest of the three global monotheistic (single-God) religious movements, the others being Judaism and Christianity.

"Islam" translates as "submission." "Muslim" translates as "one who submits." The emphasis in Islam is on submission to the will of a single God. The "five pillars" of this great and enduring religious tradition are the following:

- Confession of faith in God and in his prophet Mohammed ("There is no God but God; Mohammed is the Prophet of God.")

- Ritual worship

◆ Almsgiving

◆ Fasting

◆ Pilgrimage (See the notes on Mecca below.)

# What You Should Know About Mohammed

Here are 10 key points to keep in mind about Mohammed, one of the most important figures in all of human history.

◆ Mohammed was born in Mecca (in present-day Saudi Arabia) around the year 570.

◆ Prior to the rise of Mohammed in the early seventh century, Arabia had no prophetic tradition.

◆ Mohammed is believed to have experienced the first of a series of intense religious visions around the year 610 in a cave near Mecca.

◆ The Qur'an, Islam's central religious text, is held to record that encounter plus the later revelations of Mohammed, and is regarded as the final and authoritative word of Allah (God).

◆ After over a decade of preaching, Mohammed had been unsuccessful in converting Mecca to the new faith; in 622 he and his followers moved to Yathrib (later known as Medina, the "City of the Prophet"). This year is celebrated as the first year of the Muslim era.

◆ Mohammed was an extremely charismatic teacher and military leader who emphasized absolute reliance on a single God and a ban on idolatry.

◆ Mohammed continued to encounter resistance in spreading the new doctrine, but eventually mounted a military and religious campaign that succeeded in unifying Arabia behind a single faith.

◆ By the time he died in 632, Mohammed had set in motion both a great religious movement and an awe-inspiring military machine.

◆ Mohammed is regarded by Muslims as Allah's final prophet, and Islam is seen as the fulfillment of all previous human religious experience.

◆ Mohammed's birthplace, Mecca, is now regarded as the great Holy City of Islam and is the destination of annual pilgrimages by millions of Muslims.

# The Arab Conquest

In 634 C.E., an army of 18,000 Arab Muslims, under the leadership of Khalid ibn al Walied, defeated the Persians in a conflict known as the Battle of the Chains (so called because the Persian troops were supposedly chained together so they wouldn't run). The Persians outnumbered the Arabs, but they were routinely defeated by the Arab forces in several battles. Finally, in 636, the Arabs defeated the Persians at Al-Qadisiyah, near Baghdad, killing their leader in the process. With their leader dead, the Persians were unable to maintain effective resistance and collapsed. From there, the Arabs took the Persian-built city of Ctesiphon, effectively ending Persian influence in the region.

**Desert Diction**

The **Council of Ephesus** was a major council of the Christian church that took place in 431 C.E. The council condemned as heretical Nestorian Christianity, which viewed Jesus as two distinct but united individuals, one human and one divine. The council also deposed Nestorius, the leader of this sect.

At the time of the Arab conquest, the native people in Iraq were Christians and other non-Muslims. Most people were Nestorian Christians, a sect of Christianity that diverged from the Byzantine church after the *Council of Ephesus* in 431 C.E. The Nestorians had established a large cultural base in Mesopotamia by the time the Arabs moved in.

## Baghdad and the Golden Age

Arabs came to dominate the region, and the Arab Empire centered itself on the new city of Baghdad, in central Iraq. In 750 C.E., Abu al Abbas al-Mansur became the first caliph of the Abbasid dynasty. He created his capital city in Baghdad in 762.

Baghdad represented the physical and intellectual intersection of Arab, Hellenic, and Persian culture. It was located near old Babylon, but was still a new city, founded by the Arabs.

The city became a powerhouse of learning, religion, and culture. By 1000 C.E., Baghdad was regarded as the intellectual center of the world. As the seat of power for the caliphs, Baghdad was also to become the cultural capital of the Islamic world. In fact, by 800 C.E., Baghdad was second only to Constantinople in size with almost one million people living in its environs.

Due to its position astride major trade routes between Asia and Europe, Baghdad became a commercial center as well. Silk road routes passed through it, and the city reflected the impact of these Far Eastern products, philosophies, and innovations. For example, the Arabs introduced "Arabic numbers" to the Western world. In actuality, those numbers came from Indian mathematicians.

## You Do the Math

The story of a prominent Arab mathematician is a good representative case of the Arabs' role in taking the best of East and West and adding the best of their own to it. These scholars and scientists worked out of great schools that were founded in Baghdad. The leading Arab mathematician of the Golden Age who lived in Baghdad was Abu Ja'far Muhammed ibn Musa al-Khawarizmi. Al-Khawarizmi discovered some of the key concepts of what would eventually be known as algebra, and he presented the new invention of the zero to the West.

Al-Khawarizmi wrote several math texts, 10 of which survive. In one of them, he introduces the Hindu number system (including the zero) to his readers. Even al-Khawarizmi's name and book titles have been forever ensconced in modern mathematics. When western Europeans received translations of one of his math texts and saw the author's name, they called him "Algorismus" as a Latinized version of his given name. Modern mathematicians and computer programmers have retained the term "algorithm" to describe a step-by-step process for carrying out computations.

At its pinnacle, Baghdad had a teaching hospital, a university, palaces, and civil engineering projects that were the equal of any in the world at that time. In fact, many of the medical treatises written in Baghdad during this time were standard reference texts for European doctors for the next 600 years.

**Iraq Fact**

Al-Khawarizmi's major text is called "Kitab al-jabr w'al muqabalah" which translates to "Restoration and Balancing." The text outlines several of the key elements of algebra. The name "algebra" is derived from the book's title (a-jabr) itself.

**Increase Your Iraq IQ**

Another famous figure of the time, Abu Hamid al-Ghazzi was a professor at Baghdad's great religious school, the Madrasa al-Nizamiya. Al-Ghazzi wrote several religious treatises that blended orthodox and mystic Muslim religious opinions, and is considered one of the greatest reformers in Islam.

# Turn Out the Lights, the Party's Over

Despite a remarkable flowering of culture and thought in a very short period of time, Baghdad gradually saw its central role diminished in the face of new centers of

Islamic thought and commerce in places like Egypt, Persia, and Central Asia. On the religious front, a schism staggered the Abbasid Empire.

## The Shiite Schism

It started in 661 C.E., when Ali ibn Abi Talib, Mohammed's cousin, son-in-law, and the last of a group known as the Rightly Guided Caliphs, was assassinated, and a non-family member was made caliph. Ali's death triggered political and religious dissension among the Muslim faithful.

> **Increase Your Iraq IQ**
>
> The Fatimid dynasty wrested North Africa away from the Abbasids by 969 C.E. The Fatimids founded Cairo as their new capital. Cairo became a major center for learning and culture. Throughout the next 1,000 years, Egypt and Iraq competed for dominance in the region.

Debates regarding succession led to the development of the Shiites, a sect of Islam that recognizes Mohammed's descendants through Ali as the only legitimate leaders of the faithful.

# Rapid Ascent, Rapid Decline

Baghdad's control over the Empire steadily decreased. Almost as quickly as they had been conquered, the farthest reaches of the Abbasid Empire began to break away from the central authority of Baghdad.

# Turks and Persians Behind the Throne

> **Desert Diction**
>
> The **Mamluks** originally were Turkic slaves (not Arabs) who came from Central Asia. Initially they were slave-warriors and palace guards. Gradually, they became officers and even administrators in the Baghdad bureaucracy. Finally, they assumed actual control of political affairs in Baghdad, keeping the caliph as a front. As the power behind the throne, they determined who would be caliph, and what policies he would pursue.

The caliph's ability to rule independently was steadily eroded, as more and more territories challenged the political authority of Baghdad. The weakened caliph, coupled with internal dissent of the Shiites, allowed others to take a more prominent role in affairs of state. By the 830s, the court at Baghdad was really run by the *Mamluks*, who played king-makers. The Mamluks decided who would be caliph, and maintained the office to provide legitimacy for their rule. However, the caliph became a religious figurehead only.

In 945, the weakened Abbasid administration succumbed to the Buwayhids, a powerful military clan that originated in Shiite Persia (modern-day Iran). Like the Mamluks before them, the Buwayhids allowed the caliph to remain as a puppet. The Buwayhids, in turn, were superceded in 1045 by the Seljuks, a Turkic group from Central Asia. The Seljuks were Sunni Muslims, and so were welcomed in Baghdad as a preferable alternative to Shiite Buwayhids.

The Seljuk Empire lasted until 1155, and at its height, the area that was to become Iraq experienced a minor renaissance. Infrastructure was rebuilt, and science and cultural institutions were refounded in the major cities. However, the Seljuk line was not able to maintain its grip on power for very long. By 1100, local strongmen were already carving out states of their own within the Seljuk territories. Petty dictators rose and fell almost routinely. For example, between 1118 and 1194, nine Seljuk sultans ruled Baghdad. What's more, only one died of natural causes. The rest were killed by the one who came next. Gradually, the Seljuks gave way to local strongmen, who battled among themselves for supremacy in the region. But before anyone could solidify control in the region, the party was crashed by some very unwelcome guests.

## Mongol Destruction

In 1258, the first wave of Mongol invaders crossed into Mesopotamia. Led by Hulagu *Khan*, the grandson of Ghengis Khan, the Mongol horde took Baghdad and plundered the riches of the city.

The Mongol invaders weren't interested in adopting the best of local culture and learning. They were more interested in sacking and destroying ... and sack and destroy they did. They flattened the major cities they came through, and legend has it that the Khan made a mountain of skulls from the scholars and leaders of Baghdad. They even wrecked the irrigation canals and city walls. Baghdad and the region that would become Iraq were ruled by the Khan from the city of Tabriz, in modern-day Iran.

**Desert Diction**

The **Khan** was the ruler of a Mongol horde, or army. The Khan also become the political ruler of their empires.

As occupiers, the Mongols eventually converted to Islam, and they became some of its greatest proponents. As the Mongol Empire extended further and further, Islam spread as far as western China on one end and into Europe on the other.

The Mongols themselves were unable to maintain control over Mesopotamia for very long. After the death of the last great Khan, in 1355, the region fell to a local dynasty called the Jalayirids. The Jalayirids ruled until about 1400, when they in turn lost their grip on power by another invader from the East (coming out of Central Asia), whose military savagery rivaled that of the Mongols, themselves.

## A Lame Invader

A Turkic *atabeg*, or regent, named Timur, emerged from Samarkand, in modern Uzbekistan.

Timur rallied an army of his own and swept out of Central Asia into Mesopotamia, killing as he went. Timur was lame in one leg, and was known as "Timur the Lame" or "Tamerlane."

### Desert Diction

An **atabeg** was a regent who served a prince under the Mongol system of administration. The atabeg was usually in charge of a city or region that then was controlled by a prince, and ultimately, by the Khan. The atabegs had great autonomy within their own administrative control.

### Increase Your Iraq IQ

Today, the Uzbeks have a statue of Tamerlane in the center of the capital city of Tashkent, where he is a national hero ... one man's marauder is another man's savior!

In 1401, Tamerlane's armies captured Baghdad. Tamerlane made his own mountain of skulls in Baghdad, and succeeded in wiping out much of the culture that had survived the Mongol invasion a century and a half before.

Tamerlane was not a Mongol, but was a Turk. Tamerlane was also, at least on paper, a Sunni Muslim. However, he didn't do much for Islamic culture in Baghdad. Instead, he pillaged most of the cities he conquered and brought the riches and the scholars that survived the initial invasion to his capital. In fact, the city that really flourished was his capital of Samarkand, where magnificent building ensembles, caravanseries, and madrasas (Islamic schools) were built.

Tamerlane's empire was short-lived; it declined in the years after his death in 1405. Like the Mongols, long-term administration of an empire was not his goal, or his real talent.

## Local Bosses Reign for a Time

As Tamerlane's empire disintegrated, local strongmen again rose to fill the void of power in Mesopotamia. Islam took firm root, as the local people struggled to recover what had been lost or taken by the Mongols and Tamerlane. These local rulers were unable to consolidate much more than a small area or a single city. No one emerged to assume control over the whole region.

The area that would come to be called Iraq became a battleground between two neighbors: the Ottomans and the Persians, as you'll discover in the next chapter.

## The Least You Need to Know

- The Arabs brought Islam to Iraq.

- Baghdad flowered under Arab Islamic culture from 700 C.E. to about 1100 C.E.

- The Mongols and Tamerlane destroyed much of the accomplishments of the earlier Arab culture.

- The region languished under petty strongmen for centuries.

# Chapter 9

# Between a Rock and a Hard Place: The Ottomans and the Persians

## In This Chapter

♦ The conflict between Sunni and Shiite

♦ The discovery of oil and its importance to the West

♦ The origins of anti-Western bias

We've seen how two powerful influences on modern Iraq—Arabs and Islam—first appeared; how these influences overlaid an existing Mesopotamian culture that extended all the way from the ancient Sumerians; and how the flower of this cultural confluence was plucked by the Mongols, then trodden on by Tamerlane. By the start of the sixteenth century, the region was in chaos, and a series of small tyrants came and went in the confusion.

Into this mix, the Ottomans—about whom you'll be learning more in a minute—and the Persians began to fight for control of the region. The front line in this fight was the border between Ottoman-controlled, Arab territories (now called Iraq) and Persia (now called Iran). This fighting set a pattern that exists to this day: Iraq as the "bulwark" of the Arab world against the Persian world of Iran.

This parallel has deep historical resonance. Although both sides are Muslims, the Arabs are ethnically different from the Persians, and speak a different language. What's more, today most Arab Muslims are Sunni, while most Persian Muslims are Shiite. By the end of the sixteenth century, after the Persians converted to Shiism, the Arab-Persian struggle took on a Sunni-Shiite element as well. The region that became Iraq was a front-line in this struggle where Sunni and Shiite groups coexisted uneasily (as they do today). (To fast-forward just a few centuries: Remember that Saddam Hussein and his Ba'th party are Sunni Muslims, and that Sunnis constitute a powerful minority within present-day Iraq.)

In this chapter, we will look at the next important ingredients in the mix that is modern Iraq: tensions between Shiite and Sunni, the discovery of oil, and a complex series of relationships with Western powers.

# In This Corner ... the Persians

As we saw in the last chapter, the Shiite/Sunni split rocked the Abbasid Empire. As the empire began to weaken, outlying territories broke away from Baghdad's central control; the Shiites concentrated in Persia and southern Mesopotamia. The Sunni were just about everywhere else in the Islamic world.

When Tamerlane left, anarchy gripped the region. Other Turkmish groups moved into the vacuum left and took control of the region in 1508. These groups were known as the Safavids, and they were Shiite Muslims. They invaded, in part, because the two Holiest Cities of the Shiites, An Najaf and Karbala, are in modern Iraq.

Again: Most of the population of southern Mesopotamia was (and still is) Shiite. The neighboring Ottomans, however, were Sunni Muslims, and they were not happy about the prospect of a new Shiite state on their doorstep.

# And in This Corner ... the Ottomans

The Ottomans were a Turkic people who created an empire that emerged from the Byzantine Empire—the old eastern half of the Roman Empire. Initially Christian, the Byzantine Empire eventually gave way to Islamic forces and became the Ottoman Empire. The Ottomans saw no choice but to invade in order to repel the Persian (Shiite) threat to their Turkish (Sunni) Empire.

The Ottomans began to invade from the north and east, and eventually they took control from the Persians by 1534, led at that time by Sultan Sulyeman the Great. The Ottomans held a tenuous control of the region that would become Iraq for the next 100 years. In 1623, the Persians were able to capture Baghdad. The Ottomans drove the Persians out for good in 1638, led by Sultan Murad IV. They retained control of the region until World War I.

The fighting between the Ottomans and the Persians spread to the Sunni population in the northern part of modern Iraq, and to the Shiite population in southern Iraq. Whenever the Persians were in control, things were good for the Iraqi Shiites. When the Ottomans were in charge, things were good for the Iraqi Sunni, and lousy for the Shiites.

Notice anything interesting here? The bloody Ottoman/Persian conflicts of this era presaged both the bitter Iran-Iraq war of the 1980s … and the pattern of contemporary rule in Iraq. The (minority) Sunnis have controlled the Iraqi government in modern times, and have consistently oppressed the Shiites.

> ### Increase Your Iraq IQ
>
> The Ottoman Empire lasted from 1301 until 1918. The Ottomans renamed the Byzantine capital of Constantinople as Istanbul when they conquered it in 1453. They created an Islamic empire that stretched across the Bosporus strait into southeastern Europe (stopping at Vienna along the Danube River), and across the Middle East, eventually encompassing Mesopotamia (present-day Iraq) and stopping at Persia (present-day Iran).

# Occupying Powers and All That

So it was that the Sunnis living in the territory around Baghdad, in the center of what would soon be known as Iraq, held authority over the Shiites in the south and the Kurds (and rural Assyrians) in the north.

These Sunni found themselves running the show.

The Sunni didn't have the blessing of either the Shiites or the Kurds to be in charge, but they did have the backing of a powerful foreign occupying power—in this case, the Ottomans. Later on, the British would play a similar role in maintaining Sunni authority.

> ### CAUTION Oil Spill Ahead
>
> It's easy to get confused about minorities and majorities in the Middle East. Remember that Sunni Muslims are, and have historically been, the majority group throughout the Arab world … but they are and have been for centuries a powerful *minority* in Iraq. Iraq's dominant Sunni Muslims have been compared (by Shiite Muslims, it's worth noting) to white South Africans in the apartheid period.

# Ottoman Control, Kind Of

It's important not be confused into thinking the Ottomans had an iron grip on the region. They ruled loosely for most of the period up through 1830, when they finally solidified their hold over the region under a string of more able (and less corrupt) administrators.

For most of their time in Mesopotamia, the Ottomans were fighting in Europe and against the Persians, and they devoted little time and attention to internal improvements to the part of the region that would become Iraq. There were periods under certain *sultans* where the region would get a greater-than-normal share of attention, but for the most part the old cities languished, and power shifted to the rural tribal leaders.

The Ottomans divided the ancient region of Mesopotamia into three administrative districts, called vilayets. The vilayets were Mosul in the north, Baghdad in the middle, and Basra in the south. Mosul had a majority of Kurds, and along with Baghdad was a Sunni region; Basra was Shiite. Taken together, these three vilayets are the forerunner to modern Iraq.

**Desert Diction**

A **sultan** was a ruler in the Ottoman Empire. The sultans assumed political authority over their territories, unlike the Abbasid caliphs who claimed both religious and secular authority.

**Iraq Fact**

Midhat Pasha was a powerful Turkish figure of the nineteenth century. Having served effectively as the Ottoman governor of Bulgaria from 1864 to 1869, he was transferred to Baghdad. After three years, Midhat left Baghdad and rose to a position of prominence within the Ottoman Empire, leading a reform-driven revolution in 1876. He was eventually exiled, sent to prison, and killed.

# The Ottomans Settle In

From 1750 to 1830, the Mamluks reemerged in the south, and established a stable government in the Basra and Baghdad vilayets. (Remember that the Mamluks were the king-makers whose maneuverings at court determined who would be the next caliph.) The Mamluks were able to check the tribal chieftains, but they were not able to extend their control further northward, toward Kurdish territory.

The Ottomans put their foot down in 1831, and pulled the three vilayets together under central control. However, they were not able to exercise real governance until 1869, when Midhat Pasha took control. During his three-year reign, he cleaned up Baghdad, repaired infrastructure, and pacified the tribal chieftains. Midhat also introduced more persistent taxation on the region. (Up to then, the whole idea of taxation had been a hit-or-miss proposition once you got outside the walls of a city.)

# The Rise of Arab Nationalism

The firmer Ottoman grip on the province of Iraq resulted in growing Arab resentment toward the Turkish rulers.

The Arab Iraqi elites in the cities began to identify themselves as Arabs first—in contrast to the Ottomans who were Turkish, and the Persians who were, well, Persian ... and Shiite to boot. These tribal leaders weren't able to generate a broad sense of Arab nationalism in Iraq, but the concentrated populations in the cities began to yield a new and influential brand of resentment against foreigners ... a resentment deeply connected to one's (Sunni) Arab identity.

These elites didn't lead a popular rebellion against the Ottomans. This was due mainly to the fact that Ottoman authority over the region was still, for many people, a matter of abstract, and not particularly meaningful, political theory—rather than an important fact of everyday life.

The Ottomans, however, were not the only empire seeing to their interests in the region. There was another group of foreigners to contend with; the British invaded during World War I as part of their conflict with the Ottomans.

> **Increase Your Iraq IQ**
>
> The forerunners to the Arab nationalists (who emerged in the 1930s) in the province of Iraq were wealthy urban merchants, scholars, and religious leaders. It was the members of these elites who chafed most at the presence of Ottoman (and later, British) outsiders who "administered" their lands.

## Superpowers Screw Up in Iraq: The Beginning of a Very Long Story

One of the most striking themes of life in post-Ottoman Iraq is the extraordinary series of mistakes and miscalculations made by Western superpowers seeking power and influence in the region without concern for (or knowledge of) ancient social groups and institutions. These errors compounded a steadily more irreparable "disconnect" between local peoples and the Western governments. This is the Big Theme known as the "Compound Error." We will look at this Big Theme more in Chapter 10.

The destabilizing pattern got its start under the British in the early part of the twentieth century, who viewed Iraq essentially as a geographic means to an end: the development of a land route to India. The United States would make similarly shortsighted mistakes as the years progressed, and a rising tide of Iraqi resentment against the West would be the result.

# Enter the Bulldog

By the start of the twentieth century, the Ottoman Empire was failing—and was widely known as the "Sick Man of Europe." European powers, notably Britain and Germany, began to covet Ottoman holdings. Along with the Ottoman administrators, the British began to make their presence felt in Iraq, much to the dismay of the budding Arab nationalists.

Imperial Britain was interested in protecting the jewel in its crown: India. The most obvious hurdle, beyond the sheer distance between London and Bombay, was the fact that there was no easy land route to India from Britain.

The British had set up a steamship company in 1861 that ran from the Gulf up the Shatt-al-Arab to Basra. This company would be able to transfer people and material more easily across Mesopotamia to Iran, Afghanistan, and ultimately to India.

Further, the British wanted to maintain a secure air route to India, and they needed secure refueling stops in the Middle East. Remember that airplanes in the early part of the twentieth century navigated more by ground landmarks, and flew much shorter distances between refueling stops.

## England and Germany: The Major-Power Shuffle

The British also had to contend with the Germans, who were pushing their own agenda in Iraq. The Germans wanted to build a railroad from Berlin to Baghdad that would have given Germany the commercial and strategic advantage in the region. The Germans succeeded in getting a concession from the Ottomans in 1899 to build a railroad from Konya in modern Turkey, to Baghdad. They were able to extend this concession from Baghdad to Basra by 1902. Their ultimate goal was to run the railway all the way to the Persian Gulf port of Kuwait.

The British tried to block this deal, but could do little to prevent it in the end. Ultimately, the British simply worked around the official Ottoman concession to Germany; they struck treaties with the tribal chieftains in Basra vilayet with an eye toward keeping their own steamship route open … and slowing down German rail construction.

# Black Gold: The Beginning of the Oil Economy

Then there came a fateful twist in the story. It was black and it oozed from the ground.

The British realized, around the turn of the century, that there were extensive oil deposits in the region, and their interest in the area duly increased. Over time, the problem of controlling oil reserves became as important as, if not more important than, the problem of maintaining a link to India. The problem of building good relations with the people actually living in the region, however, never seemed to rise very high on the list of priorities.

In 1901, the British obtained a concession from the Ottomans to take oil from Ottoman territories. Under the terms of the concession agreement, the British exacted favorable terms from the Ottomans for exporting the oil they took from the region. In 1912, the British created the Turkish Petroleum Company to pump oil in the Ottoman territories (including the province of Iraq), and the Anglo-Persian Oil Company to extract oil from modern-day Iran.

**Iraq Fact**

Britain has no oil of its own, and its new industries were demanding more and more of the stuff. In addition, the new Lord of the Admiralty, Winston Churchill, decided that the Royal Navy should use oil in its ships instead of coal, so oil suddenly became a key interest of the British.

These two companies quickly built up oil fields and refineries in the region. The main production areas were in modern-day Iran, but oil was also discovered around Mosul, in northern modern-day Iraq.

British oil concessions with the Ottomans and others in the Middle East typically included an agreement that Britain would provide military protection for the sheikhdoms that signed on. Of course, protecting the local kingdoms also meant protecting British investments there, so the military protection was an easy commitment to make. Even before the military protocol had been signed, Britain had had no problem sending in troops when its interests were threatened in the Middle East.

### Increase Your Iraq IQ

The sequence of events in oil concession agreements between Arab Gulf states in British "protection" usually followed a predictable order. First, there was a commercial agreement between the oil concern in question and the head of state; then there was a political agreement between British government and the oil firm, accompanied by an endorsement of the whole setup confirmed, in writing, to British authorities by the head of state. Many rulers in the region expanded their authority, power, and influence by means of this kind of military/governmental/commercial mating dance in the early part of the twentieth century.

# The Great War Brings a New Boss

The practice of Western military intervention in the Middle East to ensure the steady flow of oil to the West did not start in 1990. The British patented the idea 76 years before the Americans perfected it.

The Ottoman Empire entered World War I as an ally of Germany and Austria-Hungary in 1914. The British were deeply concerned by this development, because their Turkish Petroleum Company holdings were now in enemy territory. In response, the British landed a division of troops from Iran and India in the southern part of Iraq, at al-Faw on the Persian Gulf. This division marched north up the Shatt-al-Arab, reaching Basra in November 1914. Despite intense Ottoman resistance, the British division managed to reach Baghdad by March 1917.

Even after the armistice between the British and Ottomans was signed in October 1918, the British continued their expansion northward toward the oil-rich areas around Mosul, eventually occupying that city in November 1918. From that point forward, the Ottomans ceased to be the authority in Iraq.

After 500 years of occasionally distracted dominance in Iraq, the Ottomans were out, and Britain was in. The question was, how would this latest outsider respond to the emerging challenges of the Arab world?

# The British Stoke the Fires

In the next chapter, we'll look in depth at the nature and consequences of the British military intervention in Iraq, and we'll see how British imperial policies in Iraq helped to foster a growing Arab nationalism and an increasingly anti-Western outlook. Both developments, of course, would continue to play out for decades—intensified, not infrequently, by Western bluster and shortsightedness: what I call the "Compound Error."

## The Least You Need to Know

- ◆ The Ottomans and the Persians battled for control over Mesopotamia. The region was the border between the Arab and Persian worlds, and the Sunni and Shiite sects of Islam.

- ◆ Ottoman control over the region was never very strong. The old cities in the region lost their power. Most of the authority devolved to regional tribal chieftains.

◆ As the Ottoman Empire weakened (the infamous "Sick Man of Europe"), Britain and Germany began to extend their imperial reach into the region.

◆ The British (and other West European powers and eventually the United States) obtained oil concessions and set up oil companies in the region to export the oil at very favorable terms.

◆ The British took over from the Ottomans at the end of World War I and started a cycle of mistakes that would intensify Arab nationalism and anti-Western feeling for decades to come.

# Chapter 10

# Lines on a Map

## In This Chapter

♦ World War I

♦ The birth of the modern state of Iraq

♦ The British tend to their interests

The story of Western colonialism and imperialism in Asia, Africa, the Middle East, and the Americas is long and sordid. It involved Western powers such as Britain, France, and the United States taking economic and political control over weaker or underdeveloped countries in order to exploit their natural resources. Such practices had profound, and often negative, impacts on the weaker countries, many of which haven't fully recovered to this day.

We'll only be touching on a small part of the wretched history of imperialism by taking a look at how the British consolidated their power in the soon-to-be-founded state of Iraq.

## British Imperialism

British imperialism in Iraq accelerated three important processes that would play out for decades to come:

 ◆ Sunni control over the territory now called Iraq—despite the Shiite majority within the new country's borders

 ◆ Increasing local Iraqi resistance to non-Iraqi rulers placed over them

 ◆ The emergence of increasingly violent anti-Western sentiment

# World War I

In the last chapter, we saw how the British became interested in Mesopotamia, first as a link in their communications chain to India, and then as a source of newly important oil.

However, things got messy for the Brits when the Ottomans entered World War I on the German side. The Turkish Oil Company holdings in Mesopotamia were immediately threatened by the Ottoman action. In response, the British moved troops into the region to protect their oil operations and their link to India.

The military action in the province of Iraq was fierce. In 1916, the Ottomans captured an entire British unit after a bloody 140-day siege at Al Kut.

General Maude, who led the British troops, declared that the British would support Arab independence after the end of the war, in return for their support against the Ottomans during the war. The Arabs agreed, throwing their support behind the British to fight off the Ottomans who ruled over them. The British regrouped and took Baghdad and Mosul by 1918.

## Lawrence and the Arabs

British military fortunes were aided by the efforts of T. E. Lawrence, also known as Lawrence of Arabia, who organized Arab tribal fighters into an effective force. In 1918, Lawrence and his Arab allies succeeded in capturing Damascus before the British army even got there.

An idealistic and energetic man in his 20s, Lawrence embodied the promise of British imperial support to the Arabs in the region. Like the Arabs, he grew disillusioned when the British did not make good on their promises of Arab independence after the Great War ended. The concept of "Arabism" was a relatively recent invention of the late nineteenth and early twentieth centuries, one that paralleled the emergence of other national identities. The British appealed to this sense of being "Arab" to help rally support against the Germans.

> **Increase Your Iraq IQ**
>
> Thomas Edward Lawrence (1888–1935) was a British Military Intelligence Service officer stationed in Cairo at the start of World War I. Lawrence cultivated a strong bond with Prince Faisal (later King Faisal of Iraq), a member of a powerful Hashemite family. During the war, Lawrence organized and fought alongside these Arab allies against the Ottoman armies in the region. After the war, Lawrence remained in the region, in the Middle East division of the British Colonial Office. Disillusioned when the British did not grant independence to their former Arab allies, Lawrence resigned his commission and spent the next few years out of the spotlight. Probably looking for new adventures, he enlisted in the Royal Air Force under an assumed name in 1925. After his discharge, he died in a motorcycle accident in England in 1935. His story was the basis of a number of popular works, including the Oscar-winning film *Lawrence of Arabia*.

# Mandate, Not Independence

At the end of World War I, the Ottoman Empire was defeated, and the British were in control of former Ottoman holdings in the Middle East. In Iraq, British imperial troops occupied the main cities of Basra, Baghdad, and Mosul (these three cities were the capitals for the Ottoman valiyets that bore their names).

After the Treaty of Versailles that ended World War I was signed, the future of the Middle East (including Iraq) was settled at the San Remo Conference. The League of Nations took over the administration of the territories of the defeated German and the Ottoman Empires. These territories were called Mandates, and were placed under the control of a European ally until the country could govern independently.

## Europeans Divide the Spoils and Draw (Dumb) Borders

The French got control of what was soon to be called Syria, while the British got Palestine, Saudi Arabia, and Iraq. They already had control of Persia (later known as Iran).

The borders of these regions were drawn in blissful ignorance of local realities. The Europeans drew straight lines for most of the boundaries, assuming that the deserts they were drawn through were unpopulated. They were wrong on that account, and the new countries were immediately saddled with tribal strife as members of the same clan were divided by national boundaries, while rival clans were joined within the same region.

The boundaries that were drawn for Iraq were particularly disruptive of traditional trading and tribal patterns. To the south, the border between Saudi Arabia, Kuwait, and Iraq was a series of straight lines. The border included a diamond-shaped "Neutral Zone" between Saudi Arabia and Iraq, and an almost diamond-shaped Kuwait next to that.

The line between Iraq and Kuwait separated the city of Basra from its long-time trading partner, the coastal city of Kuwait (for which the new country of Kuwait was named). Furthermore, the Neutral Zone became a source of friction over potential oil reserves there. Further northward, the boundary between Saudi Arabia and Iraq sliced through the old Baghdad vilayet, and divided traditional tribal territories with an international border.

> **Superpowers Screw Up in Iraq:** If the British had set up a formal committee to find a mistake that would amplify their initial alienating approach to Iraq—treating it, in essence, as a convenient doorway to India—that committee couldn't have come up with a more high-handed alternative than the British policy choices that immediately followed World War I. Arab leaders were denied the independence they had been promised as incentive to fight alongside British forces, and borderlines that ignored social and cultural were instituted. As a result, local aspirations and cultural allegiances were effectively ignored.

The British also cobbled together the Sunni Baghdad vilayet and Shiite Basra vilayet. At first, the Mosul vilayet was not part of Iraq—but the British became alarmed by Turkey's claims to the Mosul vilayet—Turkey had recently been formed from the remains of the Ottoman Empire—and so included Mosul in the Iraq Mandate by 1925. The boundaries, ethnic, and religious makeup of modern Iraq was set.

The Iraqis received "Class A" Mandate status according to Article 22 of the League of Nations Covenant, which meant that it was intended to become an independent country in a few years' time.

# Iraqi Reaction

The Iraqi leadership—the wealthy elites in the cities, who were Ottomans (non-Arab), and the tribal leaders—who were Arab, were dismayed by the broken promises of the British. They had expected that the 1919 Paris Peace Conference that resulted in the Treaty of Versailles would also result in the immediate creation of independent Arab states. Instead, the Paris Peace Conference left it to a later conference, at San Remo, to define borders of the Arab Mandates that would eventually become modern states.

The British appointed Sir Percy Cox to serve as high commissioner, or leader, of the Iraq Mandate, and he was assisted by Colonel Arnold Talbot Wilson. Cox was soon embroiled in all the local problems of the Iraqi state, from infrastructure repair to tribal conflict. Cox eventually was dispatched to Iran from 1918 to 1920, leaving Wilson in charge. Wilson originally came from India's imperial administration, and he promoted a number of Indians to responsible positions in the Iraqi government. This was a foolish and high-handed choice that further alienated the Iraqis.

**Iraq Fact**

Prince Faisal, one of the Hashemite Arab heroes of the rebellion against the Ottomans, attended the Conference expecting to participate in the planning of Arab independence. Instead, Faisal was largely ignored.

> **Superpowers Screw Up in Iraq:** The British failed to incorporate local Iraqi elites into their new government in Iraq. Instead, they imported still more foreigners (this time Indians) to assume roles in the new bureaucracy. Needless to say, this move did nothing to endear the British commissioners to the local population.

The Mandate was strained from the beginning. A British officer, for instance, was ambushed and killed in the Shiite Holy City of An Najaf, leading to bloody reprisals.

# Repercussions

The Iraq Mandate was finalized at the San Remo Conference, on April 25, 1920. In July 1920, the local Iraqi nationalist leadership learned of the Mandate's final adoption, and they attacked the British troops still stationed in Iraq.

**Desert Diction**

The **Rebellion of July 1920** was an important event in modern Iraqi history. The British ultimately put down the rebellion, but the uprising featured Sunni and Shiite leaders, and cities and rural dwellers, working together against the occupying British.

Led by secret societies made up of scholars, religious leaders, and merchants, the *Rebellion of July 1920* started in Mosul and soon spread across the territory.

The rebellion failed, but that was almost beside the point. The new state was bringing tribal leaders together, but hardly in the way the British had hoped.

# The British Abandon the Mandate

After the Rebellion, the British decided, for both logistical and financial reasons, that the Mandate period had to end, and that the time had come for Iraq to be in charge of its own affairs. (In name, at least. Britain still hoped to be able to control Iraqi policy from behind the scenes.)

---

### Increase Your Iraq IQ

Hussein ibn Ali (not related to Saddam) was sharif of Mecca. The sharif was considered to be the descendent of Mohammed, and his family was powerful and well respected in the hijaz (the area that would later become part of Saudi Arabia). Hussein's son, Faisal, was a prince alongside Lawrence during the march into Damascus. This same Faisal later became King of Syria (for a year) and then King of Iraq. Faisal's son Ghazi and his son Faisal II also ruled in Iraq.

---

To lead the new nation, the British selected Prince Faisal, the friendly son of the Hashemite Hussein ibn Ali. Prince Faisal had become King Faisal of Syria in 1920, but was removed from that role by the French when they assumed control of the Syria Mandate in 1920. The British plucked Faisal off the bench, and put him in charge of Iraq in 1921. The British arranged a plebiscite, with only one question on the ballot; it resulted in Faisal's "election," with 96 percent of the vote.

**Desert Diction**

The **Hashemite** royal family installed in Iraq was, not surprisingly, pro-British. The family included the sharif of Mecca, and claimed to be descended from Mohammed. The British assumed, somewhat naively, that this fact would somehow legitimize the monarchy. However, the Hashemite kings not Iraqi, and this fact alone doomed the monarchy from the start.

While the Hashemite claims of descent from Mohammed probably helped with the Sunni portion of the population, they didn't inspire allegiance from the Shiite majority in Iraq, who did not recognize the authority of the sharif of Mecca, anyway. The British, however, decided that it was more important to appeal to the Sunnis.

The new Hashemite monarchy immediately entered into a treaty with Britain that guaranteed the monarchy would "consult" with the British on foreign affairs, and any affairs that related to British oil concessions.

# The British Make a Fateful Choice

When the British determined to set up a king in Iraq, they also decided to prop him up with a locally recruited army, rather then rely on British imperial troops. This decision was critical, as the Iraqi army became a vital force in the decades leading up to the overthrow of the Iraqi monarchy (see Chapter 13).

In an attempt to accommodate the Sunni majorities in the countries surrounding the new Iraq (every other Arab country and Turkey), the British set up Sunnis in leadership positions in the army and government bureaucracy. The Shiites, the majority in the new state of Iraq, made up the rank and file of the army—but they were commanded by Sunnis.

Guiding principle: The British weren't particularly big on listening or inclusiveness at this point in their imperial history.

> **Superpowers Screw Up in Iraq:** The British didn't bother to discuss important matters with affected local Arab leaders when Iraq was formed. Instead, the British allied themselves to the old Ottoman elites who remained in the area. This disregard for local Arab desires eventually contributed to open rebellions against Britain and the governments it maneuvered into place in Iraq.

The army would prove to be a critical force in modern Iraq. First, the new army officer corps provided stability to the (foreign) monarch the British selected. (Later in Iraqi history, however, the military would provide the leaders of a series of coups.)

**Iraq Fact**

The British took care not to fully enfranchise the Shiite majority. The British figured that a Sunni-controlled state was more palatable to Iraq's neighbors, and would ultimately support the uninterrupted flow of oil.

# Faisal's Uneasy Rule

King Faisal ibn Hussein I ruled from 1921 to 1933. As you might imagine, Faisal suffered from a chronic legitimacy problem. He was not granted full authority (the British also created a national parliament), he was not Iraqi, and he was considered (with some justification) to be a British puppet. Faisal's regime was wracked by outside pressures from Turkey (still coveting Mosul) and internal resistance from tribal leaders who had never really been totally subdued during or after World War I. (Remember that during the Ottoman period, the tribal leaders were essentially left to their own devices.)

The treaty that Faisal signed with the British basically dictated that Iraq would remain economically and politically dependent on Britain. The treaty also earned the disdain of the Iraqi elites, who considered their leadership to be traitors to the Iraqi nationalist cause.

# Leaving the Kurds Out in the Cold

Flashback time: During World War I, British victory in the Middle East was far from certain, and British policy makers were looking for support wherever they could find it. The British had told the Kurds that they would get Mosul vilayet as part of an independent Kurdish state.

However, once oil was discovered in the Mosul area, and with the Turks threatening the Mosul vilayet from the north, the British incorporated Mosul into the new Iraqi state in 1925.

> **Superpowers Screw Up in Iraq:** In yet another compound error, the British made conflicting promises that could never be honored. During the height of the fighting in World War I, the British had promised the Kurds that they would have an independent state in return for their support against the Ottomans. However, the British had also promised the Arabs that they would gain their independence. It was, of course, impossible to give the same land to two different groups of people.

The Kurds were left out in the cold, and were denied their independence. Indeed, the disgruntled Kurdish minority found itself subject to a new (and utterly alien) monarchy.

The Kurds found themselves spread between Iran, Iraq, and Turkey, with no homeland of their own. This "solution" was to have profound consequences for modern Iraq.

Including Mosul meant oil wealth for the Iraqi state, but it also meant a large group of angry Kurds inside Iraq's borders. This situation further necessitated a powerful domestic (Sunni-led) army to help keep the country together.

# Leaving the Assyrians Out in the Cold, Too

Like the Kurds, the Assyrians in northwest Iraq had been promised independence if they supported the British against the Ottomans. The Assyrians were Christians, and because of this, the British assumed that they were somehow superior to the Muslim Iraqis.

The Assyrians were formed into separate army units and allowed to keep their weapons after the British dissolved the old Iraqi *levies* in place of the new Iraqi army. Assyrians fleeing from a brutal Turkish regime were given lands in the historic Kurdish homeland to settle on. The Assyrians, armed and hostile to the Kurds, relied on the British to help them gain their own homeland. However, like the Kurds, the Assyrians were shut out during the country-creating San Remo Conference.

**Desert Diction**

**Levies** were indigenous troops considered part of the British armed forces. The levies were not considered as fully skilled as their British counterparts.

# Iraq and a Hard Place

It all added up to a nearly impossible-to-manage domestic political situation.

Faisal I did his best to moderate between British demands and local realities. He was mindful of how the French had tossed him out of Syria, and he wanted to stay in power in Iraq as long as possible. He made sure the British wishes were carried out, and that the oil kept flowing. The nationalists were too busy competing amongst themselves for power to mount effective resistance to the monarchy.

The treaty with Britain called for a nationally elected assembly, a first for Iraq. The elections were held, and the National Assembly convened in 1925. As it turned out, the Sunnis and some Kurds held authority in the executive branch and the army, while the Shiite tribal leaders held power in the National Assembly. As a practical matter, the National Assembly enacted laws that did little more than create prolonged, regional debates.

The British maintained their control through the divide and conquer policy: a semi-strong monarch, an ineffective parliament, and internal power struggles among the potential opposition. While this policy might have appeared to make sense at the time, it didn't address the growing resentment of the British role in Iraq.

# Independence, at Last

After years of lobbying and negotiations between the British and the Iraqi monarchy, Iraq was finally admitted to the League of Nations on October 13, 1932, as a fully independent nation. Of course, the British still had a stranglehold on the economy and the political organization of the state, but Iraq had won its place in the community of nations.

In 1933, however, the picture changed dramatically. The pro-British Faisal I died, and his son, Ghazi ibn Faisal, an Arab nationalist and anti-British, took the throne. Ghazi was an adherent of pan-Arabism (discussed in Chapter 1), and he favored an alliance of Arab countries. The new king signed a nonaggression treaty with Saudi Arabia in 1936. (Remember that Ghazi's family was related to the sharifs of Mecca, so the agreement with Saudi Arabia was easily signed.)

Even Ghazi's Arab nationalism didn't save him from the same illegitimacy that haunted his father's regime. In fact, Ghazi continued his father's practice of making decisions behind closed doors. Rather then reach out to the local elites, he excluded them from policy making.

# The First Coup

Ultimately, Ghazi's regime was rocked by a *coup d'e'tat* (Iraq's first of many) in 1936. The army officers, led by Bakr al Sidqi, staged the coup that put in place a coalition government that included Kurdish and Shiite leaders, along with the Sunni elites.

Ghazi had no choice but to accept the new government in order to keep his throne. This coalition government was the first truly pluralist government in Iraq. It wasn't popularly elected, but it did include the main constituencies that comprised the new state. The post-coup coalition had two factions: the Shiite and Kurdish leaders who wanted to focus on internal reforms to land ownership and laws, and the military leaders, who wanted to expand the power of Iraq. There were no pan-Arabs in the new government to argue for brotherhood with fellow Arab states.

The coalition government reached a treaty with Iran that recognized the border between Iran and Iraq to be the middle of the Shatt-al-Arab channel. Up to that point, the border was the Iranian shore, an arrangement that had given Iraq at least nominal control of the waterway.

The coalition didn't survive very long. The Shiite leadership simply could not tolerate Sidqi's policies, and eventually he was assassinated by a group of army officers in 1937. The new nationalist government also made plans for the first Iraqi invasion of Kuwait in 1939. The Iraqi leadership saw Kuwait as a former province of Iraq—even though the British

**Desert Diction**

Coup d'e'tat is French for "state stroke." A coup, or change of government, is initiated by a small group and almost always involves military officers. This small group suddenly takes power, displaying and using enough force to remove (usually kill or exile) the current leaders, and inserts a new leader instead. Coups occur by surprise; coup leaders don't consult with the general population before taking power.

had created an independent monarchy there as well. In the Ottoman days, the region had been closely connected with the Basra vilayet, and the Iraqi nationalists felt that the British had unjustly withheld Kuwait from their new state.

The Ghazi regime was preparing the invasion of Kuwait when the king was killed in a car accident. The invasion was postponed in the confusion, and the plans were dropped altogether when World War II broke out.

## The Least You Need to Know

- ◆ The British established a Mandate in Iraq following World War I to maintain control of the oil in the region.

- ◆ The British withdrew from the Mandate in a few years' time; formal independence for Iraq, however, did not come about until 1932.

- ◆ The British set up a non-Iraqi Sunni monarch in Iraq, with a weak national assembly to check his power.

- ◆ The monarchy and the post-coup government took a decidedly anti-British bias in the 1930s.

- ◆ The British intervened in Iraq when it suited them to safeguard their oil interests.

# Part 3

# The Rise of Saddam

What made Saddam Hussein's reign possible? The answer involves at least a century of global conflict, superpower diplomacy, ancient rivalry, and modern geopolitics. (There are some disagreements about oil along the way, too.)

In this part, you'll get an introduction to the world that made Saddam possible—and get an understanding of the man himself.

# West Is West: The British and the Americans

## In This Chapter

- ◆ The errors and weakness of the pro-British regime in Iraq
- ◆ The rise of anti-British political and revolutionary groups
- ◆ The push to keep more of the oil riches in Iraq
- ◆ The Americans step in

Nationalism can take odd forms in a newborn country whose borders are determined by centuries of overseers from other lands, and whose residents are long-antagonistic groups deeply suspicious of one another even at the best of times.

In this chapter, the uneasy balancing act that is modern Iraq comes into clearer view ... as does a deeper understanding of its steadily intensifying hostility toward the West.

# Arab Nationalism: Convenient to the West (for a Minute)

As we saw in Chapter 10, the quickening fire of Arab nationalism helped Lawrence of Arabia rally an Arab army to the British cause in World War I, when the British promised Arab independence in return for Arab military support.

In the end, however, the British did *not* deliver the independence they had promised. At the end of World War I, England was triumphant, but the people of the Middle East were still being ruled by outsiders.

The failure by the British to follow through quickly on the expectations of independence they had manipulated during World War I was among the most serious of their errors during the period. This failure, in fact, was one of the chief reasons that British policy alienated Arab nationalists in the period following World War I.

Western mistakes in the Middle East in general, and in Iraq in particular, were starting to gather a kind of cumulative force. The errors were a little bit like the old Bill Cosby routine about unpaid parking tickets: Why pay them when you can shove them in the glove compartment so they can rise in value, like savings bonds?

In this case, the escalating "value" of Western errors in the region could eventually be calculated in lost diplomatic opportunities, the alienation of key Iraqi elites, and (scariest of all) a tilt toward Hitler.

The foundation for an epic "disconnect" was being laid.

# Another War, a Different Attitude

By the beginning of World War II, a coalition government had taken control in Iraq. It was led by Premier (and Army General) Nuri as-Said.

**Iraq Fact**

Eventually, Arab nationalists in Iraq came to see the objective of getting the British out of the Middle East as similar to the earlier effort to get the Ottomans out of the region.

This coalition was the first-ever governing combination of the three groups that constitute the modern state of Iraq. There were Shiite tribal leaders, Sunni officers and merchants, and Kurd leaders in the coalition.

In March 1940, though, Said's government was replaced through election by a stronger Arab nationalist coalition led by the new premier, Rashid Ali al-Gailani. Gailani was one of an emerging group of nationalists dedicated to an independent Arab nation … and to getting the British out of the region.

As a result, Gailani's government immediately adopted an anti-British stance, and stopped implementing the full terms of the 1930 Anglo-Iraqi friendship treaty.

## Iraq Defies the British

The British pressed Gailani's government to fulfill the terms of the alliance treaty. In response to this affront to their national independence, the Iraqi military leadership (made up of Sunnis, and many Arab nationalists) revolted April 30, 1941.

The army leadership installed Gailani as the head of a new regime that was now openly pro-Axis, and defiantly anti-British. Gailani then alarmed the British by trying to impose limits on British troop movements inside Iraq. (From the nationalist Iraqi point of view, of course, limiting the troop movements of a foreign army stationed inside one's own borders seemed a perfectly appropriate exercise of national sovereignty.)

> **Superpowers Screw Up in Iraq:** The mistakes that compounded after World War I, including the failure to deliver quickly on expectations of independence, contributed to the rise of Iraqi nationalism. That nationalism, in turn, led to a decidedly pro-Axis government in Iraq at the start of World War II. The British were faced with the same problems they had encountered in Iraq in World War I: a hostile government threatening both the flow of oil and communications with India.

# The Bulldog Barks

Britain responded to Iraqi resistance in the same way it had during World War I: British troops from Iran and India were dispatched to Iraq.

They arrived at Basra, and on May 2, 1941, war broke out between British and Iraqi forces. In a remarkably quick capitulation, the Iraqis surrendered on May 31, 1941, just four weeks after the fighting began. (Sound familiar?)

Compounding a by-now familiar error, the British perpetuated a local government that was not led by locals. Instead, the British continued to throw their weight behind a Hashemite, non-Iraqi, monarch whose biggest political handicap, among a torrent of competing handicaps, was probably his age. (More on that in a moment.)

---

**Increase Your Iraq IQ**

On June 1, 1941, in the aftermath of the British victory, a campaign of terror by Iraqi "soldiers and civilians" was unleashed against a small delegation of Jews who had journeyed to Baghdad to greet the regent there. The violence followed an abortive attempt by one Yunis Al Sabawi, a Nazi sympathizer, to slaughter all Jews in central Iraq. (He was deported before he could carry out the plan.)

The spasm of violence was part of a two-day descent into chaos now known in Iraq as the *Farhud* (dangerous collapse of order).

## A Foreign Monarchy

Remember, the Hashemite royal family installed in Iraq when the British abandoned the Mandate was, not surprisingly, pro-British. However, the Hashemite kings were Saudi, not Iraqi, and this fact alone doomed the monarchy from the start.

Look once again at the situation the British had engineered: An artificial country found itself with artificial leadership imposed from the outside—leadership incapable of commanding the respect of the majority of its citizens.

During World War II, the defects of the puppet-show became steadily more obvious … and steadily more difficult for nationalist forces in Iraq to stand.

**Iraq Fact**

The British were willing to fight in Iraq in World War II when there were so many other battles raging because Iraq was important to the Allied War effort as a source of oil, and as a transshipment point for war materials going to the Soviet Union.

## Iraq and the Allies

In addition to throwing their weight behind the Hashemites, the British installed a provisional pro-British government (excluding the recently elected anti-British National Assembly). Later the British backed a new government formed by Nuri as-Said, the long-time friend of Britain.

The Said government promptly declared war on Germany and its allies on January 17, 1943, and was touted by the Allies as the prime example of an "independent" Arab state fighting against the Axis.

## And a Little Child Shall Lead Them … Not

So: What was the biggest problem the Hashemite royal family faced during this period? It had to do with the calendar.

At the death of his father, Gazhi ibn Faisal, in 1939, Faisal ibn Gazhi (Faisal II) was informed that he was the new king of Iraq. However, at the time of his father's death, Faisal was only three years old, and only nine at the end of World War II. The monarchy was controlled by a regent, Amir Abd al Ilah, who was Ghazi's first cousin.

The authority of the regime was diminished for a number of reasons, among them the fact that until Faisal, the peoples in question had not been ruled by a king for more than 1,000 years.

Even a strong, capable, shrewd, and occasionally visible monarch would have had a tough time asserting authority in this situation. A nine-year-old boy had no chance. The national assembly, controlled by the military, commercial, and religious leadership, did its best to assert daily authority in Iraq.

This was not always easy, given the predations of the British.

# "Sure, You've Got a Government. Just Don't Do Anything We Don't Approve of …"

Most attempts at Iraqi self-government during this period were effectively undermined by the British.

Under the terms of the 1930 agreement between the two countries, the British essentially controlled the Iraqi transportation system and several key ministries, including, not surprisingly, those that oversaw oil production.

The Iraqi government was obliged to consult with Britain on foreign affairs, and were forbidden to take any foreign policy actions of which the British disapproved.

# Cracks in the Facade

Although the government was dominated by Britain, that hold was tenuous. The National Assembly had bitterly debated the 1930 Treaty with Britain—but eventually ratified it. There had been fights in the parliament chambers during the debates.

The same Iraqi elites who dominated the parliament in 1930 (Shiite and Sunni tribal leaders) and the military (Sunni city leaders and a few Kurdish leaders), and had united in the 1936 coup, were in power during the 1940s. Their affection for Britain was certainly strained, and the British could not rely on the local leadership for very much support.

The clock was ticking.

## Britain Gets the Postwar Imperial Blues

The truth was that after World War II concluded, the British found the Iraqis increasingly difficult to control. The support of the parliament and army was lukewarm at best, the monarch was a child, and the regent, Amir Abd al Ilah, turned out to be an Arab nationalist.

Here and elsewhere in the world, British imperial authority went into severe decline.

> **The Superpowers Screw Up in Iraq:** As they had in World War I, the British made conflicting promises to a number of parties during World War II. The offer: greater independence in return for support against the Axis. This time the promises were made to both the Palestinians and the Jews living in the Palestine Mandate. This promise to Arab and Zionist groups, coupled with moral revulsion at the scope of the Holocaust, led to the creation of Israel after the war, and the next defining element of modern Iraq: opposition to Israel.

# Previews of Coming Attractions: Nationalism Rises ... and a Strongman Holds Court

After the war, the leadership in Iraq was made up of wealthy merchants, scholars, clerics, and army officers. Many of them were Arab nationalists whose goal was true Iraqi independence from the West. Some nationalist groups were inspired by movements in other countries, some groups represented local divisions of international movements (the Ba'th Party was an example) and some, like the Kurds, agitated for their own independence from Iraq, and thus were against its current regime.

The prime minister, Nuri as-Said, however, suppressed virtually all overt political activity. The government didn't even allow political parties until 1946. Even afterward, the government was very heavy-handed with opposing parties, and most legal forms of dissent in the press or political arena were not tolerated. Without such avenues of protest, dissent went underground and became more revolutionary. Even the more moderate groups of the intelligentsia were radicalized by the tough tactics of the Said government, which was the ruling government for most of the post-WWII era.

The Iraqi leadership, ever conscious of its weak grip on power, responded by closing off debate and making policy decisions behind closed doors. The leadership circle effectively cut out the majority of the officials in the government who represented the Iraqi people.

This closed decision-making process was a portent of things to come.

# Tough Times for the Hashemite Monarchy

The alienation of the Iraqi elites occurred at several levels. The intelligentsia were more inspired by pan-Arabism than by any Iraqi-developed political movements. The army had attempted an abortive coup during World War II, and had suffered chronic underfunding and close scrutiny by the government ever since. Even before World War II, the Free Officers Movement—a group of officers dedicated to full Iraqi independence—had been strong among the military leadership. And the Shiite tribal leaders, for their part, were dismayed by the heavy-handed Sunni leadership.

The one thing *all* the leading Iraqi players seemed to agree on, though, was a distaste for the Hashemite (Saudi) monarchy.

The alienation of the general population went even deeper. They saw their standard of living sink by the day, with little hope for improvement. The country's economic situation had been bad before World War II and only got worse in the decade following the war, as oil revenues spurred inflation—but not real wages.

# Economic Woes, Economic Colonialism

The government's legitimacy was sorely tested by economic troubles. The domestic economy was beset by high inflation, bureaucratic corruption, and an increasing rift between the Regent (Abd al Ilah) and the Nuri as-Said government. The two could not agree on common economic policies and political initiatives that could have led to meaningful infrastructure improvements, and public works devolved into petty squabbling between the tribal factions in the parliament.

Meanwhile, marginal harvests and a land policy that allowed the tribal leaders to export most crops to the British (rather than feed their own people) compounded the misery of the rural population.

In the cities, an emerging middle class found little economic opportunity, and inflation attacked the real value of salaries.

Economic policy centered on the oil industry, which was now controlled by the British, French, and Americans. The Iraq Petroleum Company (IPC) continued to be dominated by a consortium of British, French, and finally

> **Increase Your Iraq IQ**
>
> The export economy, both for oil and food, was a signature element of colonialism. The colonial power (in this case Britain), takes raw materials from the colonized country, without compensating that country to the full value of the materials extracted. The Iraqi economy simply could not support that kind of strain, particularly in drought years, when crops failed.

U.S. oil companies. To the Iraqi resistance movements, the oil concessions that enabled these Western oil companies to develop Iraqi oil fields were just a thinly veiled form of colonialism.

This pattern was the same in the other countries in the region. Iran, Saudi Arabia, Kuwait, and the other Gulf states all had Western-dominated oil companies.

While oil revenues gradually climbed over time, they didn't help the vast majority of ordinary Iraqis. After the Said government renegotiated the Iraqi share from 20 percent to 50 percent of revenues in 1952, Iraqi oil receipts jumped from $32 million in 1951 to $112 million in 1952. The increased cash flow, however, only lined the pockets of government officials. Little was devoted to infrastructure projects or development programs. Iraq's oil boom stood in stark contrast to the poverty of its people.

> **The Superpowers Screw Up in Iraq:** High-handed Western dominance of the Middle Eastern oil industry, based on past concessions, inflamed passions in Iraq and many other countries in the region. Anti-Western feeling grew.

# Open Rebellion

The Portsmouth Treaty, signed in 1948, once again defined the relationship between Iraq and Britain in a way that was completely in Britain's favor. The agreement required Iraq and Britain to reach an agreement on all matters pertaining to Iraqi defense. Basically, Iraq could not make any defense treaties on its own. The Treaty severely compromised Iraqi sovereignty, and outraged Iraqi nationalists.

**Iraq Fact**

The **Israel War** (or Israeli War of Independence) occurred between 1948 and 1949. Egypt, Transjordan, Iraq, Palestine, and Syria waged war against the new state of Israel; the Arab states eventually negotiated separate armistice agreements after the Israelis established clear air supremacy.

Opposition openly erupted in 1948, in what came to be called the Wathbah Rebellion. The nationalists were outraged by the Portsmouth Treaty signed earlier that year; they had finally had enough of decisions being made without their agreement.

The rebellion probably had as much to do with Iraq's increasing economic woes as the lower oil revenues due to the closing of the Haifa pipeline during the *Israel War*. More than 40 percent of oil receipts that were left were earmarked for either the army or to support the Palestinian refugees who flooded into Transjordan and Iraq. There were bread shortages and high inflation. Widespread riots broke out in the cities, and there was fighting in the countryside.

Eventually, Said put down the rebellion, but his relationship with the nationalist regent became even more strained. The British supported Said and his oppressive tactics. They saw him as the best way to maintain stability (and the flow of oil) in Iraq.

# Nationalism Gets a Boost

In order to get peace with the rebels, Prime Minister Said was forced to repudiate the Portsmouth Treaty, and the nationalists were encouraged by their results.

The simple fact that factions from all facets of Iraqi society had coalesced and rebelled signaled continued trouble for the Hashemite monarchy and the British-backed parliament.

Five years later, on January 17, 1953, a direct election (the first in Iraq) took place. A new, constitutionally elected government was seated on January 29, 1953. This government was also pro-British—but it didn't last long.

# Enter the USA

U.S. oil companies had begun to take a larger and larger role in Iraqi oil industry. (You'll learn about the U.S. oil industry and Iraq in Chapter 14.) At the time, Iraq and Iran each played key roles in the U.S. policy of containment of the Soviet Union. With, at least on paper, a democratic process in place and the oil flowing, the United States was able to point to Iraq as a model ally in the Middle East.

The Eisenhower Doctrine, instituted by the United States in the early 1950s, promised U.S. aid to any country that resisted communism, and the Eisenhower administration decided that Iraq fit the bill. However, this was a surface perception: the Communist and Socialist Parties did exist under the surface in 1950s Iraq. They were never as powerful as the Nationalists, but the Communist Party persisted into the 1960s, until it was outlawed by the Ba'th Socialist Party. Nonetheless, the Eisenhower administration decided to provide military aid to Iraq in 1954.

Like the British before them, the Americans' interest in the region was not welcomed by the Iraqi elites who ran the parliament. By the summer of 1954, a new parliamentary election resulted in anti-U.S. groups gaining the majority, threatening the military aid package—and the power of the seated, pro-Western Said government.

Before the new government could take control, Said dissolved the parliament on August 4, 1954, and new elections were held. This time, the main opposition party, the National Democratic Union, found itself suppressed by the government. This led the Socialist Party to walk out of the elections in sympathy. When the new elections were held in September 1954, the pro-Western government won in a landslide.

At this time, the United States took the baton from Britain in Iraq. Unfortunately, as we shall see, the Americans also took on the British propensity for superpower mistakes.

## The Least You Need to Know

- For much of the twentieth century, Iraq was governed by a shaky, pro-British monarchy and heavy-handed government.

- The combination of Sunni-controlled parliaments and a Hashemite regent challenged the legitimacy of the government, which was largely ineffective.

- Western oil concessions, treaties, and maneuvering by Britain, and later the United States, only increased simmering anti-Western sentiment.

- The United States took over for Britain in the mid 1950s, as the Eisenhower Doctrine (and U.S. thirst for oil) pulled the United States into the region.

# The Enemy Principle: Iraq's Foreign Policy

## In This Chapter

- ◆ Iraq and Turkey
- ◆ Iraq and Israel
- ◆ Iraq and Egypt
- ◆ Iraq and Iran
- ◆ Iraq and the United States

British and U.S. errors in policy toward Iraq certainly strengthened Iraq's anti-Western outlook. Those errors, however, are not the only reason Iraq has developed and reinforced the kind of culture, outlook, and leadership history that it has.

Iraq's own policies in the modern era, particularly those of its Hashemite and Ba'th rulers, reflect another important trend—namely, the tendency of autocratic Iraqi rulers to unify the (fragmented) country against a common enemy.

# Dictators Need an Enemy

Dictators, especially those faced with the task of unifying social groups with extremely diverse interests and outlook, often search for outsiders to blame. Put plainly, dictators often decide that they need to focus the attention of the public on an enemy.

---

### Increase Your Iraq IQ

In literature, George Orwell explores the dictators-need-an-enemy theme in his classic *1984*, in which the residents of Oceania hold a daily "Two Minutes Hate" against the enemy, Emmanuel Goldstein. In the end, Goldstein turns out to be a fiction invented by the ruling dictatorship.

---

The fight against the enemy rallies the people of the country to a single cause. The dictator's leadership abilities are highlighted in the fight against the enemy. The privations that the population must endure can be blamed on the fight with this enemy. If the dictator defeats the enemy, his prestige is increased.

Hitler and Stalin come to mind, of course; each demonized domestic political opponents and foreign rivals, and each built huge PR campaigns around conspiracies that existed only in their own imaginations, conspiracies that often drew attention away from the details of military or economic failures.

# Focusing on the Enemies: A Long Tradition in Iraq

In this chapter, we will see how this theme "Dictators Need an Enemy" has played out for decades against Iraq's rivals in the region: Turkey, Iran, Israel, and Egypt. We will see how Iraq's kings and later its dictators, have consistently latched on to these enemies—and the United States—in an attempt to bolster their own shaky authority at home.

This is not to suggest that actual conflicts and disagreements with these countries do not exist—only that the legitimacy of the Iraqi leadership is often deeply invested in an adversarial relationship with *some* enemy, and that the struggle against that enemy serves an important unifying (and distracting) purpose.

Specifically, we will look at Iraq's rivalries with …

 ◆ **Turkey.** The rival claimant for former Ottoman territories that would make up the modern state of Iraq. In addition to territorial rival, the Turks are not Arabs and represent the old Ottoman oppressors.

 ◆ **Israel.** A long-standing focus of the Iraqi leadership, and the main rallying cause of the collective Arab states. Iraq's Ba'th Party tenets include a stated objective of destroying Israel and establishing a Palestinian homeland in its place.

◆ **Egypt.** A rival for about 1,000 years for leadership of Abbasid culture and commerce, Egypt is the chief rival for control of the pan-Arab movement. (See Chapter 2 for a quick overview of the pan-Arab movement, and Chapter 15 for more details.)

◆ **Iran.** The ancient enemy to the east. The Iranians are Farsi-speaking Persians, not Arabs. Also, Muslim Iran is Shiite, like the southern majority in Iraq. This Shiite connection makes Iran a neighbor who can (and perhaps does) create a destabilizing influence in Iraqi internal affairs. During the Ottoman Era, the Iraqi vilayets of Basra, Baghdad, and Mosul were the bulwark of Arabism against the Persians. We will look in greater depth at the on-again off-again hate affair with the Iranians in Chapter 17.

◆ **The United States.** The latest Western imperialist (taking the place of Britain). We will look briefly at the role the conflict with the United States has played in recent years. (The United States' status as enemy number one in Iraq is covered in greater detail in Part 4.) The United States had been following the British lead in compound errors since the end of World War II. U.S. companies began to get serious about Iraqi oil and, using the vehicle of the Eisenhower Doctrine, the U.S. government had become increasingly involved in Iraqi internal affairs.

# A Common Thread

Over the years, Iraqi leadership (Hashemite kings, regents, prime ministers, and dictators) have been repeatedly frustrated in their foreign policy forays. Their foreign policy efforts were usually intended to increase their domestic stature.

(Warning: Strategically selected historical flashback ahead.) Consider, for instance …

# Turkey, the Kurds, and the Contest for Mosul

In the period immediately following World War I, you may recall, the modern nation of Turkey was carved out of the Ottoman Empire.

The former Ottoman vilayets of Basra (now southern Iraq) and Baghdad (now central Iraq) were combined to create the Hashemite Kingdom of Iraq. The vilayet of Mosul (north of the Baghdad vilayet, bordering Turkey and Iran) was not originally part of the post-WWI state of Iraq. Mosul's status was undetermined at that time, as the British tried to figure out what to do about the Kurds (who occupied a significant portion of the Mosul vilayet).

When large amounts of oil were discovered in the Mosul region, the British were keen to control those assets. The post-WWI country of Turkey began to make serious claims for Mosul, however, and the Kurds also were arguing for this territory.

## Faisal Finds a Unifying Cause

King Faisal, the Saudi clan member, and newly installed king of Iraq, was looking for some cause to rally the people of his new country (new as a state, and new to him). The aggressive rhetoric of the Turks over Mosul was the perfect opportunity.

Faisal used this issue to create a sense of rivalry with Turkey, and by so doing, hopefully ingratiate himself to the Iraqi Sunni elite in Baghdad.

He was only marginally successful. Many of the Baghdad elites were enamored by the Young Turks movement (a progressive group of army officers in Turkey, dedicated to reforming the Turkish government and breaking away from Western dominance), and saw it as a blueprint for their own independence from British authority. Furthermore, most of the people in the Baghdad vilayet had more in common with the tribes in Syria and Jordan, than with the people (including a lot of Kurds) up in Mosul. For that matter, most of the people in the Basra vilayet in southern Iraq had more in common with the people in Kuwait and the Shiite in Iran.

## A Hollow Victory

As noted in Chapter 10, in 1925, alarmed themselves by Turkish overtures regarding incorporating Mosul into Turkey, Britain had the League of Nations agree to assign Mosul to Iraq. So Faisal had his foreign policy "victory" over the enemy (Turkey).

Unfortunately, most Iraqis never bought into the argument that Turkey was the enemy, or that Mosul was worth fighting for in the first place. In fact, given the way the British forced the solution through the League of Nations on behalf of Iraq, most Iraqi elites (the people Faisal was trying to impress) saw the annexation of Mosul as a sign of Faisal's weakness, not as a sign of strength.

(End strategically chosen historical flashback. We now return to our regular programming.)

# The Cold War Comes to the Desert

At the end of World War II, Britain became concerned by the Soviet Union's increasing attention to the Middle East. In a rekindling of the old "Great Game" played by the British and Russian Empires in Central Asia, both sides made moves to shore up partners in the oil-rich Middle East.

---

### Increase Your Iraq IQ

The "Cold War" is the name for the competition between the West (mainly the United States) and the Soviet Union for primacy in the world. While the United States and Soviets never fought directly, they battled each other through foreign aid, propaganda, and technology. The Cold War lasted from the end of World War II, to the collapse of the Soviet Union in 1989.

The "Great Game" is the name for the maneuvering between the British and Russian Empires in the late nineteenth and early twentieth centuries. The British wanted to protect their northern frontier in India, and the Russians wanted to extend their southern frontier toward India. The two superpowers invaded, plotted, and spied throughout Central Asia during this period.

---

# The Bulldog Brings in Uncle Sam

As the Cold War deepened, Britain did its best to prop up pro-Western Arab governments in its former Mandates, and promoted their participation in the United Nations.

Iraq joined the UN in 1945. Even before World War II, Britain had maneuvered to promote a stronger Iraq in the region—the better to contain other rivals. In 1945, one of those rivals was the Soviet Union. However, after the end of World War II, Britain's resources were exhausted, and the old British Empire was crumbling. Britain found itself spread too thin to manage the growing Soviet threat. The United States emerged as the leader of the Soviet *containment* effort.

The first real test of the containment policy (and thus the beginning of the Cold War) occurred in 1947, when the Soviet Union became involved in a civil war in Greece. Communist rebels were attacking the pro-Western monarchy there, and the Soviet Union was backing the rebels. Also, the Soviets were pushing Turkey to grant them naval base concessions on the Bosporus. (Remember that the only route Soviet ships had to get into the Mediterranean was to exit the Black Sea via the Bosporus.) The Soviets were offering cash to Turkey, which Turkey sorely needed.

**Desert Diction**

The **containment** concept, which is credited to George Kennan, a senior diplomat at the U.S. Embassy in Moscow in 1946, outlined the need and methods for containing Soviet expansion.

Britain was unable to match the Soviet offer, but U.S. President Harry Truman could. So Truman trumped up the Soviet threat to something greater than it actually was. By "scaring the hell out of the country" (as Senator Arthur Vandenberg so eloquently put it at the time), Truman was able to get the U.S. Congress to appropriate a $400 million aid package for Greece and Turkey. The Greek communists were defeated, and the Soviets never got their naval base on the Bosporus. The Cold War was on, and it quickly reached into Iraq.

# The Arab League

Although weakened after World War II, Britain continued to maneuver to protect its position in the region. They moved to contain the Soviets by encouraging the formation of a coalition of Arab countries into a larger, unified entity. This concept eventually became embodied in the "Arab League."

---

### Increase Your Iraq IQ

The Arab League (formally called the League of Arab States) includes Egypt, Transjordan (now Jordan), Lebanon, Saudi Arabia, Syria, Yemen, and Iraq. The League exists to this day, but it doesn't represent all the Arabs in the region, and it has not worked toward a unified Arab state in decades. Its mission now focuses more on issues that affect the collective Arab states.

---

The British favored the Arab League, as it represented a bulwark against Soviet expansion into the region. Over time the Arab League would become less sympathetic to Britain, but early on, the League was pro-British.

Iraq was a founding member of the Arab League in 1946. As an Arab League member, Iraq became an active proponent of the pan-Arab movement. Iraq's Premier Nuri as-Said went so far as to suggest that Iraq and Transjordan (now Jordan) should be united. While the idea did not go very far at that time, the Said government signed a treaty of mutual defense and friendship with Transjordan in 1947.

# Pan-Arabism's First Test

The first test of the pan-Arabism, and the new alliance treaties, came in May of 1948, when the State of Israel was proclaimed. Anti-Zionism had been a long-time tenet of Arab leaders, and the Arab League member countries all adopted the same policy.

## The Hashemites Find a Unifying Cause

The Hashemite monarchy in Iraq saw the founding of Israel as an opportunity to bolster their own domestic position. The Hashemite regent Abd al Ilah seized the opportunity to put Iraq in the forefront of the fighting against Israel. (The king, whom the regent represented, was 12 years old in 1948.)

Immediately after the creation of the Israeli state in 1948, Iraq and Transjordan invaded Israel. Even after the other Arab forces had withdrawn from the fighting, the Iraqis stayed on. The Iraqis fought with particular fury all that summer and into the fall.

Finally, when it was apparent the Israeli defense forces were going to win (or at the very least, the Iraqis were not going to win) the Transjordanians negotiated a cease-fire with the Israelis on behalf of themselves and the Iraqis. Even after the cease-fire agreement was signed on May 11, 1949, Iraqi troops continued to fight against Israeli troops in central Palestine. On April 3, 1949, the Transjordanian army replaced the Iraqis, and the fight finally stopped.

**Iraq Fact**

The Hashemite monarchy had, of course, been created by the British. Britain had also led the way in the creation of the state of Israel from the Palestine Mandate. The British did not want the Arab states to attack Israel. Ironically, it was their own creation—the Hashemite monarchy in Iraq—that became one of the most violent opponents of Israel.

## A Hollow Defeat

Back at home, the regency had failed to score the points it wanted to with the Iraqi elites. The engagement in Israel was a failure, and the prominent role that Iraq played was a source of embarrassment at home, not pride. While the Iraqi military would participate in the 1967 and 1973 wars against Israel, the Iraqis didn't play the leading belligerent role they had in 1948.

Given that the attempt to prevail against Israel, or to even assume a leadership role in the fight against Israel, had fallen flat, the Iraqi leadership needed a new enemy to fight, the better to rally support and gain prestige.

They found the competition they needed within the arena of the pan-Arab movement, in a renewed rivalry with Egypt.

**CAUTION**

**Oil Spill Ahead**

The Iraqi government's continued antipathy to Israel would emerge again during the Gulf War, when the Iraqis launched missiles at Israel in an attempt to draw Israel into the war, and turn the conflict from a U.S.-Arab coalition vs. Iraq to an Arab coalition against a U.S.-Israeli alliance. Again, the attempt failed. We will look at this event further in Chapter 22.

# Competing with Nasser

What country would lead the Arab world? In the late 1940s and early 1950s, the most prominent candidates were Egypt and Iraq.

In 1948, Abd al Ilah (the regent for the Iraqi boy king) proposed an Iraqi-Syrian union. Nuri as-Said, the prime minister, opposed the idea, and a rift between the two Iraqi leaders began to widen. The matter was settled by the Syrians, themselves, when Syrian strongman Adib Shishakli took over that government in a coup in 1949.

Shishakli was opposed to a union with Iraq. Even though he was overthrown (with Iraqi help) in 1954, the plan was dropped. By then, Syria was closer to Egypt, anyway.

Under Gamal abdel Nasser, Egypt was presenting itself as the alternative to Iraqi leadership of the Arab world. A dominant personality, with ambitious international goals of his own, Nasser moved away from Britain early and often.

As part of his own anti-British leaning, Nasser targeted Iraq's policy parallels with Britain, and used them to win greater credibility for himself within the Arab world.

Consider, for instance …

## The Baghdad Pact

In 1955, Iraq was a founding member of the Baghdad Pact, a mutual defense treaty with Iran, Pakistan, and Turkey. The simple fact that the treaty was signed in Baghdad indicates the leadership position that Iraq was trying to maintain.

Nasser saw the Pact as a clear challenge to Egyptian dominance in the Arab community. The Baghdad Pact was supported by Britain, and was signed with non-Arab states. The British and Americans assembled the Baghdad Pact nations as an anti-Soviet coalition. The British did not think they needed Egypt to participate, and this troubled Nasser.

Nasser knew that if more Arab states joined the Pact, Egypt's standing would suffer. He responded to its creation by calling on the Iraqi military to overthrow the monarchy.

This call was not as far-fetched as it may sound. Remember that the Iraqi monarchy was ruled by a Hashemite family from Saudi Arabia—they were not Iraqis. Consider, too, that the king himself was only 16 at that time. The monarchy was run by a regent, the king's uncle, Abd al Ilah. The government was run by Nuri as-Said, who owed his position to the British and almost always carried out their wishes regarding foreign policy. Nasser's call cannily appealed to the growing anti-Western sentiment in Iraq.

The Iraqi military didn't actually rise up at that time, but the Pact wasn't a popular treaty with the Iraqi elites, who identified more with Nasser's style of Arab nationalism over their own government's notions of international relations.

# And Then There Was Suez

Things only got worse for the Iraqi government during the Suez Crisis.

The crisis started when the Egyptians nationalized *the Suez Canal.* The British responded by invading the Sinai, supported by the French ... and the hated Israelis. As an ally of the British (at the government level, if not among the country's elites), Iraq had to stand by and not openly oppose the British initiative.

Before war could break out, the United Nations brokered a truce, and the British, French, and Israelis withdrew. After the settlement, Nasser's standing only increased among the Arab world, at the expense of Iraqi prestige. After all, the Iraqis had done nothing (except be the lapdogs of the British) while Egypt (led by Nasser, of course) had struck a blow for Arab autonomy and prestige.

**Desert Diction**

The **Suez Canal** connects the Mediterranean Sea to the Indian Ocean. The canal is located in Egypt; transit through the canal saves ships the much longer and more arduous journey around the Cape of Good Hope and the African continent.

# Struggles for Pre-Eminence

The competition over leadership of the Arab political world carried over into the pan-Arab movement. Nasser promoted the United Arab Republic (UAR), as we saw in Chapter 2. The UAR was intended to become a single Arab power, and was supposed to incorporate the Arab nations in the Middle East (under Egyptian moral leadership, of course).

Syria and Egypt joined up in February 1958, and Yemen tentatively joined soon after. However, no one else joined, and the UAR fell apart a few years later. Yemen never completely joined in, and Syria dropped out. Egypt kept the UAR as its name, even though it was the only member of the Union after the Syrians dropped out.

# The Iraqi Leadership Searches for a Unifying Cause

Iraqi leaders were not to be outdone by the Eqyptians. They responded by forming their own version of the UAR, the Arab Union (AU), in 1958. Iraq and Jordan joined up (there was a Hashemite monarchy in Jordan), and Iraqi Prime Minister Nuri as-Said was brought off the bench to head the new state. Said had been in retirement at that time.

The newly crowned king, Faisal II, was only 22 (he had formally assumed the throne at the age of 18 in 1954) at the time, and he was still taking orders from his uncle, the regent. The Arab Union was formed with British and American blessings. Like the Baghdad Pact, the AU was a controversial move, initiated almost exclusively by the government of Iraq instead of the Iraqi people, and it didn't have unanimous support from the Iraqi National Assembly.

Egypt's (the UAR) Nasser portrayed the Arab Union as another Western affront to the Arab world. The Egyptians argued that the only reason the AU was created was because the British were trying to defeat a true Arab union, the United Arab Republic. Nasser called again for the Iraqi people to overthrow the new Arab Union government.

## Good-Bye to the Hashemites

This time, Nasser's ploy worked. On July 14, 1958, Iraqi General Abdul Karim Kassem led a coup d'état. Ostensibly, Iraqi troops were moving into Jordan as part of a joint military exercise. Instead, the battalion stopped in Baghdad and seized control of the government.

King Faisal II, Abd al Ilah, and Nuri as-Said were all killed. The next day, on July 15, 1958, the new government declared its support for the UAR and announced the termination of the Arab Union.

**Iraq Fact**

Prime Minister Nuri as-Said was captured trying to escape Baghdad dressed as a woman.

The pro-British Hashemite monarchy was gone, and it would not be replaced. Its repeated attempts to gain sufficient legitimacy for survival through foreign policy victories had failed. There were in fact very few Iraqi foreign policy victories in the decade following World War II.

With the successful coup, Iraq had entered the next phase of its journey to the twenty-first century. Iraq was now a self-governing state, Arab-focused, and run by a Sunni military elite more than willing to focus public attention on an external enemy (such as Israel or the United States) to bolster its legitimacy.

This structure would survive to the present. It is the formula that rules Iraq.

## The Least You Need to Know

- The Iraqi monarchy never had the support of the Iraqi elite or people.

- The Iraqi monarchy attempted to legitimize itself by finding an enemy. (The Turks, Israelis, and Egyptians all played that part.)

- The Iraqi monarchy ultimately failed in each of its major foreign policy initiatives.

- The British, following the principle of Compound Error, repeatedly placed the monarchy in no-win situations, and abandoned them in the end.

- The Hashemite monarchy ultimately fell to a coup lead by the Sunni-controlled Iraqi army leaders.

# Three Coups

## In This Chapter

- ◆ The 1958 coup
- ◆ The 1963 coup and the first Ba'th government
- ◆ The 1968 coup that entrenched Ba'th rule in Iraq

The Arab Ba'th Socialist Resurrection Party gained power through a series of coups over a 10-year period between 1958 and 1968. All the coups were led by Iraqi generals, who were just as alienated from the common Iraqis as the Hashemite monarchs had been.

## We're Closed!

An important theme that unites all three of these coups is the notion of the *closed society*.

In a closed society, power is concentrated within a small group. Other groups that manage to maneuver their way into a position to challenge the ruling group can quickly take over power from the ruling group, without the rest of the society being able to do much about it.

**Desert Diction**

A **closed society** is one where information, power, and decisions are controlled by a small central authority and are only shared within a tiny ruling circle. Closed societies don't allow for a pluralist government or meaningful open debate on issues. Open societies, by contrast, share information, power, and decision-making across a much broader spectrum of the population.

Open societies take longer to make fundamental political changes, are less likely to undergo coups and revolutions, and are less prone to rapid changes in the central authority group. In an open society, more groups share power and wealth. Each group holds some power—and no one group has virtually *all* the power.

In closed societies, changes in leadership and policy may happen in sudden, violent shifts (like a coup d'état). Open societies, on the other hand, tend to process social change more easily, with fewer violent spasms and fewer dramatic, unexpected political upheavals.

In Iraq in the 1950s, power resided with a very few groups—the fragile leadership structure set in place by the British excluded important sections of the population.

# Demagogues, Dictators, and Chaos

To understand Iraq's political situation in the 1950s and early 1960s, it helps to understand power shifts in other closed societies in the twentieth century.

One of the ways a *demagogue* becomes a dictator is by promising to bring order when there is chaos. This is the technique that Hitler, Stalin, Mussolini, and others used to justify taking total control in Germany, Russia, and Italy, respectively.

Hitler's Nazi Party, for instance, actually joined forces with the communists (even though the two groups were complete opposites on the political spectrum) in order to destabilize the Weimar Republic government in the 1920s and 1930s. By joining voting blocs with the communists, the Nazis were able to help bring about vote after vote of "no confidence" in the seated government in the Reichstag (parliament).

**Desert Diction**

**Demagogues** are leaders or prominent figures within a society who preach a specific philosophy. They gain prominence by preying on the fears or prejudices of the population.

The combined efforts of the communists and the Nazis resulted in dissolved governments, hectic reelection campaigns, and ineffective decision-making, creating an atmosphere of chaos within the government— and deep resentment in a population facing economic crisis.

Hitler was finally given the opportunity to form a government in 1933. In the name of stability, he then cracked down brutally on all opposition (including the communists, who had been the Nazis' partners in chaos).

Similarly destabilizing maneuvers were in evidence in Iraq in the 1950s and 1960s.

# The Army Elite Gains Power

Emerging as a power center to challenge the unpopular, foreign-born monarchy and the ineffective parliament was an increasingly powerful officer corps.

You'll recall that the British had created a local, Iraqi army to prop up the Hashemite monarchy. This was because the British realized the Hashemites might have a tough time of it—not being Iraqis and all—and would need a tool to help maintain control of the country. Remember that the tribes in the countryside, and the Kurds in the north, were essentially operating independently within Iraq. The army, the British reasoned, was needed to control these restless and potentially destabilizing groups.

Recall, too, that the British wanted to maintain ties with other Arab leaders in the region; hence the Sunni (minority) monarchy. The Sunni monarch, of course, would need Sunni support in the army. So even though the majority of the population in Iraq was (and is) Shiite, the British made sure the officer corps was made up of Sunnis, while the rank and file was Shiite.

It was this Sunni military elite that became the key lever in prying out existing governments and setting up new ones in their place. The principal method of change was the coup d'état.

# Times Change

Power in Iraq in the 1950s was concentrated into the hands of the British-leaning monarch (Faisal II), and the prime minister (Nuri as-Said) and his immediate circle. The other power elites, including the Iraqi officer corps, were not included in the decision-making process, and they were becoming increasingly unhappy at this state of affairs.

**Oil Spill Ahead**

The coups of the 1950s, while important, were not the only leadership spasms in Iraq; there had been several coups and rebellions over the preceding 20 years, including the 1936 coup, the 1941 military takeover, the 1948 Wathbah Uprising, and smaller uprisings in 1952 and 1956.

The officers, in particular, were unhappy over several things. They were Arab nationalists who resented the pro-British puppets who ran their state. The officers didn't necessarily identify themselves with the rest of the Iraqi population, especially the Shiite majority, the Kurds, or the Assyrians. Their interest was focused on themselves, and their pan-Arab brethren in other countries.

These officers resented the non-Iraqi monarchy, they resented the foreign policy blunders of their government, and they resented its heavy-handed approach to decision-making. Most of all, they resented the British manipulation of their nation.

# A Fateful Party

Iraq was fertile ground for the Ba'th Party in the 1950s. Founded in Syria, the Ba'th Socialist Party was pan-Arab; it had local branches in each Arab country, and its members were dedicated to a pan-Arab state.

The Ba'th Party originated during World War II, formed by two Syrian students, Michel Aflaq and Salah ad-Din al-Bitar. It was formally founded on April 7, 1947, as the Arab Ba'th Socialist Party.

Aflaq and al-Bitar were keenly aware of British and French imperialism throughout the Middle East. They were fans of the pan-Arab ideal, and they were enamored with the political ideology of *socialism*.

**Desert Diction** _____

**Socialism** as a concept was first described by Friedrich Engels, and then extended by Karl Marx in the end of the nineteenth century. Both were reacting to the situation that early industrialization had created. Workers (labor) were paid subsistence wages and had little to no hope of social advancement. Owners (or the capitalists) controlled the means of production and exploited workers. Socialism argued that workers should own the fruit of their labors, not the capitalists. The ideology envisioned workers owning the means of production, with higher living standards for all.

Socialism had emerged as a vibrant political ideology in the 1920s and 1930s, and a wide range of socialist parties became powerful before and immediately after World War II. Socialism took many forms depending on where it took root, but its emphasis on equity, political rights, and state ownership of property had a strong pull on young idealists in universities around the world.

## The Ba'th Party in Iraq

The Ba'th Party emerged as a viable organization in Iraq in 1952, when a charismatic leader named Fu'ad ar Rikabi, a Shiite, founded the Iraqi branch of the Arab Ba'th Socialist party that year. Rikabi was still able to attract Sunnis to the party. However, over time, the Sunni took control of the party.

The Ba'th Party tenets included adherence to socialism (including state ownership of the key segments of the economy), political freedom (an inclusive process), and pan-Arab unity. These tenets took root amongst the Iraqi intelligentsia, who were suffering from the poor economic environment in Iraq, and who were alienated by British imperialist policies and the closed decision-making style of the Iraqi leadership.

The members of the Iraqi intelligentsia drawn to the Ba'th Party were generally Sunnis of some privilege. Like the officer corps, they identified more with other Sunni intelligentsia in other countries, and less with their own countrymen who represented far different religious and economic realities than their own.

During the next five years, some army officers joined the party ranks, but membership was still very small within Iraq. Like the national socialists in Weimar Germany, and the communists in Tzarist Russia, the Iraq branch of the Ba'th Party started as a small group on the outside, looking in.

> ### Increase Your Iraq IQ
>
> Across the Arab countries, memberships in local Ba'th Party branches grew rapidly.

# Wathbah, Revisited

Look once again at the challenge that *preceded* the coup that swept away the Hashemite monarchy described in Chapter 12.

Prime Minister Nuri as-Said and the Hashemite regent, Abd al Ilah, negotiated the Portsmouth Treaty with Britain. The Treaty stipulated that Iraqi leadership had to consult Britain on any military matters, through a board of Iraqi and British "advisors." The nationalists were outraged, and without a legal political option, they rebelled. The rebellion spread quickly and tapped into popular unrest over high bread prices, and continued economic malaise.

The Wathbah uprising was violent. It was suppressed violently, and the rebel groups were all but eliminated (at least in the forms they had taken at that point). However, the strife didn't end until the Said government openly repudiated the Portsmouth Treaty.

The result: The rebels were defeated and repressive measures were heightened, but a segment of the rebels' wishes were granted (namely, the treaty was abandoned).

In order to retain power, the ruling government had accommodated some opposition demands, but had redoubled its efforts to avoid any further challenges to its authority. Such challenges, however, would prove impossible to avoid.

## Rumblings

What have we got so far? A state of general political chaos, economic hardship, resentment of the British, and widespread alienation of Iraqi elites excluded from participating in policy decisions. All of this was bubbling in the pressure cooker of a closed society.

Something had to give.

# July 14, 1958

And give it did, on July 14, 1958. On that morning the Iraqi army toppled the royal regime. According to official Iraqi accounts of the event, the regime the army overthrew "had opened the door wide for monopolies to plunder the country's oil wealth under unjust concessions, tied Iraq to imperialist alliances, especially the Baghdad Pact, and turned the country into a center of conspiracy against the revolutionary movement of the Arab homeland."

Was the 1958 coup a just uprising by an oppressed people ... or, a coup staged by members of the Sunni officer elite to topple the Said government they despised?

However it's categorized, the July 14, 1958, coup followed the Hashemite monarchy's creating the Arab Union with Jordan (in response to the Egyptian-sponsored United Arab Republic, or UAR). The Iraqi parliament ratified the union on May 12, 1958—but the Sunni officers got together enough supporters to bring the union—and the Iraqi government—down only 60 days later. They were led by General Abdul Karim Kassem.

King Faisal II, the regent, and Said were all killed immediately. The next day, July 15, the new government (now calling the country the Republic of Iraq) abandoned the Arab Union, and announced its intention to forge closer ties to the UAR.

Kassem continued the new government's anti-British policies by withdrawing from the Baghdad Pact in March 1959 and pulling out of the *sterling bloc* in June 1959. Remember, the Baghdad Pact was a mutual defense treaty that included Iraq, Turkey, and Iran. It was sponsored by the British, and was intended to stave off the Soviet expansionism.

Kassem was forced to carry out a delicate balancing act. A child of Sunni-Shiite parentage, Kassem tried to keep the various groups happy, but he wasn't always successful.

For example, under pressure from the nationalists, Kassem's government revoked about 99.5 percent of the Iraq Petroleum Company (IPC)'s concession rights. However, this move didn't really change much, as the existing IPC facilities were located on the remaining 0.5 percent of the original concession area. So by nationalizing the concession, Kassem looked like an Arab nationalist to the nationalists by defying the foreign powers, and he looked like a socialist to the Iraqi Communist Party by nationalizing a key industry. His action helped him gain prestige from both groups at home. At the same time, he really did not seize any physical plant from the IPC, though he did take value from the IPC by taking away its concession areas.

**Desert Diction**

The **sterling bloc** was the group of nations who tied their currencies to the pound sterling. Iraq withdrew from this group in 1959.

## Red Bedfellows

Kassem wasn't really pro-Communist, but his government did reach an aid agreement with the Soviet Union. Because of that agreement, Kassem was diplomatically obliged to tolerate the Iraqi Communist Party (ICP)—a rival of the Ba'th socialists—in order to get the aid the Soviets were promising. The ICP was a more established party than the Ba'th Party, and it had successfully agitated against previous governments. The ICP was, in a way, much less

**Oil Spill Ahead**

Once Iraq pulled out of the Baghdad Pact, the treaty group really couldn't refer to itself that way anymore ... after all, there was no Baghdad in the pact! So, the remaining countries (including Turkey and Iran) called themselves the Central Treaty Organization. This name was safer, in case anyone else decided to drop out.

violent than the Ba'th, and more extensive. The ICP had, in a sense, paved the way for the Ba'th Party in Iraq, even though the Ba'th were ideologically opposed to the ICP.

The issue of the UAR membership involved another balancing act. The Ba'ths wanted to join the union, but Kassem and the Communists did not.

## The Kuwait Conflict (1960)

The Kassem-controlled Republic of Iraq wasn't done throwing off the British yoke. In June 1960, the British ended their protectorate over Kuwait, and declared it an independent state.

With the British out, Kassem's troops moved into Kuwait. The Iraqis claimed that Kuwait had been part of the old Basra vilayet, and so it really belonged to Iraq. The British rejected this claim, stating that the League of Nations had sanctioned the current borders, and that the vilayet borders were not material to the current situation. Justified or not, the Iraqis used the ancient vilayet boundaries to justify their claim (and they would do so again).

The British sent troops to Kuwait in July 1960. Kassem tried to get the United Nations to order the British to leave what he claimed was Iraqi territory. (You'll recall that the Iraqis were poised to invade Kuwait in 1939, as well.)

The United Nations refused, and even the Arab League rallied to support Kuwait. (Does any of this sound familiar?)

The Iraqis backed off. Like the Hashemite monarchs before him, Kassem saw his prestige (and his grip on power) suffer a debilitating blow through a failed foreign policy initiative. Kassem responded by cutting of relations with most of his Arab neighbors, deepening his isolation.

## Pressure from the Kurds

The Kurds saw their chance during all the confusion. They initiated a rebellious uprising in northern Iraq. Kassem responded brutally, and unsuccessfully, continuing the previous regime's protracted campaigns against the Kurds. His inability to contain the Kurds only hastened his own demise, as his prestige with the army took another blow.

# February 8, 1963

So in the environment of internal chaos and foreign policy failure, the Iraqi officer corps decided to try again.

They first attempted a coup in March of 1959, but Kassem got wind of it, and rallied the Communists to his side. Iraqi Communists organized a huge rally in Mosul; it got out of hand, and members of the Iraqi Communist Party attacked and killed well-to-do Mosul families and nationalists.

Later, the Iraqi Communist Party led attacks on upper-class Turkoman groups in Kirkuk during another rally. Kassem finally responded by cracking down on the ICP, and jailing some of the rank and file membership. Despite these actions, the Ba'th officers attempted to assassinate Kassem in 1959, having concluded that he had lost effective control of the country and was letting their enemies, the Communists, get too powerful.

> ### Increase Your Iraq IQ
>
> "Thus, the 14th July Revolution was a historic event, but it soon suffered a set-back when it was dominated by the dictatorial rule of Abdul Karim Kassem. The Arab Ba'th Socialist Party therefore had to continue the struggle to restore the revolution to its genuine path."
>
> —*Official Tourist Guide to Iraq*

## Saddam Takes Aim

General Saddam Hussein (yes, *that* Saddam Hussein) attempted the assassination, but he only wounded Kassem.

Predictably, Kassem responded by cracking down on the Ba'th Party. Undeterred, the Ba'th tried again on February 8, 1963. Despite his enormous popularity with the vast majority of his country's population, Kassem was alienated as a leader from the ruling elites, and so was removed and killed. According to the official Iraqi account of events:

> On this day the Arab Ba'th Socialist Party carried out its great Revolution, which brought down the dictatorial regime. It was a socialist, democratic and nationalist revolution in which all the civil and military formations of the Party took part, which elicited the hostility of imperialist forces. The latter combined in conspiring against it on 18th November, 1963, while it was only a few months old.

This coup involved the Ba'th elements of the Iraqi officer corp. They succeeded in killing Kassem, but the Ba'th were not strong enough to hold onto power.

## The Backlash

There were about 1,000 members of the Iraqi branch of the Ba'th Party at that time. Now, this seems like too small a number to mount an effective government, but remember that in a closed society, relatively small numbers of well-placed people can topple a shaky regime.

However, when Kassem was overthrown, millions of Iraqi urban poor and rural peasants rallied to his support in a fruitless attempt to save his life and restore him to power. Kassem's own poor origins had made him a hero to the common people who made up the bulk of Iraqi society.

The simple fact that Kassem could be so easily removed from power despite popular wishes shows just how illegitimate the Iraqi political process was in the eyes of the people of the country. From the Ottomans, through the Hashemite monarchs, to the military-led republic, the leadership of Iraq had steadily moved apart from the people it was supposed to govern. This process continued with Ba'th leadership.

Moreover, the Ba'th had gone on a nine-month purging spree during their time in power. They arrested, imprisoned, and killed Communists and other political challengers to their power. Some 5,000 Iraqis, mostly ICP leaders, were killed. Increasingly isolated, and increasingly unpopular, the same factors that allowed the Ba'ths to take power allowed the next officer clique to take it from them on November 18, 1963.

# Rapprochement?

The Ba'th group was pushed out in November 1963 by a group led by General Abdul Salam Arif. The Ba'th were big enough to unseat Kassem, but were just too small to effectively run the state. Arif represented a broader base of followers who were more moderate than the Ba'th. Once in control, Arif attempted a rapprochement with the West and his Arab neighbors.

Arif was killed in a helicopter crash in April 1966, and his brother, General Abdul Rahman Arif, took over as president. The Arif(s) government was no more open or embraced than the first Ba'th or Kassem governments had been. Salam Arif was also a supporter of the United Arab Republic's Nasser, and his plan included eventual membership in the UAR. (The target date was 1966.)

Arif continued to maneuver pro-Nasser people into his inner circle, much to the dismay and concern of the Iraqi pan-Arabists, who still saw Iraq as the leader of the Arab world. For them, union with Egypt would surely mean domination by Nasser, and that was unacceptable.

The Ba'ths, meanwhile, continued to recruit new members and extend their reach deeper into the officer corp. Five years after their first attempt, they seized power again.

According to the official Iraqi account of the events: The 17th July 1968 Revolution, under the leadership of the Arab Ba'th Socialist Party, is the most important event in the history of modern Iraq. A progressive Revolution, it succeeded in liberating Iraq from all forms of subservience, in rescuing the country's oil wealth from the control of international oil monopolies by the historic decision of Oil Nationalization of June 1st, 1972.

The events that led up to the July 17 coup came to a head during the 1967 Arab-Israeli War.

# Why It Happened

In 1967, Iraq had joined other Arab countries in declaring war on Israel. Iraq had also closed pipelines used to send oil toward Western nations. Diplomatic ties were cut with the United States, which supported Israel during the conflict.

The result of the economic effects of closing the pipeline, and the anger that arose from losing another showdown with Israel, combined to encourage a group of Iraqi officers to make their move.

# The Arab Revolutionary Movement

The Arab Revolutionary Movement, comprised of a group of young army officers, were increasingly disillusioned by the Arif government's reliance on Nasser supporters within the government.

Led by Colonels Abd ar Razzaq an Nayif and Ibrahim ad Daud, the Arab Revolutionary Movement ousted the Arif government.

# Taking Over Someone Else's Coup

The Arab Revolutionary Movement officers acted independently from the Ba'th when they launched the coup. However, it quickly became clear that Nayif and Daud did not have the backing within the army to remain in power. In less than a month, the Ba'th levered Nayif and Daud out of power, and took over the government again.

The new Ba'th government was led by General Ahmed Hassan al-Bakr. Official Iraqi accounts of events claim that the Ba'ths united the competing constituencies within Iraq, but this is far fetched. The al-Bakr government was just as isolated as the Arif and Kassem governments had been. It was still a case of closed-society, leading groups fighting amongst themselves.

The stage was set for the Ba'th government's consolidation of power, and for General Saddam Hussein's rise from would-be assassin to leader of Iraq.

## The Least You Need to Know

- The coups that led up to the Ba'th seizure were a result of shaky provisional governments taking over for the ones that preceded them.

- The coup governments took increasingly anti-Western positions.

- All the coups were led by Iraqi generals, who were just as alienated from the common Iraqis as the Hashemite monarchs had been.

- The Ba'th Socialist Party persevered against Communist rivals during the 1950s and 1960s.

- The Ba'th Socialist Party attempted to take power in 1963, but was edged out; they themselves did the edging out in 1968.

# Chapter 14

# Oil, Guns, and Money: Iraq's Role in the World Economy

## In This Chapter

- ◆ Socialism in Iraq
- ◆ The oil industry gets nationalized
- ◆ The ins and outs of OPEC

The Arab Ba'th Socialist Resurrection Party took control of Iraq on July 17, 1968. The Ba'th Party has continued some of the policies of the post-Hashemite coup leaders, and added its own brand of socialism and foreign policy to the mix.

To understand Saddam Hussein—and current Iraqi policies toward their people and the rest of world—we have to understand how Ba'th-led Iraq dealt with its economic challenges, its Middle Eastern neighbors, and its role in the international community in the years following the 1968 coup. These issues all dovetail—and finally result in Saddam's emergence on the scene.

# Socialism, Iraqi-Style

As we've seen, the Arab Ba'th Socialist Resurrection Party was founded by Michel Aflaq and Salah ad-Din al-Bitar, a pair of Syrian students who were steeped in the concepts of socialism, which included the following:

◆ Land reforms

◆ Trade unions

◆ Public ownership of natural resources

◆ Public ownership of factories

◆ Worker involvement in the management of companies

◆ Inclusion in the political process

Socialism in Europe in the post World War II era has applied many of these concepts to daily life. As a general rule, the brand of socialism that emerged in Eastern Europe was much more centrally controlled than the brand that emerged in Western Europe, primarily because the eastern European countries were under the political, military, and economic domination of the Soviet Union.

Which brings us to a fascinating set of parallels worthy of a brief digression: the similarities between the emergence of Ba'th rule in Iraq and the emergence of Soviet rule in Russia.

**Desert Diction**

In Marxist theory, the **dialectic** is the concept that change occurs through the struggle between opposing forces of labor and capital, or workers and owners. The outcome of the struggle results in the next "higher" form of society (for example, socialism evolving into communism).

# Ba'th Rule, Soviet Rule

The Soviet Union called itself Communist, but in reality it was not communist in quite the way that Karl Marx had originally envisioned. In fact, Marx predicted that communism would "take root" in an advanced industrialized country, like Germany, Britain, or the United States. Marx believed communism would develop as the ultimate state of human social and economic evolution. The historical *dialectic*, as he termed it, would culminate in communism, but there was a long way to go before we would get there.

---

**Increase Your Iraq IQ**

Karl Marx (1818–1883) was born in Germany and connected with fellow radical economist Freidrich Engels while living in Paris. Together, they are credited with developing the tenets of socialism and communism that found a broad audience in the 1830s and 1840s in Europe.

After the socialist revolutions that swept Europe in 1848 failed, Marx turned to a more "radical socialism" that became known as "communism." Marx determined that the inevitable laws of history (as determined by dialectic materialism) would eventually result in a "dictatorship of the proletariat." These concepts were eventually put forth in Marx's *Communist Manifesto* in 1848, and his seminal work, *Das Kapital* (1867), that was edited by Engels and republished in 1894. Marx is considered a leading economic theorist even by non-Communist country economists.

---

Like the Ba'th, the Bolsheviks of pre-Soviet Russia seized a leadership opportunity. Like the Ba'th, the Bolsheviks were really not equipped to run a complex state, in large part because few Russians were Bolsheviks when the 1917 Revolution occurred in Russia.

## Knocking Out Rivals by Making the Most of Chaos

There were two competing Communist parties in Russia in 1917, the Bolsheviks and the Mensheviks. Bolshevik means "majority" and Menshevik means "minority." In reality the Bolsheviks were the more radical minority of the Communists in Russia. Led by Lenin, the Bolsheviks seized power and claimed to be the majority of the Communists, but they were hard pressed in the beginning to maintain control.

The chaos that reigned after the Russian Revolution was an asset to the Bolsheviks, because it meant that no other group could rally enough support to topple them.

Almost immediately upon assuming power in Russia, the Bolsheviks began to revise Marx's original theories of communism to their reality in Russia. As a result, the economic and political system that emerged in Russia was never really Communist in the classic sense. The Russian economy was not industrialized to any great degree, and the society had not passed through a socialist phase, which Marx felt was necessary for a successful Communist state.

Two key points are worth bearing in mind here: Russia was a closed society when the Bolsheviks took over (not unlike Iraq), and it was far from an industrial powerhouse economically (ditto).

## Socialism in Open and Closed Societies

Historically, socialism has evolved very differently in open societies than in closed societies. The socialism that emerged in countries like Britain, Germany, and Sweden was based on a much more inclusive political process than the socialism that was practiced in the Soviet Union. The Western European model involved steady but sure politically mandated reforms to an existing (and thriving) economic system. The governments created socialist institutions and nationalized various industries and services, but they did so as a result of the mandate of the voters in those countries.

In other words, socialism did not occur outside the democratic process. These countries had a vibrant democratic process that was essentially stable. No coups took place.

Socialism in closed societies, on the other hand, looks very much like another code-word for dictatorship. The Soviet system had only one political party (the Communist Party of the Soviet Union); and although the system claimed universal suffrage, there was no tolerance, dissent, or political challenge to the ruling party. Power and decision-making was concentrated in the Politburo, which consisted of fewer than 20 people. Changes were mandated from the top, not from the will of the populace. Consider, for example, the Collectivization campaign of 1929, where the Soviet state brutally took private farms away from the peasants and "collected" them into large state farms. Hundreds of thousands died resisting that process, and millions died in the famines that came afterward.

# Socialism in Iraq

The socialism that emerged in Iraq resembled the Soviet version far more than it resembled the West European model. Like Tsarist Russia, Iraq was a closed society prior to the coup in 1968. The Iraqi populace was almost completely alienated from the process of governance. Any socialist institution-building (nationalization of industries, collectivization of agriculture) happened *to* the people, not *by* the people.

## Iraqi Socialism and Marx's Model

Industrial society in the late nineteenth and early twentieth century was a battleground of labor and owners. Trade unions emerged and led the cause for improving working conditions and garnering more pay. Apart from the ballot box, labor resorted to the strike as a potent weapon in the ongoing competition for wealth. In most European countries in the first half of the twentieth century there were a large number of industrial workers.

Marx had argued decades before, that socialism, and then eventually communism, could only successfully grow in an advanced industrial society. Socialism is driven fundamentally, according to Marx, by the alienation of the worker from the finished product. Industrial workers, he predicted, would drive the process of socialism in their desire to realize the fruits of their labor. Labor would control capital, instead of capital (concentrated in the hands of a few "capitalists") controlling labor.

In both early-twentieth-century Russia and in 1960s Iraq, though, there was a relatively small number of industrial workers. In two classic cases of life failing to imitate political theory, the army of industrial workers required to "build socialism" simply didn't exist in these two countries. Therefore, in each case, socialism as Marx envisioned it had to be modified to reflect the reality of the state in which it emerged.

> **Increase Your Iraq IQ**
>
> In industrialized economies, Marx assumed that socializing industry would lead the state toward communism, because most people would be industrial workers. When this wasn't the case, the blueprint for socialism had to be improvised. How effectively this was done is a subject for debate. The Soviet model lasted about 70 years; the Chinese version has lasted for more than 55. The Iraqi model has lasted, so far, about 35 years.

# And Now, a Word from Your Friendly Neighborhood Economic Theorist ...

Industrialization is the process of creating specialized production processes in a centralized location, like a factory. In an industrialized society, workers perform specific functions that contribute to a complete product or service. Each function is a specialized activity that is unique and separate from the other specialized activities that also make up the product.

Industrialization requires capital formation. In other words, people need to have excess capital (money) to invest in factories and machinery, or to buy stock in companies that make things.

The standard theory about industrialization runs something like this:

♦ Agricultural resources are concentrated into efficient farms.

 **Oil Spill Ahead**

Until recently the agricultural sector in Iraq could support the population. The combination of wartime damage to irrigation infrastructure and increased urban population means that Iraq must now import food.

- The increased farm output generates excess capital for the farm owner—money that the farm owner later invests in industry. The more efficient farm frees up people to move from farm work to factory work.

- The key ingredients—extra money and extra people (and, incidentally, extra food to feed them)—all have to be in place for industrialization to take place.

The underlying assumption to this theory is that investment in industry yields higher results for the landowner than investment in agriculture. However, in Iraq at the time of the Ba'th Party takeover, it had long been more profitable for landowners to continue to invest in agriculture than in industry.

**Desert Diction**

A **shaykh** was the traditional tribal leader in Iraq. Tribal groups were made up of families, and the leader of the family groups was the shaykh. The position was hereditary.

Landowners had to pay the rural peasants very little, and infrastructure improvements (such as new irrigation systems) greatly increased output, and thus money. So most ruling *shaykhs* were content to continue to plow their profits back into farming, rather than into industry.

## Flashback: Private Sector Growth (Or Lack of It) in Iraq

At the turn of the twentieth century, Iraq was not a particularly good place to build a factory. Transportation was primitive, electricity was rare, and local demand was small. So most manufacturing remained at the artisan level, with work done in small shops.

During World War II, local demand for manufactured goods increased, as deliveries from other countries were curtailed. Local industrial investment took off in the post-World War II era, when state oil revenues were devoted to investments in private industry. From 1950 to 1959, the output of manufactured goods grew at a brisk 10 percent annually. Of course, that was from a very small initial base, but the numbers still signified the potential for Iraq to develop a significant value-added industrial sector.

A common pattern in socialist economies is that private sector investments tend to slow down as state investment picks up. The same happened in the post-1958 coup Iraq. As the new leaders invoked socialist principles and began to return land to the peasants, private money began to flee the country.

The process was gradual at first. The Abdul Karim Kassem government focused on returning land to the peasants, and initiated the first phases of nationalizing the oil sector. Still, beyond these few measures and allowing trade unions, he basically ignored the industrial sector, which was hardly the orthodox Communist approach to economic planning. Communist orthodoxy included complete control over industry.

However, the emphasis changed in 1964, when the post-1963 coup government of Abdul Salam Arif, taking its cue from Nasser's Egypt, nationalized (that is, established government control of) the 27 largest private industrial companies in Iraq. The Arif government also instituted other socialist concepts similar to those the Ba'th espoused. These included limiting private ownership in nonnationalized industries, mandating worker participation in governing boards of factories, and requiring a 25 percent profit-sharing program. Under such a plan, 25 percent of the profits from the enterprise would be allocated to a workers' fund, for distribution to the workers at some later date, in some future determined manner (direct payments, investments in worker's health and recreation facilities, etc.).

The result was predictable: Most able administrators and factory managers left Iraq, and they took a lot of capital with them. Industrial output slowed compared to earlier years.

**Iraq Fact**

The Iraqi version of socialism was at first heavily influenced by Egyptian socialism, as developed by Gamal abdel Nasser. The Arif government that took control during the 1963 coup followed Nasser's lead; it began the process of nationalizing industries, starting with insurance companies and banks, and moved on to assume state control of many other industries.

## The Whys and Wherefores of Socialism in Iraq

Why did Iraq's leaders pursue these policies? There were a number of reasons.

For one thing, many Iraqi officials truly believed in the socialist doctrines they preached. For another, leaders had convinced themselves that they should follow suit with what was happening in Egypt and other countries. There was also an attempt to appeal to popular sentiment by exacting some degree of retribution against those who had prospered under British protection. Once political power had been attained, nationalization of industry was seen as the remedy to ongoing economic domination by the old British-backed power elites. Land redistribution was used to break the stranglehold of the monarchies the British had established, and to displace the groups who had benefited from the system and kept largely landless peasants in servitude.

Probably the main reason for the nationalization, though, was that by removing a class of well-educated, well-off industry owners, the government was eliminating a significant threat to its tenuous authority.

# The Ba'th Regime Keeps on Nationalizing

The Ba'th regime continued previous governments' socialist policies, and extended the nationalization reach to just about all industry during the 1970s.

Iraq was not (and is not) an exporter of industrial goods to any large extent. The total size of the Iraqi nonoil industrial sector is basically limited to serving domestic demand. The part of the Iraqi industrial economy that doesn't produce oil isn't particularly efficient; it has been subsidized by oil revenues for years.

The Ba'th government uses the five-year plan method for managing Iraqi economy, but that system has been disrupted by the Iran-Iraq War, the Gulf War, and the subsequent sanctions.

---

### Increase Your Iraq IQ

Many communist and socialist regimes include a "central planning" agency where a single ministry directs all economic activity. In the Soviet Union, this organization was called GOSPLAN (State Planning Agency). In Iraq it is called the Ministry of Planning. The central planning agency creates a five-year plan that sets targets for production and investments during the following five-year period. In general, Iraq's five-year plan goals are usually not met, and much economic development still occurs outside the scope of the plan itself.

---

It is true that, in the 1980s, due to the tremendous economic strains of the Iran-Iraq War (see Chapter 16), Saddam Hussein allowed more private enterprise to meet domestic demand. (In a similar way, Lenin launched the New Economic Program in the 1920s to stimulate local industry that had been devastated by socialization in the years before.) Still, the main way that Iraqi industry continued to function was by means of an infusion of subsidies from oil revenues.

# Iraqi Oil: From Concessions to Nationalization

The timeline showing the movement toward nationalization of the oil industry in Iraq is as follows:

**1912:** Turkish Petroleum Company (TPC) formed

**1914:** Anglo-Persian Oil Company (British owned) takes 50 percent stake in TPC

**1925:** Hashemite monarchy grants first oil concessions for TPC in Iraq; oil-rich Mosul vilayet added to modern state of Iraq

**1928:** Gulf Oil Company joins TPC; the first U.S. oil company to enter Iraqi oil fields

**1929:** TPC changes its name to Iraqi Petroleum Company (IPC)

**1932:** Mosul Oil Company formed to manage northern IPC concessions

**1938:** Basra Oil Company formed to manage southern IPC concessions

**1966:** Iraq government repeals 99.5 percent of original IPC concession; Mosul Oil nationalized

**1972:** Al-Bakr government repeals remaining IPC concessions

**1973:** Iraq nationalizes Basra Petroleum Company

 **Iraq Fact**

The concessions granted to the British in 1901 resulted in only 5 percent of the country's oil revenues remaining in Iraq. The Hashemite monarchy managed to improve terms somewhat, but not much; Iraqi elites seethed for years about concessions granted to the Iraqi Petroleum Company (IPC), and this resentment was a major impetus toward nationalization.

# Pipeline Politics and the Road to Nationalization

Formed in 1938, the Basra Petroleum Company (BPC) had responsibility for the southern portion of the IPC concessions. The BPC opened a pipeline to al-Faw on the Persian Gulf in 1951. In 1952, another pipeline was laid across Syria, linking the huge Kirkuk fields to the Syrian port of Baniyas. With these two pipelines working, Iraqi oil exports doubled from 10 million tons in 1951 to 20 million tons in 1952. The increased oil revenues to the Iraqi government went to industrial investment, military expenditures, and (last but not least) the cause of lining the pockets of the ruling group.

Up to this point, the ruling Iraqi group did not interfere with the IPC, or with its foreign owners. The money was rolling in, and there was no need to rock the boat.

As oil revenues dramatically increased, however, Iraqi governmental leaders focused on domestic supplies. As part of the concession, the IPC was supposed to provide all of Iraq's domestic demand for gasoline and distillates. The IPC operated a small refinery near Kirkuk for this purpose, but it couldn't meet demand on its own. The IPC also relied on an Iranian refinery to help. The Iraqi leadership did not like the strategic disadvantage of this arrangement.

Their fears were proven when the Iranian government nationalized its oil industry in 1950 and cut production of the refinery used to produce Iraqi oil. The Iraqi government bought the Kirkuk refinery from the IPC and commissioned another to be built at Baghdad. This move signaled the beginning of the Iraqi leadership becoming directly involved in its own oil industry.

## Let Me Tell You How It Will Be: Oil Taxes in Iraq

In 1952, the Iraqi leadership demanded, and received, a 50 percent tax on the oil profits. The government was simply following the example of Saudi Arabia, which had increased the tax it charged on oil profits. The old tax had been around 25 percent, so the change again increased oil-related revenues for the ruling group.

Still the IPC limited overall production from Iraqi fields, because there was more than enough oil available by 1960. The major oil companies that controlled IPC lowered the prices they charged for Iraqi oil, which reduced the profit tax. Even more frustrating to the Iraqis was the fact that the IPC treated Iraq as a strategic reserve, using only a fraction of the massive oil resources available … and essentially "calling the shots" in a way that had a profound effect on the Iraqi economy.

## Enter OPEC

In response to the situation, the Iraqi leadership convened a meeting, in Baghdad, of the major oil producing nations in the region. In September 1960, this group formed the Organization of Petroleum Exporting Countries (OPEC). This single move was a critical step on the path to nationalizing Iraqi oil. OPEC membership meant the Iraqi oil production was added to that of a bloc of oil producing countries. By working together, these oil producing countries could dramatically affect oil prices by controlling oil production.

The next such step, as we have seen, occurred in December 1961, when the Kassem government repealed a huge (undeveloped) portion of the IPC concession. This move did not take over working assets, but it did signal the impatience of the Iraqi leadership with the relatively small output of the IPC.

In February 1964, the Arif government set up the Iraq National Oil Company (INOC). INOC was state-owned, and did not include any of the Western major oil companies who were invested in the IPC.

However, INOC lacked the experience necessary to effectively develop oil fields on its own, and the IPC continued to generate most of the oil revenues from Iraq at the Kirkuk field it controlled.

In 1966, despite the higher taxes, the repeal of 99.5 percent of the oil concessions, and the formation of a state-owned oil company, the foreign dominated IPC still controlled how much oil would be pumped and shipped out of Iraq. On top of this situation, OPEC member countries negotiated individually with the major oil companies, rather than as a group, so there was little benefit yet to OPEC membership.

The situation worsened for Iraq in 1966 when Syria raised its transit rates on the oil passing through the pipeline across its territory. The Arif government refused to pay, and the Syrians cut the pipeline. The loss of revenue to the state was enormous.

The Arif government felt that the IPC was selling its oil at lower prices and limiting production to punish the government for the previous repeal of the 99.5 percent of the original concession. Arif reached out to the French, and later the Soviet Union, to help develop domestic oil for itself. Eventually, these two outside players were able to help get Iraqi oil production moving without the help of the IPC.

## Nationalization Under the Ba'th

By 1972, when the Ba'th party was in power, the success of the INOC finally brought the IPC to the bargaining table. The IPC offered to increase output and raise prices if the original concession area was restored. But, by now, the al-Bakr government, emboldened by the successes of INOC in developing the huge Rumalyah field, responded by nationalizing the remaining 0.5 percent of the old IPC concession. They created the Iraqi Company for Oil Operations (ICOO) to manage the Kirkuk fields. The Basra Petroleum Company was allowed to continue operation in the south.

---

### Increase Your Iraq IQ

On October 6, 1973, the Jewish holy day Yom Kippur, the Arab states around Israel attacked. Egyptian forces drove across the Sinai, and Syrian forces attacked from the north. Iraqi troops joined with the Syrians, and Iraqi planes attacked alongside the Egyptians. After some initial success, the Egyptian forces were pushed back across the Sinai. Then the Syrian, Iraqi, and Jordanian forces were pushed back beyond Jerusalem.

U.S. and Soviet diplomacy, along with a rapidly deteriorating military situation for the Arabs, forced a cease-fire on October 23, 1973. Egypt and Israel signed a peace treaty in November, but Syria and Iraq kept fighting until 1974. As a result of the war and subsequent cease-fire discussions, U.S. ties with Egypt (that had been broken after the Six-Day War in 1967) were resumed. (U.S. diplomacy stopped the Israelis from destroying a marooned Egyptian army group during the fighting, and that may have contributed to the warming relations between the two countries.)

The IPC and Iraqi government settled their grievances in February 1973. The IPC paid $350 million to the government as compensation for charging low prices, and the government gave the IPC 15 million tons of Kirkuk crude, valued at $300 million.

The following year, the al-Bakr government nationalized the Basra Petroleum Company interests. They were reacting to the October 1973 Arab-Israeli War; they wanted to avoid shipping oil to any country that supported Israel. To do this, it was necessary to control all of Iraq's oil. By 1975, the process was complete, and Iraq controlled 100 percent of its oil industry.

Al-Bakr was the nominal leader of the Ba'th government, and gets the credit for nationalizing the Iraqi oil industry in the early 1970s. However, al-Bakr was just the front man for another Ba'th leader, who also took part in the 1968 revolution, and was steadily assuming more and more power inside Iraq.

This leader proved to be quite adept at channeling the newly controlled oil revenues to domestic infrastructure projects that increased agricultural output and improved transportation—as well as his own popularity. This new leader also succeeded in channeling more resources into internal security, otherwise known as the secret police. This enlarged security apparatus eventually became his stepping stone to ultimate power.

His name was Saddam Hussein.

## The Least You Need to Know

- The Arab Ba'th Socialist Resurrection Party is not a socialist party in the Western European or Soviet sense.

- Industry in Iraq was gradually nationalized from 1963 to 1980.

- The oil industry was nationalized by 1975.

- Oil revenues allowed the Iraqi governments to subsidize their nationalized nonoil industries.

# Meet the New Boss: Saddam's Ascent

## In This Chapter

- ◆ Saddam's early years
- ◆ His role in the Ba'th rise to power
- ◆ His campaign to consolidate his authority
- ◆ His move to the top

In the previous chapter, we saw how the Ba'th Party applied its own version of socialism to Iraq. The lack of industrial development meant the state had to look to the oil industry to finance its regime.

In order to get the necessary money from the oil industry, the government assumed full control over that industry. Iraq's first "republic" governments (in reality, coup-led regimes that were as closed and detached as the ones that had preceded them) nationalized the Iraqi Petroleum Company (IPC). By nationalizing the IPC and its Basra Petroleum Company subsidiary, the Iraqi leadership created a huge source of revenues for the state.

The oil revenues were used to prop up undeveloped and inefficient local industries in Iraq. Oil money also bought food to supplement local agriculture.

# Ba'th Party Time: The Secret Policeman's Ball

Perhaps most important of all for the Ba'th leadership, the oil money funded a strong police force. This group later grew into a force that was fiercely loyal to the man who headed the secret police, Saddam Hussein.

# Saddam's Ascent

Saddam Hussein was born into a rural farm family in the village of al-Awja, in the Tikrit region north of Baghdad. He was born into the al-Khattab clan and so, as a youth he had three blue dots tattooed onto his right hand. This tattoo was a sign of his clan roots, and marked him for life as a member of that clan and the rural community.

Saddam's career and mentality reflect far more of a clan leader's roots than those of a socialist visionary. His rise and consolidation of power followed the patterns of village power politics, where the strongest leader's family ruled the village, and so took the best for themselves at the expense of other families. In Saddam's case, the other village eventually became the entire country.

*Saddam Hussein.*

## Country Mouse, City Mouse

An enduring defining characteristic of Iraqi society has been the split between rural tribal culture and urban culture.

In the cities, people identify more with the state and with the services it provides to make life in the city possible.

In the countryside, on the other hand, state ties are less pronounced. The population is connected more directly to a number of tribes. Each tribe consists of a number of clans. Each clan is centered around a number of villages. Each village consists of several families. Each family is led by a patriarch.

The strongest patriarch's family holds sway in the village, commandeering the best resources and land. In the rural areas, one's identity is with the family, the village, the clan, and more loosely, the tribe.

## Missing in Action

Saddam's father abandoned the family prior to his birth, leaving Saddam to be raised by his mother.

In subsequent years, Saddam's mother remarried. Saddam's stepfather was abusive toward Saddam, and the little boy had an unhappy early childhood.

Saddam was sent to live with his uncle when he was 10 years old. It was (and is) not uncommon for an elder in an Iraqi tribal group to take in a young child in need of direction.

## Enter the Rich Uncle

The uncle who took in Saddam was one Adnan Khairullah Tulfah. Tulfah was a devout Sunni, and he introduced Saddam to members of the Sunni elite who were playing a leading role in Iraqi politics.

Tulfah himself eventually became the governor of Baghdad, and Saddam gained firsthand exposure to how power was gained and wielded in Sunni ruling circles.

Saddam was instructed early in two concepts that would become pillars of the Ba'th Party:

> **Increase Your Iraq IQ**
>
> The name Saddam means (aptly enough) "One who confronts."

> **Oil Spill Ahead**
>
> Saddam's uncle gave Saddam an early education in ethnic prejudice; Uncle Tulfah wrote a pamphlet titled: "Three Whom God Should Not Have Created: Persians, Jews, and Flies."

Pan-Arabism and anti-Zionism. Many young Arab men of the era, of course, were trained in the same ideas. These two concepts were deeply ingrained into contemporary Arab attitudes, and still are to a great extent. Saddam happened to have, in his uncle, a particularly able and energetic instructor.

## Contempt for the British

As a teenager, Saddam watched as Gamal abdel Nasser toppled the British-backed regime in Egypt. Nasser became the symbol of Arab power and pride to Arab nationalists in the other British-run Arab nations, including Iraq.

Saddam was 15 years old in 1952 when Nasser staged his takeover. Like many young Arab men of the period, he doubtless held the (formerly) powerful empire in contempt for its past arrogance and current influence within Iraq.

Young Saddam lived in the household of a high-ranking Sunni official in Baghdad, and thus had access to a variety of news, books, and broadcasts that brought events in the world to his doorstep.

## A Member of the Elite

Saddam was raised into the Sunni, anti-Israel, anti-British, pan-Arab, Iraqi elite. He was able to network with others in Baghdad who shared his beliefs and to learn about important new ideas and political movements in the Arab world.

One of the political movements that was captivating Iraqi urban elites in the 1950s was the Arab Ba'th Socialist Renaissance Party. As we have seen, this party synthesized pan-Arabism and socialism into one ideal, and preached the resurgence (resurrection) of the Arab nation.

| Increase Your Iraq IQ |
| --- |
| As in many countries where Communist and socialist parties vied for control against other political groups (nationalists, fascists, etc.), the Communists and socialists saved their most savage violence for each other. |

Young Saddam saw the Ba'th Party, and its dedication to overthrowing the existing Iraqi government, as a path to power. Saddam jumped onto the Ba'th bandwagon with both feet, proving himself a worthy revolutionary at every opportunity.

## Previews of Coming Attractions: A Death in the Family

At the age of 20, Saddam officially joined the Ba'th Party. He took part in Party demonstrations and was a prominent fighter alongside the street toughs whom the Ba'th used to fight their battles against rival parties.

No rival party was so detested by the Ba'th as the Iraqi Communist Party (ICP).

Saddam gained stature in the Ba'th movement by killing a Communist activist. The activist happened to be his brother-in-law.

## A Murderous Ascent

In 1959, Saddam led an attempt to kill Prime Minister Kassem. Saddam was wounded in the leg but was able to escape to Syria.

Like the unlucky Nuri as-Said (the last prime minister under the Hashemite monarchy), Saddam went disguised as a woman. (Remember that at the time, most Iraqi women wore veils, and so it was a good way for a person to hide his or her identity.) Of course, considering that Saddam is 6 feet 2 inches tall and more than 210 pounds, he must have cut a fairly striking figure in a country where most people are almost a foot shorter.

Even though the assassination attempt failed and he fled the country dressed as a woman, Saddam's stature within the Ba'th organization in Iraq grew. He had proven himself as committed as any to the success of the Ba'th Party. Saddam traveled from Syria to Cairo, where he met his hero, Egyptian President Gamal abdel Nasser. At that point, Nasser's popularity outside Egypt was extremely strong. He represented the resurgence of Arab culture against the Western imperialists, and his successful nationalization of the Suez Canal was a source of pride for Arabs throughout the Middle East.

Nasser, while not a Ba'th himself, was an Egypt-centric pan-Arabist; he was in favor of overthrowing the Iraqi government because it constituted a rival to his pan-Arab authority. (You'll recall his repeated calls to the Iraqi military to take over the government). Nasser was all too happy to give aid and comfort to the young Ba'th revolutionary. With Nasser's support, Saddam was able to enroll in a Cairo law school in 1962. Saddam's true course of study, however, was the overthrow of the Iraqi government.

## Back Home Again

On February 8, 1963, the Ba'th Party staged a coup and ran a short-lived, violent regime.

During this nine-month tenure, the Ba'th killed thousands of people and imprisoned thousands more. The Ba'th resorted to torture to punish their captives and to gain information and confessions from them. (In so doing, they were setting a precedent that would be followed in later years under Saddam's rule.)

Saddam returned to Baghdad and quickly was given command over a Ba'th prison where, not so surprisingly, most of the tortures were conducted. He again demonstrated his willingness to do whatever was needed—including murder and torture—to support the Ba'th Party's power, and by doing that, increase his own power.

You'll recall that the Ba'th Party only held power for nine months in 1963. A coalition of officers, led by General Abdul Salam Arif, threw out the Ba'th in November 1963. The Ba'th officials were all removed from power, and many were imprisoned. Saddam managed to survive the Arif sweep, however, and he began to work with the Ba'th Party leadership to prepare for the next opportunity to seize power.

Saddam himself oversaw the creation of a secret police force and an intelligence apparatus that would be used during the next coup—whenever it came—to consolidate the Ba'th grip on power. The Ba'th leadership would not leave the door open again for another group to undermine their position.

## A Tale of Two Coups

The Ba'th Party in 1963 had been heavily influenced by Nasser and less focused on domestic realities inside Iraq than it should have been. The 1963 Ba'th leadership had taken power riding popular discontent with Iraqi foreign policy moves, but they lost power because of their own clumsy dealings with domestic resistance and their inability to assume a sustaining control of the daily functions of government.

By 1968, the Ba'th Party was older and wiser. Nasser's influence had begun to wane. The Ba'th Party leaders were focused, prepared, and (thanks to a new intelligence network) better informed about their adversaries.

The next opportunity came in July 1968. By that time, the Arif government was reduced to an uneasy alliance of senior officers trying to maintain their grip on power. The disastrous economic and political results of the 1967 Arab-Israeli War, the mounting corruption in the leadership, and fracturing of the central ruling group, opened the door for the Arab Revolutionary Movement to take power from the Arif government.

However, the Arab Revolutionary Movement was just as unprepared in 1968 as the Ba'th were in 1963. In less than two weeks, the Nayif-Daud government was overwhelmed by the Ba'th, thanks in large part to their secret police and intelligence agents.

Led by Saddam Hussein, the Ba'th moved swiftly, and they did not repeat their 1963 mistakes. They took power, and they held it.

> **Increase Your Iraq IQ**
>
> Saddam Hussein was a key figure in the 1968 Ba'th campaign to take power. He was everywhere in the early days, rallying support, directing the secret police, and demonstrating his leadership.
>
> Saddam had helped build the Ba'th's secret police force, and he was a respected leader inside the Ba'th Party. He was one of the up and comers in a party that commanded the attention and the imagination of the Iraqi intellectual elite in Baghdad. Saddam was not from that crowd—as his tattooed hand betrayed—but he was still able to move among them, thanks to his uncle's teachings. More importantly, he was able to gain their acceptance through his tireless support of the socialist and pan-Arab ideals of the Ba'th Party.

## "He Took All of Us In"

Initially, Saddam's rural background was seen by the early Ba'th intellectual leadership as an asset. Because he came from the "other side of the tracks," he was even more qualified in their eyes to keep the amalgamation of peoples, religious sects, and rural/urban backgrounds together.

Dissolution of the Iraqi state was—and still is—a real fear of the elites in Iraq. They were well aware of the diversity and constant antagonisms within their artificial boundaries, and they realized that a strong hand would be needed to keep it all together. Truth be told, the elites may have been happy to have a "low-born" person (although certainly one capable of taking on refined airs) to handle their dirty work for them.

Hamed al-Jubouri, an early member of the Ba'th Revolutionary Command Council, put it this way in a recent interview in *The Atlantic Monthly:*

> In the beginning the Ba'th Party was made up of the intellectual elite of our generation. There where many professors, physicians, economists, and historians—really the nation's elite. Saddam was charming and impressive. He appeared to be totally different from what we learned he was afterward. He took all of us in. We supported him because he seemed uniquely capable of controlling a difficult country like Iraq, a difficult people like our people. We wondered about him. How could such a young man, born in the countryside north of Baghdad, become such a capable leader? He seemed both intellectual and practical.

As al-Jubouri and his peers learned, Saddam's inscrutable character and urbane manners were the poses of a ruthless clan patriarch who would do whatever was necessary to preserve and extend his own power.

# The Ba'th Party Triumphant

In late July, the Ba'th Party scooped power from the Arab Revolutionary Front and installed Ahmed Hasan al-Bakr, a former Army general, as the country's new leader. Al-Bakr was the chairman of the Revolutionary Command Council (RCC) that exercised (and continues to exercise) real political authority in Iraq. (The positions of president, and prime minister of the cabinet, while important, did not carry the authority that membership in the RCC did.) Almost all the top spots were held by military officers, increasing the likelihood of military support for the new regime.

**Iraq Fact**

The Tikriti tribe was centered in a region just north of Baghdad. They were located in and around the city of Tikrit. Saddam Hussein's village, al-Awja, was near Tikrit.

Note the clan influence: The ruling circle of the Ba'th Party was dominated by Tikritis. The Tikritis were from the town of Tikrit (close to where Saddam was born). Ahmed Hassan al-Bakr, the leader of the Ba'th Party in 1968, was a Tikriti. Three of the five-member Revolutionary Command Council were Tikritis: al-Bakr, Hammad Shihab, and Saddam Hussein. All three were related, as well. Furthermore, the president, prime minister, and defense ministers were Tikritis.

## Why Not Saddam?

If Saddam Hussein was so capable and so well positioned within the Ba'th leadership, why wasn't he placed in charge in 1968? The answer is twofold:

- In 1968, Saddam was not yet willing to take power.

- He was not strong enough to hold power if he had taken it.

Saddam probably remembered the short-lived 1963 coup; a careful man, he probably wasn't ready to stick his neck out as the head of a precarious fledging government. Saddam had managed to survive the November 1963 power transition, mainly because he was not that visible outside the Ba'th Party itself.

Saddam Hussein was, in short, the consummate behind-the-scenes man.

Another point to bear in mind is that the other Ba'th leaders, and Iraqi elites who indulged them, were still not quite prepared to have a tattooed country boy in charge. Early in 1968, before the purges that Saddam and al-Bakr pursued with a vengeance over the next five years, there were still solid power blocs outside the fledgling Ba'th regime. These power elites would have to be mollified, or destroyed, before Saddam would be able to wrest and hold on to power in Iraq.

## Saddam Repels a Counterattack

The members of the Ba'th leadership that took over in 1968 were not Nasser syco-phants, but there were still many Nasserites in the Iraqi elites. These Nasserites saw the Ba'th government as being too independent and as promoting a brand of pan-Arabism that was not espoused by Nasser. These Nasserites felt strong enough to try their own coup in September of 1968. However, this time the Ba'th secret police, under Saddam's direction, sniffed out the plotters and foiled the coup. The Nasserites were purged from the party and from any positions of responsibility. Their families were dispossessed of their homes; women and children were sent into the street, and men were imprisoned.

## Justice, Clan-Style

This style of justice was totally in keeping with the clan-type power preservation methods that were perfected by Saddam and al-Bakr in their early years. Families would take revenge ... so families had to be destroyed.

Saddam, like Joseph Stalin before him, was a master of the *purge*.

## Removing the Rivals

Using the Nasserite coup attempt as a pretext, Saddam and al-Bakr relentlessly purged com-petitors, power groups, and opponents from the government. Purges became a method of removing opposition, and instilling a state of terror that enabled the leadership to assert tighter and tighter control of the government, and through it, the people of Iraq.

**Desert Diction**

A **purge** is the removal of a set of individuals from a group. In the case of Iraqi poli-tics, purges meant imprisoning and perhaps killing groups of people who were seen as threats to the ruling circle. Typically, a purge needs a reason, such as an attempted coup. The Soviet dictator Joseph Stalin excelled at the purge; he staged elaborate show trials to justify the removal of former party favorites.

## Setting the Stage

After a decade of purging, power plays, and consolidation, Saddam had assumed an aura of populism and authority with the people, and a practical control of power within the government, that strongly recalled the position of Joseph Stalin at a similar stage in his career.

The reality was as follows: al-Bakr brought popular legitimacy and army ties to the Ba'th administration; Hussein brought a genius for counter-operations and eliminating opposition. Over time, al-Bakr and Hussein took effective control of the Party.

By most accounts, Saddam was the real driver. He organized party structures and established a Ba'th militia, which later became the Republican Guard. (This militia would grow to over 50,000 men before the end of the 1970s.)

## Troubles with the Kurds

Saddam continued to do the dirty work of the Party. He directed operations against the Kurds during the early 1970s.

**Iraq Fact**

The 1968 Nasserite coup attempt wasn't the last that Saddam Hussein batted down. He successfully oversaw the response to yet another coup attempt by a dissident Ba'th faction in July of 1973.

The Kurds were rebelling against the central government in Baghdad. After the Ba'th takeover, they continued to agitate for autonomy, if not outright independence.

The Kurds were led by Mustafa Barzani. In March 1970, the RCC (with Saddam Hussein representing the council) and Barzani agreed on an elaborate, 15-article peace plan. The agreement allowed the Kurds to keep a 15,000 man fighting force. The agreement defined these Kurdish fighters as the Pesh Merga, meaning "Those Who Face Death."

The agreement did not define the status of Kurdish territory. It was not defined as independent, or autonomous, at least on paper. However, in reality the Pesh Merga controlled a broad swath of northeastern Iraq. Provisional Kurdish governments were established in this zone. Furthermore, Barzani's faction in Kurdistan, the Kurdish Democratic Party (KDP), was appointed as the only legal representative of the Kurdish people. Not all Kurds belonged to the KDP, however, and dissenting Kurds began to assail the agreement (and Barzani's Pesh Merga). By 1973, the agreement was basically defunct, and the Kurds were as rebellious as ever.

## Saddam Seeks Soviet Support

At this point, the Ba'th government resorted to an assassination attempt against Barzani and his son, Idris, in 1974. The assassination attempt failed, and the Kurds reacted with increased fury. Saddam responded with an agreement with the Soviet Union that managed to isolate the Kurds in Iraq.

Barzani responded by getting military aid from the Shah of Iran and the United States. The United States—like the Shah—was concerned by the Soviet inroads into Iraq, and they were working together to counter that influence by strengthening the Kurds. Also seeking to weaken the Ba'th government, Syria and Israel contributed weapons to the KDP.

Seeing the forces arrayed against them, the Ba'th leadership (with Saddam again leading the way) negotiated an agreement with the Shah of Iran. Basically, the Shah agreed to stop supporting the Kurds if Iraq would recognize that the boundary of the Shatt-al-Arab Waterway was the thalweg, or mid-channel, and not the Iranian shoreline. The thalweg boundary would allow both countries to utilize the waterway equally. This was a critical—and short-lived—compromise; the dispute over the waterway would eventually be the pretext that erupted into an epic and bloody war between the two nations.

Iraq also dropped its claims to some islands at the mouth of the Shatt-al-Arab, and to Khuzestan (a region along the Iran-Iraq border in the mountains). The Shah agreed to cut off arms shipments to the Kurds. This agreement, signed on March 6, 1975, by Saddam and the Shah, was finalized in Algiers, and came to be known as the Algiers Agreement.

## A Carrot and an Even Bigger Stick

With Iranian assistance cut off, the Iraqi military moved in on the Kurds. Most of the Pesh Merga surrendered, but a significant number faded back into the hills and continued to fight—or fled over the border to Iran. Saddam offered to create three autonomous areas for the Kurds, and provide them some constitutional protections. At the same time, he ordered the Kurdish villages on the Iranian border destroyed. He also forcibly relocated Kurds out of the Kurdish homeland, and relocated Arab settlers into the Kurdish homeland.

This carrot and stick policy only led to more fighting and to the weakening of the KDP legitimacy in Kurdistan. In June 1975, Jalal Talabani created the Patriotic Union of Kurdistan (PUK). The PUK and KDP devolved into a violent internecine battle through the end of 1979, effectively ending their resistance to Iraqi counter-measures. So, Saddam by the end of 1978, was able to claim a "victory" in the Kurd campaign. Once again, Saddam's reputation increased.

## On the Home Front

In the name of socialism, the Ba'th Party unveiled an industrial modernization program in 1976. Using revenues from the newly nationalized oil industry, including the quadrupling of oil prices during the oil shock in 1973, the government plowed subsidies into Iraqi industry. The government strategically located factories to create patronage and loyalty to the ruling group.

The land reform campaigns (see Chapter 14) that redistributed much of the shaykhs' lands to the farmers who actually worked them was also an effective means of strengthening the Ba'th Party, as rural communities benefited from the land reforms. Clan leaders' power was diminished, as individual families were able to take title to lands that had belonged to absentee landlords for decades.

The Ba'th leadership also invested heavily in hospitals and infrastructure projects like irrigation and roads. By judiciously meting out the cash, the Ba'th leaders were able to secure loyalties by granting economic resources through specific projects to chosen people. More cash, from higher oil prices, meant more patronage, more loyalty, and (not incidentally) more power for Saddam, as most ordinary Iraqis credited him with making the changes given his authority over the projects.

There was also an aggressive literacy campaign, and state education reforms that resulted in an almost universal literacy rate. The number of schools increased, as the state founded a public school system alongside the existing religious ones. The United Nations even gave Saddam an award for his efforts in this campaign. The program secured more loyalty for Saddam, thanks to the careful placement of the schools and hospitals.

During this period, some wealth was redistributed, education rates increased, and health standards increased. Saddam's power also increased. Domestic unrest was at least contained, and Saddam looked to foreign policy as the next step on his path to power. Saddam started by reaching out to his neighbors.

### Increase Your Iraq IQ

Saddam Hussein was presented as the primary architect of domestic reforms (education, agriculture, and industry) for the Ba'th Party in the 1970s. Al-Bakr, the chairman of the RCC and leader of the country, allowed (and probably encouraged) Saddam to take the public spotlight and credit for these populist moves in order to set the stage for Saddam to assume a leadership role.

## The Break with Egypt

Saddam's big break on the foreign policy front came with Anwar Sadat's signing of the *Camp David Accords* with Israel in September of 1978. The Accords were reviled by the Arab countries and Egypt's stature as leader of the pan-Arab movement was immediately destroyed. Saddam seized the opportunity to convene an Arab summit meeting in Baghdad that resulted in a condemnation of the Accords. The other Arab countries imposed sanctions on Egypt. (The Egyptians, now major recipients of U.S. aid, managed to get along without Arab support.)

Still not yet a formal head of state, Saddam had nevertheless taken the lead in denouncing Egypt. Iraq's stature—and Saddam's—increased among its neighbors.

**Desert Diction**

The peace agreement between Israel and Egypt was known as the **Camp David Accords.** Israel agreed to return the territory in the Sinai that it had occupied at the end of the Six-Days War in 1967, and Egypt agreed to recognize Israel's right to exist. The agreement constituted the first time that a Middle Eastern Arab nation formally recognized Israel's right to exist.

# Saddam Takes Center Stage

By early 1978, the ties that bound the Ba'th rulers were as tight as ever. Saddam, al-Bakr, and the new Defense Minister General Adnan Khairullah Tulfah were all related to Khairullah Tulfah, Saddam's uncle and mentor. All of these men were Tikritis, and all were tied to the same clan.

Around this time, al-Bakr, older than Saddam, found himself in increasingly poor health. His own grip on power was loosening, while Saddam's was tightening. In July of 1979, Saddam made his move. He placed his relative, al-Bakr, under arrest.

Officially, al-Bakr resigned. In fact, he had been in political decline for some years. Saddam, the ultimate behind-the-scenes man was ready to step without hesitation to the forefront of Iraqi politics.

So it was that Saddam Hussein assumed control of the government and proclaimed himself the new leader of Iraq.

## The Least You Need to Know

◆ Saddam Hussein was born to a poor rural family, but he was sent to live with a rich uncle who introduced him to the elites in Baghdad.

◆ Saddam was steeped in the pan-Arab, anti-Zionist, anti-British beliefs that defined the Iraqi intelligentsia.

◆ As a young man, Saddam joined the Arab Ba'th Socialist Resurrection Party and became a capable lieutenant.

◆ Saddam gradually rose to prominence through a steady campaign of power consolidation and ruthless suppression of enemies that strongly echoes the career of Joseph Stalin.

◆ After the Ba'th takeover in 1968, Saddam steadily expanded his influence behind the scenes before assuming control of the government in 1979.

# Rivers of Blood: The Iran-Iraq War

## In This Chapter

- A brisk consolidation of power
- Saddam's miscalculation
- A crisis averted

As though eager to take yet another page from the Joseph Stalin playbook, Saddam moved swiftly, vigorously, and dramatically to neutralize people in two groups: enemies and potential enemies.

In July 1979, Saddam was vice chairman of the RCC and vice president of the Republic. He was planning to assume the chairman and president roles as a matter of course. Other Ba'th Party leaders wanted a party election to select the next leader. Saddam would not risk losing that election process.

## The Purge: Saddam Takes Charge

On July 18, two days after al-Bakr's resignation, Saddam summoned the RCC and many other senior party officials to a meeting. With cameras rolling, Saddam appeared before the group in full military regalia and declared that there had been a Syrian plot to overthrow the government. Before anyone could protest, Saddam produced the secretary general of the RCC, Muhyi Abd al-Hussein Mashhadi.

A broken Mashhadi confessed his role in the plot and started naming members of the audience as co-conspirators. As each person was singled out, armed guards descended on him and dragged him away. Later, these "conspirators" were tried in secret and executed.

At the end of it all, Saddam circulated film of the spectacle throughout Iraq, publicizing his "rightful" ascent to power. Outside of the ruling circles, the military, and the urban intellectual elites, however, it is doubtful that Iraqis were overly concerned with the leadership change. In fact, considering all the reforms Saddam had instituted, they probably were happy he was now in charge.

> **Increase Your Iraq IQ**
>
> In assuming power, Saddam was simply manifesting his tribal background and the tribal way of dealing with one's rivals. By those rules, eliminating your enemies is the only way of being absolutely sure that they are no longer a threat. By being publicly ruthless, Saddam also made it quite clear to the nation—and the world—the he was capable of, and willing to use terror in order to maintain power and authority.

# Instant Replay: All the Stuff That Led Up to That Deal with the Shah

The gradual departure of the British from the region in the decades following World War II left Iran and Iraq jockeying for dominance in the Gulf. Before 1975, the two countries had operated under the terms of a 1937 British-mandated treaty governing the Shatt-al-Arab. That treaty placed the international border at the Iranian shore, instead of in the middle of the channel. Thus, Iraq had nominal ownership of the waterway. The treaty also required Iraq to maintain the waterway for navigation, while requiring "other nations" (namely Iran) to pay a transit fee for use.

With the British pulling their military forces out of the Gulf states, Iran became bolder. The Shah said that Iraq was not fulfilling its end of the treaty and abrogated the 1937 treaty. To prove his point, the Iranians cruised the waterway and did not pay the fees. The Iraqis responded by aiding dissidents in Iran, and Iran returned the favor by aiding the Kurds in Iraq. In other words, things were getting ugly between the neighboring states.

In November 1971, Iran occupied the Gulf islands of Abu Musa and Greater and Lesser Tunbs. These islands had been controlled by the two Emirates in the United

Arab Emirates. Without British military support, there was little the UAE could do about the move. However, the Iraqis viewed the move as a clear challenge; they saw Persians trying to take over the Gulf, and threaten Iraqi oil shipments through the strategic *Strait of Hormuz.* They didn't like what they saw. But they couldn't do much about the incursion, thanks to the vexing Kurd rebellion back home, which required their full attention.

---

### Increase Your Iraq IQ

The Persian Gulf is separated from the Indian Ocean by the narrow **Strait of Hormuz.** Tankers and navy vessels going to or from the upper Gulf (where the oil loading terminals of Iraq, Iran, Kuwait, Bahrain, Qatar, and the UAE are located) must pass through this strait. Iran makes up the entire northern shoreline, and the islands of Abu Musa and the Tunbs are across the Strait. The country that controls these islands can more easily interfere with shipping through the Strait.

---

As we have seen, Saddam finally sought rapprochement with the Shah in 1975. The Shah's support for the Kurds was threatening the very stability of the Ba'th government. By agreeing to move the international boundary to the thalweg (or mid-channel) of the Shatt-al-Arab, Iraq got Iran to stop supporting the Kurds. The trade-off worked, in so far as the Iraqis were then able to suppress the Kurds, who were left hanging without Iranian arms shipments. But it was only a matter of time before Iran and Iraq would be back at each other throats.

### Iraq Fact

Born in 1900, Ruhollah Khomeini was educated in the Shiite faith. In 1950, at the age of 50, he was dubbed "Ayatollah," a title that designates status as a supreme religious leader. There are a number of ayatollahs in the Shiite legal hierarchy; the Shiite faith places great emphasis on their leadership. Khomeini, like many Shiite clerics, was outspoken in his criticism of the secular regime of the Shahs. He was exiled from Iran in 1964, and spent the next 15 years in An-Najaf, the Shiite holy city in Iraq. At the request of the Shah, Saddam Hussein deported the Ayatollah in 1978. After a year in exile in Paris, the Ayatollah Khomeini returned to Iran during the Islamic Revolution of 1979. He was proclaimed leader of the Islamic Republic of Iran in 1979. The last decade of his life was filled with turmoil, notably the hostage crisis at the former U.S. Embassy in Tehran and the Iran-Iraq War.

Relations between the two countries were cool throughout the late 1970s. At one point, however, the Iraqis granted a special request of the Shah: Saddam expelled an

Iranian Shiite cleric, Ayatollah Ruhollah Khomeini, from An Najaf (the Shiite holy city in southern Iraq) in 1978. The Shah was leery of the Ayatollah's fundamentalist influence on the Shiites in Iran. Saddam, similarly leery of the Ayatollah's fundamentalist influence on the Shiites in Iraq, was only too happy to comply.

The Ayatollah went into exile in Paris, only to return to Iran in 1979, with the onset of the Iranian revolution. The Ayatollah proclaimed the Islamic Republic of Iran and assumed absolute power in that same year, 1979. Saddam was thus faced with a resurgent Shiite ruler in Iran whom he had booted out of the most holy Shiite city scarcely 12 months before. Rather than a secular, pragmatic (if belligerent) Shah, Iraq's new leader had to deal with a hostile revolutionary cleric who commanded the religious attention of over half the population of Iraq—and virtually all the Shiites in Iran.

So what did Saddam do? He picked a fight with the Ayatollah … a fight that eventually led to an epic and bloody war.

# Why Pick a Fight with Iran?

To understand why Saddam waged war against Iran, you have to understand the challenges and the opportunities he faced once the Ayatollah assumed power in Iran.

## The Challenges

Saddam feared that the Ayatollah would resume arms shipments to the Kurds in the north, and worse, maybe even to the Shiites in the south. Already, Iraqi Shiites were rioting, thanks to the government's refusal to allow a procession of Shiites to cross into Iran to congratulate the Ayatollah. To make matters worse, Saddam's remarkably efficient secret police had uncovered a Shiite group named al-Da'wah al Islamiyah (the Islamic Call, usually referred to as al-Da'wah) that called for an Iraqi fundamentalist Shiite state—on the Iranian model. Finally, the Ayatollah's regime was every bit as despotic and aggressive as Iraq's. Already, Iranian Shiite leaders were preaching an expansionist theme. Who knew what it would do next?

## The Opportunities

Iran could have been weakened by the cataclysm of fundamentalist revolution, and therefore be a ready target for attack. Saddam could increase his stature within Iraq (meaning within the Sunni elites), and within the Arab world, by beating up on the non-Arab Shiites in Iran. Second, shutting down the Ayatollah meant shutting down the Kurds. Saddam had not really put the Kurd problem to bed, and a Kurd truce was vital to his personal hold on power. Third, the Iranian region of Khuzestan bordered

Iraq. It had an Arab (not Persian) majority, and was rich in oil. Saddam thought it possible that he could either carve that region off of Iran, or at least incite the Arabs there to join his march on Tehran.

# Countdown to Battle

In April of 1980, the al-Da'wah attempted to assassinate Iraqi Foreign Minister Tariq Aziz, and then, a short time later, made an attempt on the life of the minister of culture and information, Latif Nayyif Jasim. The attempts failed; and Saddam responded by deporting thousands of Shiites with Iranian blood back to Iran and jailing al-Da'wah leaders.

Baqir as Sadir, the al-Da'wah leader, was executed, as was his sister. Things remained tense, and in September of 1980, Saddam decided to make his move. The decision looks worse in hindsight than it did at the time; relations with Iran were bad for all the Arab states at that time, and the historical enmity between the two nations meant he could expect some support from the Arab world. What's more, he doubtless saw war with Iran as a golden opportunity to increase his power at home (remember that *dictators need enemies!*), while increasing his stature as a pan-Arab leader.

# A Pretext for War

Saddam found all the justification he needed for war in the Algiers Agreement he had negotiated with Iran. The Iraqi government took the position that the 1975 agreement—the one that had given Iran joint control over the Shatt-al-Arab—was only a truce, and not a permanent treaty.

In late September of 1980, Saddam officially rejected the Algiers Agreement and announced that the Shatt-al-Arab had reverted to full Iraqi authority. Iran was incensed at the change of terms, and almost immediately both sides prepared for war. On September 21, the Iraqis lobbed some artillery into Iran, who responded in kind. The next day, both sides sent aircraft on bombing raids into each other's territories. On the day after that, Saddam sent troops into Iran, and the serious fighting was underway.

# Act I: Iraq Attacks (1980–1981)

In the early stages of the war, it seemed as though the Iraqi army would win in a walk. They were well equipped with Soviet weapons, in high morale, and ably led. They had 12 divisions, with tanks, to throw at the Iranian army.

The Iranians, on the other hand, were suffering from low morale; most of their experienced officers had been purged during the revolution; and they were now led by clerics with no military experience. Their mechanized equipment (obtained during the Shah's rule from the United States) had not been maintained, and there was little hope of getting spare parts from the Americans in the war's early stages.

Originally, the Iranians had two divisions in the central border region, but these had been degraded to the point where they only had some poorly outfitted battalions and a handful of undermanned tank companies. The rest of the Iranian equipment was not operational, due to lack of parts. The Iranian air force still was operating some of the latest American fighters, and they had shown they could use them during the foiled hostage rescue attempt in April 1980.

**Iraq Fact**

On November 4, 1979, Islamic revolutionary "students" seized the U.S. Embassy in Tehran, taking 71 captives. After releasing 19 of the hostages on November 19, they held the remaining Americans hostage for a total of 444 days. The Carter administration attempted a rescue in April of 1980 that failed completely. Ironically, the Iranian air force intercepted the U.S. helicopters, using U.S.-made fighter jets. The hostages were released on the eve of Ronald Reagan's inauguration in January 1981.

The Iraqis attempted a massive air strike against Iranian airfields on September 22, 1980, but the strikes were ineffective, and the Iranians quickly responded with air strikes of their own.

## Saddam Gains Ground

Initially, things went well for Saddam. On September 23, six Iraqi army divisions invaded the Iranian territory of Khuzestan. This region held a sizable Arab-speaking minority, and was oil-rich. Saddam wanted at least to be able to carve out this section of Iran, and he hoped the Arab minority would rebel against the Ayatollah. The rebellion never happened; however, the initial Iraqi attack drove 8 kilometers into Iran within a matter of days.

To the north, an Iraqi mechanized mountain division took the Iranian border town of Qasr-e Shirin. In the center of the front, the Iraqis drove on Mehran, and severed the main north-south road along the Iranian side of the border.

The invasion in the south pushed more than 80 kilometers into Iran after only a few weeks of fighting. In response the Iranian president, BaniSadr, freed many of the fighter pilots who had been jailed due to their loyalty to the Shah. These skilled pilots, using the latest American aircraft, were able to blunt the Iraqi attack.

By November 3, 1980, Iraqi forces reached the city of Abadan, but were stopped there by an Iranian Revolutionary Guard unit, called the Pasdaran. At its height, the Iraqi army had secured the Shatt-al-Arab and occupied a 40-kilometer swath of Iranian border territory. However, the Iranians stopped all the talk of a quick Iraqi victory by calling on the Pasdaran military units, and a new force, called the *Basij*.

**Desert Diction**

The **Basij** were referred to as the "Army of Twenty Million" or the People's Militia. They eventually numbered in the hundreds of thousands. The Basij were poorly trained and equipped, but they were religious zealots. Many went into combat carrying their own shrouds, because they expected to die in battle and achieve martyrdom.

## Saddam Extends an Olive Branch

Iran's counterattacks finally stopped the Iraqi advance. Iran also responded by convincing Syria to close the Iraqi oil pipeline and by seizing the Iraqi oil terminal in al-Faw. The Iraqi army began to dig in, and build an impenetrable defensive line (a tactic they would employ again in the Gulf War in 1990).

Perhaps realizing that he may have overplayed his hand, Saddam offered a peace settlement to Iran early in the war. The offer was rejected, and Iran began to counterattack by January 1981. The first attacks were clumsy, and failed in part because Iranian President BaniSadr insisted on commanding the troops himself. BaniSadr did not coordinate the regular army units with the Pasdaran troops, and the Iraqis were able to push the Iranians back.

In late 1981, at the Karun River, the Iranian clerics unleashed their "human wave" tactic that used thousands of Basij to break Iraqi positions. The Basij (often unarmed, many of them children), simply ran at the Iraqi troops, absorbing whatever bullets or bombs the Iraqis fired at them. Any survivors who reached the enemy (the Basij were too numerous to be completely obliterated) would fall upon the Iraqis with whatever they had, often their bare hands. The Iranians had forced the Iraqis out of their northern and central occupations by December 1981. However, the Iraqi army proved unwilling to endure the thousands of casualties that the Basij were willing to take, and so did not mount a serious counteroffensive. To make matters worse, the Iranian air force had almost total control of the skies, and was able to bomb literally any target they could find inside Iraq.

# Act II: Iraq Retreats (1982–1984)

The Iranians launched a new offensive, Operation Undeniable Victory, in March 1982. The attack forced the Iraqi army to retreat, and it wrecked three Iraqi divisions in the process. By May 1982, the Iranians had the Iraqis on the run all over the front. Saddam ordered the Iraqi army to return to the national border. He hoped that Iran would be happy to go back to the status quo, and even repeated his offer to negotiate a peace settlement in June 1982. Iran again refused to negotiate, and instead launched a major offensive (this time inside Iraqi territory) on Basra.

Still using the human wave strategy, and after suffering enormous casualties, the Iranians succeeded in capturing a small slice of Iraq. Throughout 1983, Iran continued to use the human wave with some success. However, with their superior armor, Iraq had been able to stop the Iranians. Still, Iran was prepared to fight and win a war of attrition with Iraq.

During 1984, Iraq concentrated on defending its own territory, rather than on attacking Iran. As part of this effort, and due to the large number of Iranian attackers, Iraq resorted to chemical weapons in 1984, in an attempt to stop the Iranians. Again in April 1984, Saddam offered to meet personally with the Ayatollah, but the Ayatollah again refused to negotiate with the Iraqi leader.

**Oil Spill Ahead**

Don't overlook the element of personal animus in the war waged by Saddam Hussein and the Ayatollah Khomeini. The Ayatollah no doubt still resented Saddam for kicking himout of Iraq in 1978.

**Iraq Fact**

Iran's human wave tactic used people in huge numbers to attack the Iraqi enemy. The casualties were enormous. An east European reporter, watching the battle from February 29 to March 1, 1984, wrote that he "saw tens of thousands of children, roped together in groups of about twenty to prevent the faint-hearted from deserting" during the attacks. The Iranians made little, if any, progress despite these sacrifices.

# Act III: The War of Attrition (1984–1987)

By 1984, some 300,000 Iranian soldiers and 250,000 Iraqi troops had been killed or wounded. The Iranians were still more than willing to take the immense casualties, and the Iraqis were not; thus it was that the Iranians waged a war of attrition in the hope of pressuring the Iraqis to accept defeat.

In just two days, between February 29 and March 1, over 25,000 combatants died on both sides during one of the largest battles of the entire war. In this battle, the human wave performed a new role. They ran through the minefields, to clear a path for the Iranian tanks.

Finally, the Ayatollah started to use regular army units, instead of his Pasdaran and Basij volunteers. Still the losses mounted. During one four-week stretch, the Iraqis lost 9,000 troops, and the Iranians lost 40,000. Part of these casualties were the result of chemical attacks—though Iraq denies having used these weapons of mass destruction. (See Chapter 23 for more on Iraq's use of chemical weapons.)

On February 9, 1986, the Iranians succeeded in taking al-Faw, where Iraqi oil was pumped into waiting tankers. The Iraqis attacked furiously, and finally regained al-Faw in 1988. However, the oil facilities were out of commission.

The land fighting continued, though it was basically a stalemate. Both sides extended the war to the Gulf and attacked neutral shipping that was carrying supplies to the belligerents as well as each other's oil facilities. The "tanker war" eventually damaged or sank over 111 neutral ships in 1986 alone.

 **Iraq Fact**

In March 1986, the United Nations formally accused Iraq of using chemical weapons, namely mustard gas and nerve gas. There was little doubt about it, given the large number of Iranian burn victims who were flown to Europe for treatment. The British representative to the Conference on Disarmament estimated that more than 10,000 people were injured in chemical weapons attacks.

In January 1987, Iran launched Operation Karbala Five, aiming at Basra. By the time that battle was over, Iraq had lost 20,000 men and 45 planes. The Iranians lost more than 65,000.

Despite coming close to breaking the last ditch defense of the Iraqis, Iran called off the offensive on February 26, 1987. Heavy fighting erupted in the north in May of 1987, but no definitive gains were made by either side.

## The West Gets Involved ... Sort Of

The attacks on oil shipping were making Western countries concerned. Seventy percent of Japanese, 50 percent of west European, and 7 percent of American oil imports came from the Persian Gulf in the early 1980s. No one wanted to lose those ships or see a reduction in oil exports from the Gulf region.

While both sides attacked shipping, experts estimate that Iraq attacked three times the number of ships as Iran during this period. Iraq had anti-ship missiles in its arsenal and knew how to use them. Finally, Iraq began attacking Arab-flagged shipping that was moving Iranian oil. Kuwaiti ships were attacked at this time, and they appealed to both the Soviet Union and the United States for help.

Both countries charted some tankers, and the United States sent some naval vessels into the region. On May 17, 1987, the Iraqis accidentally hit the USS *Stark* with an anti-ship missile, killing 37 crewmen. Iraq apologized, and did not attack U.S.-flagged ships after that.

Within a few weeks of the *Stark* incident, the Americans drafted UN Security Council Resolution 598 on the Gulf War, which the Security Council passed unanimously on July 20. Resolution 598 called for Iran and Iraq to suspend hostilities immediately and return to prewar boundaries. The resolution also promised potential UN aid to help rebuild the two countries' infrastructure (a step meant to result in increased oil exports from the region and lower oil prices). Tehran rejected the resolution because it did not meet Iran's terms for ending the war, and instead insisted that Iraq should be punished for initiating the conflict. By the beginning of 1988, 10 Western navies and eight regional navies were patrolling the area.

---

### Increase Your Iraq IQ

In 1985, the United States had been arming Iran, to counter the earlier Iraqi successes. (These clandestine arms shipments eventually came to be known as the Iran-Contra Affair.) But as fortunes shifted, so did superpower support. After Iran began to make progress through 1986, the United States and the Soviets became concerned about regional stability. Both countries started to arm the Iraqis during 1987, and stopped arming the Iranians. The superpowers were concerned about the possibility of a pro-Iranian Shiite state forming in southern Iraq. Such a state, they reasoned, could create serious instability in the region, and result in a further protracted war.

---

# Finale (1988)

As the land war remained static, and the superpowers were putting a damper on tanker attacks, the Iranians resorted to missile attacks on Baghdad. In what would later be called the War of the Cities, Iraq launched some 190 missiles into Iran in response to the Iranian missile attacks on Baghdad. The ongoing stress of these missile attacks, and the fear that the Iraqis would launch chemical warheads next, brought the Iranians to the negotiation table at last.

The Iranians came to the table for another reason, as well: The Iraqi army, now reequipped with Soviet and French equipment, was a much more effective fighting force than the same group four years earlier. During the first half of 1988, Iraq defeated Iran in four major battles. In the battle to retake al-Faw, the Iraqis used chemical weapons yet again. Facing those defeats, the continued missile terror, and the threat of chemical weapons, the Iranians agreed to negotiate a peace settlement with Iraq. The Iraqis, by this time, had regained some Iranian turf, but Saddam had had enough.

The Iran-Iraq War lasted nearly eight years, from September of 1980 until August of 1988. It ended when Iran and Iraq accepted UN Security Council Resolution 598, resulting in a cease-fire on August 20, 1988.

# A Bloody Toll

Iraq had about 375,000 people killed or wounded in the war, a staggering figure for a nation of 16 million. This ratio equates to about 1 casualty for every 42 people in Iraq. Iran may have endured as many as one million dead or wounded. To put those numbers in perspective, consider that Iran had 60 million people in 1988—meaning there was 1 casualty for every 60 people.

When it was all over, the issues that led to the war were still unresolved. The borders were the same, and the combatants were bloodied, but unbowed. Iraq did come out of the war with a military superiority over Iran, but that superiority was lost after Iraq's Gulf War defeat three years later.

At the end of the Iran-Iraq War, Iraq had an army of one million well-equipped, hardened fighters, with extensive combat experience. It had the largest Arab army in the region (and was second only to the Israeli Defense Forces in terms of overall power). By contrast, neighboring Kuwait had virtually no army or air force to speak of, and certainly had no combat experience.

At the same time, Iraq emerged from the war in dire economic trouble. It was supporting an army of one million men. Oil deliveries had been dramatically reduced, so money wasn't coming in. In fact, Iraq owed billions to Arab neighbors who had loaned Iraq money to battle the Iranians. It owed the most money to tiny Kuwait … and had little prospect of making its payments.

What to do?

## The Least You Need to Know

♦ Saddam picked a fight with Islamic Fundamentalist Iran for a variety of reasons, among them a desire to increase his own stature at home and in the Arab world.

♦ Iraq began the war well, but almost lost it all during the mid 1980s.

♦ Finally, when the war began to threaten oil shipments, the United States and the Soviet Union got involved and mandated a ceasefire that took place in August of 1988.

♦ When the war was over, Iraq faced enormous debts to its neighbors, most notably Kuwait.

♦ It had also built the largest, most experienced army in the region.

# Chapter 17

# Shifting Sands: Iraq Between the Wars

## In This Chapter

- ◆ Saddam's debt
- ◆ The quest for Arab leadership
- ◆ Iraq's idle, but powerful, military machine

The years that immediately followed the end of the Iran-Iraq War were fateful ones. The policies that Saddam Hussein followed during that period put the country on a collision course with the United States—and with history.

## Iraq's Economy: Black Gold, Red Ink

By the end of the Iran-Iraq War, Iraq's economy was in shambles. The country owed more than $50 billion to a range of countries that had loaned Iraq the money to fight the grinding, increasingly desperate war with Iran. Iraq had taken weapons on credit from the Soviet Union and France; it had borrowed heavily from Saudi Arabia, Kuwait, and the other oil producing Gulf states.

**Oil Spill Ahead**

Iraq owed $30 billion to Saudi Arabia and Kuwait alone. It owed the most to Kuwait, their tiny neighbor to the south.

Most of Saddam's industrialization plans had been delayed, and finally abandoned altogether, as the shockingly bloody war steadily drained the government coffers. By 1989, investment in nonpetroleum-related projects had practically stopped. There simply wasn't the money to finance projects, and wartime lenders turned off the spigots when the fighting stopped. As he surveyed the postwar wreckage, Saddam's plans for a robust, independent manufacturing sector were just a memory.

# Twisted Pipes, Twisted Dreams: The State of the Oil Sector

It all came down to the oil industry. Saddam needed oil revenues to finance the reconstruction of his shattered economy and to pay back his creditors. Saddam was well aware of the animosity of the Kurds and the Shiites toward his government. Besides using terror tactics to quell revolution, before the war Saddam had relied on relatively steady improvements in the standard of living for everybody—including the Shiites (whose loyalty was questionable given the Shiite regime in Iran)—to mollify the people and thus safeguard his position. Now that prosperity was a memory.

**Iraq Fact**

In 1988, oil generated more than one third of Iraq's GNP and constituted 99 percent of export revenues.

During the war, Saddam could blame the decline in living standards on the necessities of war. Now that the fighting was over, he was under pressure to deliver some improvements, or face the prospect of instability and an increasingly hostile Shiite majority.

## Infrastructure Blues

The problem was really quite simple: Even if Saddam could get the oil out of the ground, he couldn't get it out of the country very easily. Oil production and exports had fallen off dramatically due to war-related damage to the oil production and trans-shipment infrastructure.

In 1979, prior to the outbreak of hostilities, Iraq had produced 3.5 million barrels per day (bpd) and exported 3.2 million of them. Almost all the oil produced was exported, because Iraqi domestic demand was fairly small. Almost at the very start of the war, Iran had crippled Iraq's two main offshore terminals at Mina al Bakr and Khawr al

Amayah, where oil was loaded onto tankers. These terminals were still not open by the end of the war. Thus, the major Iraqi outlet to the world markets was closed in 1980, and two years later, in April 1982, Syria turned up the pressure by closing the pipeline that ran from Iraq, across Syrian territory, to the Mediterranean.

Why did Syria do this? Recall that Syria was led by a Ba'th regime under Hafiz al-Asad. The Asad regime was almost diametrically opposed to the Iraqi Ba'th regime, and the two countries' relations were strained even in good times. During the Iran-Iraq War, Syria was an ally of Iran. In fact, Iranian martyrs' families were given vacations in Damascus.

With the Syrian outlet cut off, and its own terminals in shambles, Iraq resorted to tanker truck convoys through Jordan and Turkey as an alternative way to get oil to market. About 250,000 bpd were exported via this method from 1983 through 1989. Iraq also expanded an existing pipeline that connected to Turkey, and by 1984 the country was exporting 1 million bpd through that channel. By 1987, the pipeline's capacity had been increased again to 1.5 million bpd. The Iraqis were also expanding a pipeline through Saudi Arabia to the Red Sea at Yanbu that would allow them to export an additional 500,000 bpd.

By 1987, despite the loss of the Gulf oil terminals and the wartime damage to other oil facilities, Iraq was still able to produce 2.8 million bpd (compared to 3.5 million bpd prior to the war) and export 1.8 million bpd (compared to 3.2 million bpd prior to the war). In short, oil production was down, and exports were just over half their prewar levels—but the exports were still reaching the foreign markets.

> ### Increase Your Iraq IQ
>
> During the Iran-Iraq War, Saudi Arabia and Kuwait, along with other Arab Gulf states, "donated" oil to Saddam Hussein's government in Iraq in order to make up for production shortfalls due to war damage. Throughout the war with Iran, Iraq received almost 300,000 bpd from Saudi Arabia and Kuwait.

# Adding Insult to Injury: Crude Oil Prices Plummet in 1988

The crash in world oil prices in 1988 made Iraq's internal economic situation even worse. *Spot prices* in 1988 were less than $13 per barrel—compared to prices over $35 per barrel in 1979.

So, let's review the situation: To attempt to improve domestic economic conditions, and to mollify a population that had endured eight years

> ### Desert Diction
>
> **Spot prices** are the current trading price of products in markets where the material is available for immediate delivery. Oil spot prices are standard measurement of current oil product values.

of war-related privation, Saddam had to get more money. His only realistic strategy for getting money was to sell oil—99 percent of Iraq's export revenues depended on oil.

The only way to sell oil was to get it out of Iraq, either by pipe or truck overland, or by ship through the Persian Gulf, past the Iranian-dominated Strait of Hormuz. (Remember that Iran had occupied Abu Masul and Greater and Lesser Tunb—islands on the south side of the Strait—and Iran also constituted the entire northern shoreline.) Unfortunately for Saddam, the main facilities for getting the oil to market were wrecked, and he could only get out about half of what he could before the war started.

Even if oil prices had remained the same as they had been in 1979, Iraq would only have been able to generate half the money it could have made if its facilities were working at full capacity. But, oil prices at the end of the war were half the levels they had been before the war, so Iraq's export revenues were only at about one-quarter of their pre-war levels.

## The Bottom Line

At a time when Iraq needed more money to rebuild its economy, it was making even less. One solution to the problem was to continue to increase export capacities and pump even more oil out of the ground to sell.

The only problem with increasing the amount of oil to sell (assuming it could regenerate its production and export capacities) was that, as a member of OPEC, Iraq was constrained by a quota on its export levels. OPEC instituted quotas to ensure that too much oil was not produced. Too much oil would create a surplus, and that would drive down prices even further. So OPEC members adhered to set quotas for production. The quotas were, and still are, based upon two main factors: negotiations, and a complex formula relating to proven reserves, capacity, and size.

If Iraq felt constrained by its quota, it could try to increase the quotas during OPEC negotiations. However, Iraqi credibility was limited on this score. Given the desperation of its situation in the middle years of the war, Iraq had unilaterally announced in 1986 that it would produce oil at whatever levels it

**Iraq Fact**

Iraq has proven reserves of around 140 billion barrels. Proven reserves are oil that we know to be in the ground. Given that amount, Iraq could pump oil for 100 years at its 1987 rates. On top of that oil (literally) is 850 billion cubic meters of natural gas. Iraq could capture that energy source as well, and had been working on that capability with Soviet assistance in 1989.

needed to prosecute the war. In 1987, facing pressure from other OPEC members (countries who were not only loaning Iraq billions of dollars, but also donating large amounts oil), Iraq had said it would stick to its quota … if Iran would reduce its quota to Iraq's level. Predictably, Iran refused the offer because the Iranian quota was twice the Iraqi level. For the remainder of the war, Iraq had produced oil inside the quotas—simply because it didn't have enough working oil production capacity to exceed them. However, as time went on, and as Iraq continued to invest in its oil infrastructure, it had begun to bump up against the quota limits.

**Oil Spill Ahead**

While still powerful, OPEC's ability to effectively manipulate world oil prices has been diminished since the oil shocks of 1973. The reason is simple: OPEC controls less of the world oil market. The biggest wild card has been the entrance of Russian oil into the market. Russia is not an OPEC member, and sells as it needs and as it pleases.

By the middle of 1989, Iraq was becoming increasingly belligerent within OPEC, demanding an increase in quotas. Saddam needed the money, and the other OPEC members were standing in his way. Quota limits are negotiated at OPEC meetings, and as in any negotiations, other factors can be brought into play, such as emergency need, or the veiled threat of using force.

# No Respect: Iraq as International Citizen

In 1988, Iraq was looking for respect, and the benefits that came with it. However, that respect was in short supply.

Any gains in prestige that Iraq had made as a leader in the Arab world during the war were tempered by the fear that its army now inspired in its neighbors. Iraq had been struggling to assert its leadership in the Arab world against its long-time Arab rival, Egypt. Saddam Hussein had seized the opportunity of Egypt's détente with Israel to increase his own stature by leading the chorus of Arab outrage over the Camp David Accords. By 1979, Iraq had normalized its relationships with the oil-producing Arab Gulf states, and the other Arab countries in the region.

For years, relations with the West—particularly the British and the Americans—had revolved around the issues of oil and Soviet containment. While not as solidly pro-West as the Shah, Saddam had been careful to be more friendly to the United States after the Islamic Revolution in Iran, and had leveraged animosity between Iran and the United States to his own advantage.

---

**Increase Your Iraq IQ**

While Iraq and the United States did not have formal diplomatic relations during the 1980s, there were established communications between them through a U.S. Interest Section Saddam opened up to U.S. companies who wanted to sell their services and products in Iraq. (Remember that power plant that the Israelis bombed in Chapter 1? It was rebuilt—not as a nuclear plant but as an oil-burning steam-generating power plant—by General Electric, a U.S. company.)

When two countries have formal diplomatic relations, they typically open an embassy in each other's country. When the two countries do not have formal diplomatic relations, they resort to the device of an "Interest Section" that is housed in a neutral country's embassy. During the 1980s, the United States had an Interest Section in the Belgian Embassy in Baghdad. A U.S. executive who worked in Iraq during the early 1980s described the building as "a U.S. Embassy with a Belgian flag over it."

---

Iraq had also been warm toward the Soviet Union in the period immediately prior to the Iran-Iraq War, but not too warm. The Soviet invasion of Afghanistan in 1979 had alienated most of the Muslim countries in the world, including Iraq. However, the ties between the countries became closer during the war: Iraq bought a significant portion of its armaments from the Soviet Union, and the Soviets were providing technical assistance to Iraq for the development of gas processing and transmission infrastructure.

Of course, the Soviets had looked at Iraq as an element in their larger Cold War struggle with the United States during this period. Anything to weaken the U.S. position in the Middle East fit their strategy, and developing closer ties to Iraq certainly fit the bill.

# Changes at the End of the War

Most Arab nations had been happy to see Iraq fulfill its ancient role as bulwark of the Arab world against the Persians. They figured that a strong Sunni-controlled Iraq was better than an expansionist, Shiite-controlled Iran in the region. Support was ample, as we have seen, and by the end of the war, Iraq owed Arab nations in general, and Kuwait (its largest lender) in particular, a very large amount of money. Iraq would pay this debt back in a way that nobody expected.

The loans had been used to buy arms from the Soviet Union, France, and the United States during the war. As a result, Iraqi relations with France were fairly strong during the 1980s. Relations with the Soviet Union and the United States warmed when the war went badly for Iraq, and got cooler when the war went better for Iraq. The superpowers, as we have seen, were working toward maintaining a prewar status quo, and in the end, they got more or less what they wanted: Neither Iran nor Iraq had emerged as a clear winner or loser, and both sides had been taken down a peg or two.

In the Arab world, however, the end of the war brought not satisfaction, but concern. By the end of the war, the other Arab countries were increasingly alarmed by Iraq's resurgence and its massive army. At over one million battle-tested men, it was the largest army in the region.

With the Iranians beaten back, there was no other country in the region that could even begin to match the Iraqis for size, experience, and fire power. Without the Iranian threat, what was to stop Iraq from embarking on an expansionist campaign at the expense of other countries in the region?

# Exit the USSR, Enter the USA

The Soviets had continued to play an active role in oil industry investment projects in the period immediately following the Iran-Iraq War, but that all came to a halt in 1989—along with the Soviet Union itself.

The Russians had economic and political problems of their own to attend to, and the Iraqis soon learned that the fading USSR was in no position to continue foreign investment in Iraq.

The U.S.-Iraqi connection continued to develop toward normal relations. However, the United States was not forthcoming with post-war financial aid to Iraq, which is what Saddam most needed in 1989. Still, Saddam acted like a man who believed that the United States was a country he could bargain with. Encouraged by the steady thawing of relations during the war, U.S. diplomats expected that the American relationship with Iraq would continue to blossom. But there was a surprise in store for the Americans—a surprise that grew out of the nearly incomprehensible levels of debt Saddam Hussein had amassed.

> **Iraq Fact**
>
> By 1989, the Soviet Union was crumbling. Central authority in Moscow was unable to maintain its tight grip on the 15 Republics that made up the Soviet Union. With the culmination of declining economic conditions, increased political and personal freedom, and nationalism, the Soviet Union formally ended on August 26, 1991.

# A Sea of Debt

By the end of the war, Iraq owed France $1.3 billion and the Soviets about $5 billion for arms purchased during the fighting. On top of that, Iraq owed about $9.3 billion to various export credit agencies (who had financed additional purchases of weapons on behalf of the governments who controlled those agencies). Iraq also owed private companies about $7 billion. These private companies were generally from countries like Turkey and India, who did not have export credit agencies to support their companies in foreign trade. Iraq also owed Western banks about $6 billion.

The most extraordinary debts, however, were owed to the Gulf states. Iraq owed these countries about $80 billion, and Kuwait was the largest single creditor. Countries who had loaned massive amounts of money, like Saudi Arabia and Kuwait, had wanted a "friendly" country between them and the Shiite Islamic Republic of Iran, and they had seen Iraq as that country.

In all likelihood, the Gulf states did not expect full repayment on the original schedules they negotiated with the Iraqis; they were, however, expecting some repayment, according to some schedule. At the end of the war, Iraq found itself in the position of having constantly to reschedule its debt payments and promise increasing amounts of its oil production to barter deals and debt repayment. This practice left less and less oil available for infrastructure investments and consumer goods imports.

## Caught in the Sinkhole

In the years following the war, Saddam found himself trying, without success, to deal with the economic implications of a conflict that had cost far, far more than he had anticipated.

**Iraq Fact**

On the home front, Saddam had offered a pension and benefits package worth more than $30,000 to each family that lost a soldier killed in action. Saddam had also compensated each Iraqi property owner in full for any property that was destroyed during the fighting.

When the war had started, Saddam appears to have assumed that Iran would surrender quickly, and that Iraq could enrich itself with Iranian land and oil at a fairly low cost. Saddam had plenty of money in the bank (about $35 billion in reserves). He figured he could pay for it all, and not risk his position by depriving his people of material comforts.

Saddam had believed that he could shield the population from the heavy casualties, and he spent heavily on expensive material and munitions in an effort to lessen the Iraqi casualty count.

The result: As the casualties had mounted surrealistically, the costs of the war had, too. This is one reason why the borrowing had mushroomed to such fantastic levels.

## Building a $300 Billion Tab

As the war progressed, Saddam also continued to invest in domestic infrastructure and factories that could produce consumer goods. As more and more men went to the front, Iraq had been forced to import foreign labor from countries like the Philippines to complete these investment projects, many of which would eventually be abandoned anyway.

In addition to these expenses, the war had cost Saddam something like $25 million each and every day. The act of keeping the army equipped and at the front had drained the country's wallet at a rate that no one, least of all Saddam, had anticipated.

By the end of it all, the total cost of the war had been truly mind-boggling for a country Iraq's size. One estimate placed the total cost of the conflict to Iraq at more than $300 billion.

Saddam simply couldn't afford to pay off the fight he had picked with Iran.

**Oil Spill Ahead**

The Kurds were not significantly represented in the Iraqi army, as they had resisted the draft throughout the war.

# The Army: All Dressed Up with No Place to Go

By the end of the Iran-Iraq War, a major transformation had taken place concerning the status of the Iraqi army. You'll recall that this army had been fighting a grueling, savage war with the Iranians for eight arduous years. Over one million Iraqis (out of a population of 16 million) were in uniform, and most were battlefield survivors.

The army had earned an even more powerful role in Iraqi government and society. It was considered honorable to be in the infantry, and honorable to fight. Even the Shiites, who made up 85 percent of the army rank and file (but not the officer corps) took pride in their role fighting against the Persian aggressors, despite the shared religion. The officer corps seemed satisfied with being officers, rather than political leaders—as long as Saddam kept the army supplied with goodies—and they did nothing to impugn the honor of the military. Saddam returned the favor by praising his army as the victors in what was essentially a stalemate.

Saddam was in the position of having fully 6 percent of his people in uniform. One out every 16 people was in the army. Iraqi society was fully militarized by the end of the war, and the citizenry was repeatedly told that they had won the struggle against the hated Persians.

Now that the war had been "won," Saddam would have to produce results for these soldiers, and the folks at home. If he did not, further rebellion was likely from the Kurds, and maybe even the Shiites.

So it was that, at the end of 1989, Saddam faced some extremely difficult choices. He needed money, stature, a way of dealing with his massive debt, and some role for his huge military machine. He looked around the region and saw a ripe plum to be picked just next door.

He set his sights on his chief creditor—the tiny kingdom of Kuwait.

## The Least You Need to Know

- At the end of the Iran-Iraq War, Iraq's economy was in shambles, and the oil production was down to half its prewar levels.

- Iraq did not get the assistance and respect it felt it deserved after the war.

- Iraq's ties to the United States were slowly warming, and Saddam felt he could work with the U.S. government.

- Iraq owed billions to other countries, foreign banks, and foreign companies, and had little prospect of meeting its payments.

- Iraq had over one million men under arms in the years just following the war.

# Part 4

# The Gulf War

In this part, you find out about the origins, the key events, and the aftermath of Iraq's conflict with the U.S.-led coalition. Here you'll find out how and why the coalition formed, how the war unfolded, and how Saddam lost the war ... but won the peace.

Chapter **18**

# The Gambit: Iraq Invades Kuwait

## In This Chapter

- ◆ The limited options open to Saddam at the end of the Iran-Iraq War
- ◆ Iraq and Kuwait: the history
- ◆ Persistently low oil prices
- ◆ Kuwait's relative weakness
- ◆ The détente with Iran
- ◆ The United States sends mixed signals

On August 2, 1990, the Iraqi army rolled into Kuwait and occupied the country. Seven days later, on August 9, 1990, Iraq formally annexed Kuwait, calling it the nineteenth province of Iraq.

# Saddam's Big Bad Idea

Considering (with the benefit of hindsight, of course) that …

- ◆ The (first) Bush administration reacted immediately and forcefully, stating that the invasion "will not stand"

- ◆ Within weeks, an Arab-Western coalition had arrayed itself against Saddam

- ◆ The United Nations quickly instituted a series of biting sanctions that cut Saddam off from the revenue of Western oil markets

… Saddam's decision turns out to have been a very bad idea.

It's possible, of course, that Saddam Hussein completely misread the tea leaves on the question of Kuwait. By the same token, it's also possible that he knew precisely the kind of reactions his action would bring about. In either case, the big question—given the forceful reaction of the international community—was and is: "What was he thinking?"

# A Method to the Madness?

As with many other wars, the causes of the Gulf War appear to be rooted deeply in the misunderstandings of key players. One can certainly make a convincing argument that Saddam misread the United States—and an equally convincing argument that the United States misread Saddam.

As we have seen, the aftermath of Saddam's last invasion attempt had not been good. He had just concluded a surrealistically costly war (in terms of people, resources, and lost oil revenues) with Iran. His country was badly damaged, domestic industrial production was down, and oil revenues were down. The price of oil was very low, and Iraq's wartime lenders were now lining up with their hands out. Saddam was forced to constantly reschedule his mounting debt payments, and he continued to delay much-needed domestic investments. His international stature, instead of growing, was diminishing, and the pending demise of the Soviet Union and the end of the Cold War had minimized U.S. attention—and the prospect of aid from the Americans.

To put it bluntly: The man needed money.

## The Russians and the Iranians Make Life Even Tougher

Unfortunately for Saddam, world oil prices continued to stay well below their 1979 levels into the year 1990. Production was up, Russian oil was flooding the market, and Iran, too, was pumping as much as it could to rebuild its war-shattered economy.

The prospects at that time for driving oil prices higher seemed poor. Only a serious crisis in the region, where a significant portion of production was threatened, would drive up oil prices again. It's possible that Saddam's thinking may have proceeded along these lines: If he himself could not deliver the goods at home, then he had to find someone to blame. (Remember: Dictators need an enemy.)

From Saddam's perspective, there were few obvious options. What could he do to get more money from his own limited oil capacity? What could he do to increase the price or the amount of oil he controlled?

One thought that may have crossed Saddam's mind was that any kind of a military crisis in the Persian Gulf would cause oil prices to spike. By threatening Kuwait, and by moving troops in (even if only for a little while) he could force oil prices up from their historically low levels.

# Target: Kuwait

Kuwait was right next door, and it appears to have seemed like the perfect target to Saddam Hussein. The country was much smaller than Iraq in terms of population (less than 1 million native Kuwaitis compared to the 16 million Iraqis) and geographical size. Kuwait's military was tiny when compared to the Iraqi military machine; Kuwait had only about 20,000 men under arms. At that time, the total size of the Iraqi army is estimated to have been one million men overall.

> **Increase Your Iraq IQ**
>
> Kuwait was founded on June 19, 1961, when the British withdrew and set up a sovereign state. In 1989, there were 826,586 Kuwaitis, and 1,316,014 foreign workers. Kuwait's economy is dependent on oil, and it is one of the richest oil producing nations in the world. The country is ruled by Shaykh Jabir Al Ahmad and his royal family.

## File Under "It Seemed Like a Good Idea at the Time"

Why take Kuwait? The main answer, of course, has to do with control of oil resources. Kuwait had fully functioning oil facilities, which would have allowed Iraq to get its oil to market. Kuwait also had enormous reserves of oil. If Saddam was to control Kuwait, he would control a larger share of the world's known oil reserves. Increased control of that much more oil would have the twin effect of increasing the OPEC quota for an enlarged Iraq—meaning more oil revenues for Iraq—and more influence within OPEC and more leverage in dealing with the organization's heavyweight, Saudi Arabia. Furthermore, if Iraq controlled more oil, and had more influence in OPEC, Saddam would have a greater opportunity to manipulate world oil prices.

Another reason for invading Kuwait, of course, was equally as pragmatic. Saddam owed Kuwait more than $13 billion, and he had little prospect of paying that money back any time soon. Saddam could wipe out a large portion of his debt by taking over Kuwait.

Of course, Kuwait was only one of many Arab countries that had lent Saddam money. Saddam needed those countries to temper their demands for repayment, to give him more time and more flexibility in making his payments. By showing that his military was powerful, and that he was not afraid to use it to get what he wanted, he may have felt he could (for instance) frighten the Saudis into backing off … and perhaps then win territorial concessions from them in the *Neutral Zone* or elsewhere.

**Desert Diction**

When the British created the countries of the Middle East following the breakup of the Ottoman Empire at the end of World War I, they could not settle the border between Iraq and Saudi Arabia. Rather than worry about it, the country makers simply created a buffer zone between the two countries, called the **Neutral Zone**. Later, oil was found under the zone, and the two countries agreed to share the development costs and revenues from that region. During the Iran-Iraq War, Saudi oil donations to Iraq were pumped from oil fields in the Neutral Zone.

In the end, however, the move into Kuwait may simply have been a gambit … a ploy that seemed to Saddam, for reasons that may not ever be completely clear to outside observers, well worth the risk involved.

# A Deadly Housekeeping Agenda

Before Saddam could safely invade Kuwait, he needed to tend to some housekeeping chores at home. First, he had to make sure that the Kurds would stay in check in the north. Second, he needed to be sure the Iranians would not interfere. Third, he needed to be sure the United Sates would not object, and if they did, that they would not do anything to stop him.

Saddam appears not to have been particularly concerned about the potential reaction of the other Gulf Arab states; he may have concluded (correctly) that none of them had the military resources to stop him.

# A Flip-Flop to End All Flip-Flops

To minimize the possibility of problems with the Kurds as he marched into Kuwait, Saddam needed to keep the Kurds militarily weak. To do that, he had to make sure that they would not be re-armed by the Iranians. (You'll recall that the Iranians were the traditional supporters of the Kurds.)

If he planned to keep the Kurds quiet as he made his move in Kuwait, Saddam would have to give the Iranians something. What he decided to give them was nothing short of mind-boggling.

The one thing that the Iranians really wanted from Saddam was equal control of the Shatt al-Arab waterway. So despite eight years of bloody fighting to *keep* the Iranians from controlling this waterway, Saddam handed it over with a stroke of his pen. In 1990, Iraq agreed to the mid-channel boundary between the two countries, thus yielding something that hundreds of thousands of Iraqis had died to prevent.

## You Might Well Ask ...

How could Saddam do this without incurring the wrath of his own people? The reaction of the Iraqi people was not his main concern. Saddam seems to have assumed that better living conditions were the public's main interest at that time, and that the people would have little objection to some form of foreign policy maneuvering that they had never had any say over, anyway. This, of course, is one of the by-products of a closed society. The dictator can (and often does) reverse policies almost overnight, without concern for public reaction.

The only reactions that Saddam appears to have concerned himself with were the Iranians, (who were satisfied for now) and the Americans, whose attitude he now set about to discover.

# Testing the Waters

Saddam began by making some extremely aggressive demands of Kuwait. He accused Kuwait and the UAE of producing too much oil and keeping market prices artificially low. Kuwait, of course, denied these accusations, and it is doubtful that Kuwait and the UAE together, even if they wanted to, could have produced enough oil to depress prices without the rest of OPEC knowing about it. Somehow, though, only Saddam was able to divine this supposed violation of OPEC solidarity.

Saddam also accused Kuwait of illegally pumping oil from the Iraqi half of the Rumalyah oil field—one of the largest proven oil deposits in the world—that both countries shared. During the Iran-Iraq War, Iraq had not been able to pump oil from their side, but the Kuwaitis had been able to continue pumping unabated. The Iraqis accused the Kuwaitis of having pumped from the Iraq half of the field by using *horizontal drilling* techniques. The Kuwaitis denied this charge, but Saddam continued to insist on it. There is no clear evidence that the Kuwaitis ever did as Saddam claimed.

**Desert Diction**

Horizontal drilling is a technique by which an oil rig sends out drills to the side, instead of straight down. This technique allows a single well to extract much more oil than it might otherwise be able to.

Saddam also pressed old claims that significant portions of Kuwaiti territory actually belonged to Iraq. These included the entire Rumalyah oil field, a band of territory along the Iraq-Kuwait border, and the Persian Gulf islands of Bubiyan and Warbah which bordered Iraq's Persian Gulf coast. Like the Iranians on the Strait of Hormuz, the Kuwaitis had the ability to interfere with Iraqi Gulf shipping if they really wanted to.

When the British created the borders between Iraq and Saudi Arabia and Kuwait and Saudi Arabia in 1922, they did not clearly delineate the exact location of the line between Iraq and Kuwait at that time. The area was considered to be empty desert, even though local tribes did live there. Later, the British *did* define the border, in a memorandum written in 1923, Iraq explicitly referred to this memo when applying for membership in the League of Nations. By referring to the memo, Iraq was acknowledging that the border with Kuwait was indeed defined. In 1990, however, Saddam insisted that the border was never formally identified, and no treaty between Iraq and Kuwait defined that border. Therefore, according to Saddam at least, a significant portion of Kuwait territory actually belonged to Iraq.

Finally, Saddam invoked the age-old Iraqi claims that all of Kuwait was really a part of historic Iraq. The claim was tenuous, but persistent. The Iraqis claim that Kuwait was at one point a part of an Ottoman Empire district that was actually governed as a part of the administrative area that became part of Iraq. The reality was somewhat different, in that the Ottomans never formally included Kuwait in their Basra vilayet. In fact, the British had insisted on this last point (that Kuwait was *not* a part of the Basra vilayet) when they agreed to let the Ottomans take nominal control of the Kuwaiti region in the early 1900s. Still, the Iraqis used this argument repeatedly through the years. Various Iraqi rulers had raised the argument about Kuwait in 1961, 1973, and now in 1990.

Thus, with a combination of fact, fiction, and good old-fashioned bluster, Saddam began to lay the foundation for his case that Kuwait was actually the nineteenth province of Iraq. He made it clear that Iraq considered Kuwait's alleged oil-pumping intransigence a threat to Iraq, and that Iraq would eventually deal with the situation in an appropriate manner.

## A Deafening Silence

The other Arab countries, as Saddam no doubt had anticipated, didn't rally to Kuwait's support during the OPEC meetings, or in other Arab forums. Kuwait was effectively isolated in these arenas.

With the Arab countries apparently willing to let Saddam do what he wanted, the Iraqi leader moved on to the task of gauging the American reaction to his attentions toward Kuwait. Many analysts now feel that a clear and forceful U.S. objection, or a U.S. warning not to proceed down the path he was beginning to follow, might well have dissuaded Saddam from outright invasion and annexation of Kuwait. This is not to say Saddam would not have continued to bully Kuwait or have stopped demanding concessions from them. However, it might have staved off an actual, troops-on-the ground invasion by the Iraqis. Whatever the case, that strong, clear U.S. warning was never made.

In fact, official statements from the Bush administration offered a very different impression. On July 31, 1990, Assistant Secretary of State for Near Eastern Affairs John Kelly testified before Congress on the situation with Iraq. By now, members of Congress were becoming concerned by Saddam's threats against Kuwait. (As it turned out, they were right, Saddam would invade Kuwait in about 48 hours.) Kelly testified that, "… the United States has no commitment to defend Kuwait and the U.S. has no intention of defending Kuwait if attacked by Iraq."

Back in Baghdad, a similar message had been conveyed directly to Saddam Hussein in a July 25 meeting between the U.S. representative in Iraq, April Glaspie, and Saddam. (This was a little over a week before Saddam invaded Kuwait.) Glaspie and Hussein met at Saddam's Presidential Palace in Baghdad. By this time, Glaspie and the U.S. government were well aware of Saddam's bluster and bullying toward the Kuwaitis. In fact, there was real concern about the recent tenor of Saddam's tirades. He had increasingly spoken about the Kuwait "situation" in terms of Iraq's survival. While most other people in the world did not make the connection between the continuation of the Iraqi state and the continued existence of an independent Kuwait, Saddam somehow did. (In a way, given his need to get money to prop up his position, if one substituted the word "Saddam" for the word "Iraq," the claims may have made more sense.) If Saddam was deliberately sending messages about his ultimate intentions in order to test the waters, he received no corresponding messages from the Americans to back off.

By the middle of August 1990, Iraq had massed more than 30,000 troops on the border with Kuwait. This move was one of the first real indications that Saddam was doing more than just rant in his Palace. Glaspie was dispatched to Saddam to find out what, precisely, he intended to do. After the war, the BBC obtained a transcript of the meeting, an excerpt of which is provided here:

> **GLASPIE:** I have direct instructions from President Bush to improve our relations with Iraq. We have considerable sympathy for your quest for higher oil prices, the immediate cause of your confrontation with Kuwait. (pause) As you know, I have lived here for years and admire your extraordinary efforts to rebuild your country. We know you need funds. We understand that, and our opinion is that you should have the opportunity to rebuild your country. (pause) We can see that you have deployed massive numbers of troops in the south. Normally that would be none of our business, but when this happens in the context of your other threats against Kuwait, then it would be reasonable for us to be concerned. For this reason, I have received an instruction to ask you, in the spirit of friendship—not confrontation—regarding your intentions: Why are your troops massed so very close to Kuwait's borders?

> **SADDAM:** As you know, for years now I have made every effort to reach a settlement on our dispute with Kuwait. There is to be a meeting in two days; I am prepared to give negotiations only this one more brief chance. (pause) When we [the Iraqis] meet [with the Kuwaitis] and we see there is hope, then nothing will happen. But if we are unable to find a solution, then it will be natural that Iraq will not accept death.

> **GLASPIE:** What solutions would be acceptable?

> **SADDAM:** If we could keep the whole of the Shatt-al-Arab—our strategic goal in our war with Iran—we will make concessions [to the Kuwaitis]. But, if we are forced to choose between keeping half of the Shatt and the whole of Iraq then we will give up all of the Shatt to defend our claims on Kuwait to keep the whole of Iraq in the shape we wish it to be. [Note from the author: Saddam's definition of Iraq obviously included Kuwait as its nineteenth province; he was arguing that he gave up full control of the Shatt-al-Arab in order to focus on Kuwait's "intransigence," unimpeded by Iran.] What is the United States' opinion on this?

**GLASPIE:** We have no opinion on your Arab-Arab conflicts, such as your dispute with Kuwait. Secretary [of State James] Baker has directed me to emphasize the instruction, first given to Iraq in the 1960s that the Kuwait issue is not associated with America.

This transcript indicates that, at the very least the Bush administration's official representative in Iraq did not firmly communicate any U.S. intention to defend Kuwait if Iraq attacked. While the Bush Administration's intention all along may have been to firmly defend Kuwait (as it ultimately did), that intention certainly was not communicated clearly to Saddam Hussein during this meeting.

Some Western analysts have compared Saddam's preoccupation with Kuwait at this time with Hitler's similar preoccupation with the Sudetenland in the late 1930s. There is an interesting parallel here, in that Saddam was clearly predisposed to annexing Kuwait and that probably only the strongest opposition would have stopped him from attempting to do so.

---

### Increase Your Iraq IQ

The Sudetenland was a stretch of territory that originally had been part of the new German state prior to World War I. The people of the Sudetenland spoke German and were of Germanic origin. After World War I, the Sudetenland was given to the new state of Czechoslovakia. However, in a notorious decision—the Munich Agreement—Britain and France agreed to let Hitler annex the Sudetenland in 1938, at the expense of hapless Czechoslovakia. In fact, the Agreement, touted by British Prime Minister Neville Chamberlain as "peace in our time," actually helped start World War II. An emboldened Hitler soon attacked Poland, despite British and French warnings, perhaps because he believed their warnings would never be backed up.

---

# All Systems "Go"

Perhaps to Saddam, the road now seemed free of obstacles, and the lights all seemed to be shining green. The Iranians had been bought off with the Shatt-al-Arab agreement. The Arab states were ambivalent about support for Kuwait, and could not really do much to stop Iraq even if they really wanted to. To all appearances, the United States was—or at least seemed to be—aloof about the possibility of an Iraqi invasion. The Iraqi troops were in place, well armed, and in high spirits.

Perhaps most important of all, Saddam himself was ready to take action. Anyone who dismissed his recent moves as empty bluster or political theater was about to get an unpleasant surprise.

# "Radical Saddam" Makes His Move

At 6 a.m. on August 2, 1990, George Bush sat in the Oval Office den and made the following entry in his diary:

> Brent [Scowcroft] came over at 5 confirming that Iraq had moved into Kuwait … they're trying to overthrow the Emir. Yesterday evening about 9 I met with Scowcroft and there were scattered reports that Iraq had moved …. I'm moving the fleet up early from [the Indian Ocean]. Saudis are concerned, and in my view all the [Gulf] countries must be quaking in their boots. This is radical Saddam Hussein moving …

"Radical Saddam" had indeed stepped to the center of the geopolitical stage. He has been there ever since.

## The Least You Need to Know

- Saddam felt increasingly boxed in as time went by after the Iran-Iraq War. He was running out of money to subsidize his position in Iraq.

- Saddam owed a tremendous amount of money to Kuwait, his weak next-door neighbor.

- Saddam began to bully Kuwait and make serious accusations about "provocative" Kuwaiti behavior.

- Saddam then bought off Iran to keep the Kurds from being armed and satisfied himself that the Arab countries would not step in to help Kuwait.

- U.S. diplomats failed to send a signal that an Iraqi invasion of Kuwait would be vigorously opposed.

# 19

# The Reaction: Isolating Saddam

## In This Chapter

- ◆ The U.S. reaction to Saddam's invasion of Kuwait
- ◆ The U.S.-Arab coalition
- ◆ Iraq's attempt to widen the Arab-Israeli war
- ◆ Diplomacy and bloodshed

On August 2, 1990, the world awoke and found Iraqi troops in Kuwait City—and heard the fading echoes of Kuwaiti military resistance to the invasion. In the face of the most massive army in the region, Kuwait had been overrun.

## The Rebellion That Wasn't

Saddam claimed that Iraqi troops went into Kuwait in support of a rebellion against the Kuwaiti royal family. This claim was shown to be false when Iraq was unable to form even a puppet pro-Iraqi government to run Kuwait. Like the other Gulf states, Kuwait is ruled by a royal family. This family didn't indulge in democratic institutions, but at the same time, the Kuwaiti royal family wasn't dealing with domestic dissent at any significant level. There are only about one million Kuwaitis, and they enjoy a fairly high standard of living.

A cynic might suggest that the Kuwaiti ruler "buys off" his population with oil revenues. However you look at it, there was no indigenous rebellion of the kind that Saddam was claiming in 1990.

The Iraqis had moved in after midnight on August 2 and caught the Kuwaitis off guard. About 120,000 soldiers and 2,000 tanks had reached Kuwait City within hours. The 20,000 Kuwaiti military put up some resistance, but were taken by surprise and completely overwhelmed. Many Kuwaiti soldiers were killed or captured in the initial assault. Eventually about 7,000 Kuwaiti military made it to Saudi Arabia with about 40 tanks. The Kuwaiti air force attacked the invading Iraqis and then retreated to Saudi Arabia as well. This remnant of the Kuwaiti military would regroup in Saudi Arabia and eventually would participate in the Alliance counteroffensive in Kuwait.

After consolidating their hold on Kuwait City, the Iraqi mechanized troops and divisions of Saddam's elite Republican Guard pushed on southward to the Saudi Arabian border. Saddam did not press forward into Saudi Arabia, apparently content with his takeover of Kuwait and the oil resources there. He would be able to exert more pressure on Saudi Arabia and other Gulf states through his enlarged territory, increased oil control, and the mere fact that he had used his army to invade another nation.

# American Reaction

In his diary, U.S. President George Bush wrote of the "enormity" of the Iraqi crisis that was now unfolding, of the emerging Western consensus, and of his determination to isolate Hussein economically. He also wrote of preparations for a military campaign in Iraq.

On August 5, Bush made an important public statement: "This will not stand, this aggression against Kuwait." This commitment to reversing the Iraqi invasion was a clear statement of U.S. resolve. The Bush plan was to isolate Hussein completely, not only from the West, but from the Arabs and the rest of the world as well.

# Saddam, the Arabs, and the West

Whether or not that resolve came as a surprise to Saddam Hussein is hard to say. He had no doubt expected objections, and even outrage, from other countries, including the United States. It seems likely, however, that he simply expected the crisis to blow over and Kuwait to remain in his hands. How likely was it, after all, that the Arab world would allow itself to be allied with countries like the United States and Great Britain?

Saddam may also have assumed that Western powers would not back the United States fully in any response to the Iraqi invasion. The French and Japanese had been conducting a large amount of business with Iraq, and Saddam seems to have counted on that fact, plus the historic lack of cohesion among the Western powers, to result in stern words but no real action in response to his invasion of Kuwait.

Finally, Saddam may have figured he could thwart any ultimate alliance by taking advantage of the ongoing Arab-Israeli conflict. Any Western-Arab alliance, if it were to form against him, could perhaps be ruptured by drawing Israel into the fight. The Arab countries would split from the Western powers (who would stand by Israel). Here was the reasoning: By escalating the conflict from a world vs. Iraq conflict to an Arab vs. Israel conflict, Saddam could hold on to his new conquest, because the vital element of the Arab country participation in any anti-Iraq coalition would be gone. And Saddam would emerge as the Arab-uniting leader of a long-sought conflict with the Israelis.

Such, at any rate, appeared to be the thinking in Baghdad: Divide the opposition and raise the stakes.

# The West Stands with Bush

The Western powers, however, rallied behind the United States almost immediately; even France and Japan joined in. The next step for the Bush administration was to build an Arab-West coalition strong enough to isolate Saddam and push him out of Kuwait.

**CAUTION**

### Oil Spill Ahead

The presence of U.S. troops in Saudi Arabia (these troops remain even to this day) was (and still is) a source of frustration and anger for many Muslim militants. Saudi Arabia is the land of Mecca and Medina, the two holiest cities in Islam, and the presence of non-Muslims in these holy lands was (and still is) seen as an affront to many Muslims.

### Increase Your Iraq IQ

Turkey, a Muslim country, was and is a critical U.S. ally in the region. The people of Turkey are Muslim, but they are not Arab (they are Turkic). Like Iraq and Iran, the Turks also have a Kurd minority within their borders. Turkey is a member of NATO, and in general has been a steadfast partner to the United States in its maneuvering against Saddam.

Saddam was correct if he thought that the Arab countries would have a difficult time falling in behind U.S. leadership. However, the fear that his military move had engendered with the other Arab states outweighed the Arab leaders' aversion to working with the West. On August 6, Bush received permission from Saudi Arabia's King Fahd to base U.S. troops in his country.

The Arab world had begun to join the Western powers against Saddam. The Saudi ruling family decided to work with Bush, and shortly thereafter the other Gulf states came on board. Egypt, Syria, Saudi Arabia, and Kuwait all signed onto the Coalition. King Hussein (no relation) of Jordan decided not to join the coalition, but he did not come out in support of Iraq, either.

# One Man Against the World

Turkey offered its full support to the anti-Iraq coalition, and Iran stayed on the sidelines. In an ominous turn of events for Saddam, the Soviet Union gave its tacit blessing to the anti-Iraq coalition. Ultimately, 38 countries joined the Coalition, and a total of 650,000 troops were arrayed against Iraq.

Saddam could not find any other allies to his cause. He was on his own.

# Action at the United Nations

The Bush administration then turned to the United Nations to generate a legal mandate to expel the Iraqi military from Kuwait. On August 2, the same day that Iraq was discovered in Kuwait, the *United Nations Security Council* passed a resolution calling for Iraq to leave Kuwait immediately and unconditionally.

**Desert Diction**

The **United Nations Security Council** includes five permanent members (the United States, the United Kingdom, France, China, and Russia) and 10 rotating members (made up of other nations in the United Nations) who are elected by the General Assembly to serve 2-year terms on the council. The chairmanship of the council rotates among all the members. Only the Security Council can mandate a UN-sponsored military intervention on behalf of a UN member country. All Security Council decisions must be approved by a vote among its members. The five permanent members can veto any measure under Security Council consideration.

Along with a series of resolutions, calling for Iraq's withdrawal from Kuwait, the United States also led the United Nations in creating economic sanctions against Iraq as well. As a result of this diplomacy, the United Nations also passed an array of economic sanctions blocking the exports from Iraq, as well as any imports to Iraq. Now, Saddam's only revenue source—oil sales—was cut off. Rather than enrichment from the occupation of Kuwait, Saddam was even more impoverished.

## Trying to Cut a Deal?

Facing a united coalition of Arab and Western states, forced to deal with a steady buildup of troops in Saudi Arabia, and cut off from making money, Saddam may have had second thoughts about the invasion. He tried to talk his way out of the problem, while holding onto the gains of the invasion of Kuwait.

On August 23, 1990, Saddam offered to withdraw from Kuwait in return for the UN sanctions being lifted, guaranteed access to the Gulf, and full control of the Rumalyah oil field. These conditions were rejected by the Bush-led coalition.

It's not hard to understand why. To the West, rewarding unilateral military action against a sovereign state with diplomatic concessions smelled an awful lot like appeasement, an approach that had helped to encourage the tyrannies of Adolf Hitler in the 1930s. And caving in on "guaranteed access to the Gulf," some analysts reasoned, could set the stage for future Iraqi aggression against Kuwait. The islands of Bubiyan and Warbah were located immediately off the Iraqi Gulf coast. Iraq could claim that control of those islands was part of the "guaranteed access" to the Gulf.

## The Coalition Says "No, Thanks"

Instead of agreeing to the proposal, the Bush administration sent in 230,000 American troops to defend Saudi Arabia, in "Operation Desert Shield." Saddam responded to the American buildup by sending more Iraqi troops into Kuwait. Bush responded by sending in an additional 200,000 soldiers. The buildup was on for both sides.

The United States was sending a huge number of troops to Saudi Arabia—far more, it would seem, than were needed simply to defend that country.

# Saddam Counters: The War of Words

Now that it had been made clear that he could not expect to withdraw and maintain control of at least part of Kuwait, Saddam tried to break the Arab-West coalition. If he could do that, then perhaps he could hold onto Kuwait.

Saddam may have sensed that the Coalition, while firm, was not long-lived. Eventually it would have to crack. His hope could have been to break that coalition apart before any military action took place.

In early September 1990, Saddam accused President Bush of being a criminal and demanded he stand trial in Baghdad. By making these accusations, Saddam was trying to pry the Arab states from the West. He charged President Bush with the crimes of:

♦ Sending U.S. troops into the areas of the holy Muslim shrines (remember that Saudi Arabia is the home of Mecca and Medina).

♦ Threatening to attack Iraq (there were 430,000 U.S. soldiers in or en route to Saudi Arabia).

♦ Imposing economic sanctions against Iraq. (Saddam was referring to the fact that the United States had led the approval of UN sanctions.)

♦ Ordering the CIA to plot against Iraq (an unproven, but seemingly obvious U.S. move considering the situation in the region).

By making these accusations, Saddam was trying to insert a wedge between the United States and the key Arab nations with which the Americans had established alliances after 1973: Egypt, Jordan, the other Gulf states, and Saudi Arabia.

# Playing the Israel Card

Saddam also tried to draw Israel into the stand off, as he would again do during the actual fighting. Apparently in the hope of getting President Bush to make public statements in support of Israel—statements that would alienate the Arab coalition members—Saddam and his ministers, notably his foreign minister, Tariq Aziz, began to bluster about Israel.

Saddam threatened to launch missiles at Israel in the event of hostilities. By making these claims, Hussein was attempting to show himself to be an outspoken anti-Israel leader, and trying to rally other Arab countries to that cause. He was attempting to remind the Arabs of what bound them all together against Israel and its ally: the United States.

Iraqi officials had been making bellicose statements about Israel in the months leading up to the Kuwait invasion. On April 2, 1990, Reuters news agency quoted Saddam as saying: "I swear to God we will let our fire eat half of Israel if it tries to wage anything against Iraq." Saddam went on to boast of the size of his chemical weapons arsenal, and promised to use those weapons on any country that would threaten Iraq with nuclear weapons. On June 18, 1990, the Baghdad Domestic News Services quoted Saddam, "We will strike at [the Israelis] with all the arms in our possession if they attack Iraq or the Arabs."

After the August 1990 invasion of Kuwait, Saddam stepped up the rhetoric. Saddam threatened again to attack Israel if the Coalition attacked Iraq. According to Reuters, on December 26, 1990, Saddam said, "Tel Aviv will receive the next attack, whether or not Israel takes part" in a coalition attack on Iraq. Tariq Aziz went a step further when he had a meeting with Secretary of State James Baker on January 9, 1991 (just six days prior to the start of fighting). When asked if Iraq would attack Israel in the event of a coalition move against Iraq, Aziz responded, "Yes. Absolutely, yes."

**Iraq Fact**

Tariq Mikhail Aziz is the deputy prime minister of Iraq. A long time ally of Saddam Hussein, Aziz is generally the primary spokesperson for the Iraqi government and the main point of contact between the United States and Iraq at senior government levels.

**Increase Your Iraq IQ**

In April 1990, British intelligence had discovered that an Iraqi-chartered vessel was loaded with large tube sections. These sections were part of a "super gun" that could fire projectiles at Iran or Israel. The British thwarted the attempted delivery.

(Later, during the actual fighting, Saddam would keep his promise, firing missiles at Israel in an attempt to draw the Israelis into the struggle.)

# The Waiting Game

Finally, on November 29, 1990, the UN Security Council passed a resolution approving the Coalition to use force to get Iraq out of Kuwait. The 15-member Security Council voted 12 to 2 in favor of the resolution. China abstained, and Cuba and Yemen voted against the measure, known as Resolution 678.

Resolution 678 had a deadline of January 15, 1991. The clock was ticking on Saddam. As the year turned from 1990 to 1991 and the deadline approached, he stood fast in Kuwait, and played a waiting game.

## The Least You Need to Know

- ◆ Saddam may have been surprised by the forceful and immediate response by the Bush administration following the August 2, 1990 occupation of Kuwait.

- ◆ Iraqi offers to withdraw, keeping some of the gains of taking Kuwait, were rejected by the Coalition.

- ◆ The United States responded by building an Arab-West coalition against Saddam, getting UN cover for sanctions against Iraq.

- ◆ Saddam attempted to break the Arab-Western coalition arrayed against him by means of divisive rhetoric, much of it designed to draw Israel into the conflict.

# Chapter 20

# The Assault: The Alliance Holds

## In This Chapter

- ◆ A storm in the desert
- ◆ The air war
- ◆ The war on the ground
- ◆ Saddam stays in power

In the last chapter, we saw how the Bush administration had assembled an international coalition to isolate Saddam—a coalition that included Arab countries. It was vital that Arab states participate; failure to win their support could have made it easier for Saddam to transform his invasion into a wide-ranging conflict between the Arab and Western worlds—with destabilizing consequences for both sides.

The Bush administration's immediate response to Saddam's move was known as "Operation Desert Shield." It quickly escalated into a full-scale military build-up of troops, material, planes, armor, and bases. The coalition partners joined in, sending their share of troops and/or money to support the effort.

The coalition nations shared the Bush administration's goal of removing Iraq from Kuwait unconditionally. Despite the troops and resources arrayed against him, Saddam refused to leave Kuwait unconditionally. It became increasingly apparent that military force would be required.

The Coalition prepared for the attack; the Bush administration got the United Nations to approve the action, and even set a deadline for withdrawal. Saddam still did not budge; however, attack became inevitable.

When the assault on Iraqi troops in Kuwait began, Operation Desert Shield turned into "Operation Desert Storm." The storm that was unleashed on Saddam was formidable. The campaign used the planes and troops of 38 countries, and had a war chest of more than $53 billion pledged by coalition and noncoalition countries alike.

# What Was the Goal of the Campaign?

According to President Bush's National Security Directive 54, issued on January 15, 1991, the goal of Operation Desert Storm was to evict Iraq from Kuwait, period. The text of Section 2 of the directive reads as follows:

> Pursuant to my responsibilities and authority under the Constitution as President and Commander in Chief, and under the laws and treaties of the United States, and pursuant to H.J. Res. 77 (1991), and in accordance with the rights and obligations of the United States under international law, including UN Security Council Resolutions 660, 661, 662, 664, 665, 666, 667, 669, 670, 674, 677, and 678, and consistent with the inherent right of collective self-defense affirmed in Article 51 of the United Nations Charter, I hereby authorize military actions designed to bring about Iraq's withdrawal from Kuwait. These actions are to be conducted against Iraq and Iraqi forces in Kuwait by U.S. air, sea and land conventional military forces, in coordination with the forces of our coalition partners, at a date and time I shall determine and communicate through National Command Authority channels. This authorization is for the following purposes:
>
> a. to effect the immediate, complete and unconditional withdrawal of all Iraqi forces from Kuwait;
>
> b. to restore Kuwait's legitimate government;
>
> c. to protect the lives of American citizens abroad; and
>
> d. to promote the security and the stability of the Persian Gulf.

# Target: Saddam?

If the National Security Directive is read at face value, the Bush administration wasn't directly targeting Saddam as an individual. But make no mistake, the Bush administration did want Saddam gone. Although there was no formally stated objective to remove Saddam from power, the Bush administration appears to have hoped (or even assumed) that Hussein would be overthrown as a by-product of a military defeat in Kuwait.

If getting rid of Saddam was a goal of Desert Storm, why was it not explicitly stated as one? The most likely answer is that the coalition that the Bush administration assembled agreed only on the goal of getting Saddam out of Kuwait. The members did *not* agree on the difficult question of whether Saddam himself should be overthrown.

Kicking Iraq out of Kuwait was a clearly defined goal, with a clean ending everyone in the Coalition could endorse: The Iraqis moving back across the Kuwait-Iraq border. The end point was unambiguous, and the morality of the goal was generally acceptable to the international community. Iraq had unilaterally invaded an independent neighbor and taken away its right to exist as a state. This type of naked aggression had to be stopped, no matter who did it, no matter where it was.

**Iraq Fact**

The debate that occurred between Western (mainly the Bush (Sr.) administration) and Arab states over what to do with Saddam in 1990 and 1991 has been echoed by a similar debate in 2002. The Bush (Jr.) administration is engaged in the same dialog, with the same Arab partners, over what to do about Saddam.

On the other hand, a commitment to overthrow Saddam could have meant more casualties, a protracted coalition occupation of Iraq, and a less certain outcome to that occupation. Also, the morality of overthrowing a sovereign ruler of an independent state, no matter how reprehensible, was much less clear as a universally moral goal of freeing an occupied state. Furthermore, the Arab states, while willing to participate in a coalition to defend one of their own (Kuwait), would be far less willing to participate in a coalition to oust the leader of one of their own (Iraq).

In short, getting an Arab-Western coalition to agree to getting Iraq out of Kuwait was one thing, getting them to agree what should happen to Iraq afterward, was quite another.

**Desert Diction**

**Operation Desert Shield** was the name of the military buildup operation in Saudi Arabia. Its nominal purpose was to set up a deterrent military force, strong enough to defend the Arab Gulf states.

**Operation Desert Storm** was the follow-up to Desert Shield. It was the name of the coalition attack on Iraqi troops in Kuwait. Its purpose was to expel Iraq from Kuwait.

# " Mother of All Battles"

The stage was set, and the pieces were in place. The UN Security Council set a deadline of January 15, 1991, for a complete Iraqi withdrawal from Kuwait. When the deadline passed, and Saddam stayed put, President Bush ordered the action to begin on January 17, 1991.

This date was six and a half months after the August 2, 1990, UN Security Council Resolution demanding Saddam leave. Rather than leave, Saddam had dug in and exhorted his soldiers and his people to prepare for the "mother of all battles" that was soon to come.

## The Air Assault Begins

On January 17, 1991, coalition forces began bombing targets in Kuwait and Iraq.

Helicopters, fighters ,and cruise missiles were all used over the next five weeks to destroy Iraqi military targets, from artillery and anti-aircraft positions, to troop concentrations and command and control centers in Iraqi cities like Basra and Baghdad. Despite some losses to Iraqi anti-aircraft batteries, coalition aircraft essentially controlled the skies and could fly their sorties at will.

The bombing campaign was carried out first against major targets; when these were obliterated, bombing proceeded against secondary targets; and the bombs were dropped on anything that *looked* like a target in a military zone.

> **CAUTION**
>
> **Oil Spill Ahead**
>
> Despite all of the intense bombing, a surprising number of Iraqi weapons facilities survived the bombing campaign, and continued to produce weapons. These facilities would soon become the focus of international weapons inspectors, and a source of international tension.

## Civilians Suffer

Although overthrowing Saddam was not a stated goal of the air campaign, certain coalition bombing efforts were clearly aimed at doing just that. Coalition bombing targets also included parts of the Iraqi infrastructure, such as oil facilities and power plants. Granted, destroying these targets did impair Iraqi capabilities on the front lines (at least indirectly), but the immediate impact was economic disruption and physical suffering among the Iraqi people.

It's possible that coalition planners sought to foster domestic unrest against Saddam, by showing his weakness to his own people, and by increasing their misery under his rule.

This raised a fateful question that continues to play out today: If the lights go out and the food runs low, would the Iraqi people eventually blame Saddam for the darkness and the hunger—or would they see the West (rather than Saddam) as the architect of their misery?

> **Increase Your Iraq IQ**
>
> After he invaded Kuwait, Saddam had prominently housed "guests" at strategic sites like power plants and munitions depots. These "guests" (read: hostages) were foreign nationals who were unlucky enough to be in Iraq after the Iraqi invasion of Kuwait. Eventually, these "guests" were released, probably because Saddam realized he was not winning the PR war by keeping them.

# Saddam Hussein, Media Mastermind

Saddam's actions during the bombing period alternated between attempting to position the Iraqi people as the victim of a heartless Western-led military campaign and making unsubtle threats.

He tried to turn world public opinion against the Coalition by showing the effects of the bombing campaign on civilians, both Western and Iraqi. (Had he yielded to protracted appeals from all around the globe, including the Arab world, to withdraw from Kuwait, those casualties would, of course, never have occurred.)

Saddam's war of words now included a war of reporters, as he used CNN for all it was worth. At one point, CNN ran Iraqi footage of a "Baby Milk" factory that had supposedly been destroyed by coalition bombing. The CNN footage included a battered sign that read "Baby Milk" in English. Of course, it seems improbable that a factory that produced a product in the middle of Baghdad would have an English sign over it, or that a factory producing infant formula would call its product "Baby Milk." Granted, CNN did indicate that their footage was subject to Iraqi censorship, but the messages got through to the viewing audience nevertheless.

---

**Increase Your Iraq IQ**

On February 13, 1991, Saddam's campaign to manipulate world opinion was aided by an errant strategic bombing strike on the Al Firdos bunker in Baghdad. More than 200 Iraqi civilians were killed in that attack. Saddam presented the bodies on TV for all the world to see. The public outcry induced the Coalition to reduce its strategic bombing in Baghdad. In a small way, Saddam had helped assure his own survival by showing the effects of coalition bombing on Iraqi civilians. He did this by causing the Coalition leadership to limit the strategic bombing, lessening the civilian suffering, and weakening support within the Bush administration for a (quiet) plan to oust or eliminate Saddam.

---

**Desert Diction**

The **SCUD missiles** that Iraq launched at Israel were made by the Soviet Union in the 1980s. Iraq had bought them from the Soviets during the Iran-Iraq War, for use against targets in Iran. Fired from a mobile launcher, the SCUD was capable of reaching targets hundreds of miles away.

# SCUDs over Israel

As he had threatened, Saddam responded to the bombing by attempting to split the Coalition. Shortly after Iraq came under attack, Iraq started bombing Israel.

On January 18, 1991, the day after the Coalition first struck, Iraq launched its first *SCUD missiles* at Israel. Saddam's goal was simple: induce the Israelis to strike at Iraq, which would make it increasingly difficult for the Arab countries to remain part of the Coalition. Saddam had made this intention clear in late 1990, and President Bush, in his National Security

Directive 54, had acknowledged this threat openly: "The United States will discourage the government of Israel from participating in any military action. In particular, we will seek to discourage any preemptive actions by Israel. Should Israel be threatened with imminent attack or be attacked by Iraq, the United States will respond with force against Iraq and will discourage Israeli participation in hostilities."

The United States sent Patriot missile batteries to Israel, to shoot down the incoming SCUDs. The Patriots were very effective in this task, although Israel was hit by a number of SCUDs. Ultimately, Saddam's plan failed, as the combination of U.S. diplomacy, Israeli forbearance, and Patriot missiles restrained an Israeli military response. The Coalition continued to hold throughout the month of January and into early February 1991.

The diplomacy that the Bush team conducted in keeping Israel on the sidelines, while all the time they were being attacked, is impressive. The efforts of the diplomats were only surpassed by the courage of the civilians who sat through the SCUD strikes.

While international attention was focused on Baghdad bunkers, "Baby Milk," and Israeli SCUD craters, the Coalition continued to rain tens of thousands of tons of munitions on unfortunate Iraqi soldiers along the front in Kuwait. The impact of B-52 bombings on Iraqi forces could be felt 20 miles away across the desert. Away from the spotlight, the Iraqi army was being pummeled into submission.

The Iraqis didn't sit completely still, however. On January 29, 1991, Iraqi units moved into Khafji on the Saudi Arabia-Kuwait border. Initial gains by the Iraqis were reversed, and two days later they were forced back out of Khafji. Although Saddam's intentions are not clear (as he didn't organize for a full-scale assault), the initial setback was a sort of wake-up call for coalition forces that Iraq's military would be a tough opponent in the coming fight. Of course, the opposite generally proved true, but that wasn't clear from the Khafji incident.

**Oil Spill Ahead**

Surprisingly, Saddam also fired SCUDs at Saudi Arabia. This practice seemed to fly in the face of his "draw in Israel" strategy, but launch them he did.

**Iraq Fact**

The Coalition (read: United States) military commanders released very little current information on the Coalition bombing campaigns and the attacks on the front-line Iraqi units. Most of the media information that was released came from Saddam and tended to show the results of errant bombs on Iraqi civilians. The news blackout was a source of great frustration and quiet outrage for Western journalists.

# An Offer from Saddam

On February 15, with Soviet diplomat Yevgeni Primakov working the halls in Baghdad, Saddam offered to withdraw from Kuwait. President Bush called the offer a "cruel hoax" and refused to consider the offer.

Why did Bush refuse Saddam's offer? Saddam had once again put conditions on the withdrawal, conditions that could have meant noncompliance with the various UN resolutions. What's more, the Iraqi offer was for a gradual withdrawal, not an immediate one. Bush wasn't willing to grant Hussein any conditions, nor give him time on the ground in Kuwait. The president's reasoning was apparently based on pragmatic considerations as well as logistical ones: Once the initial offer was accepted, the Arab-West coalition would begin to dissolve.

> **Increase Your Iraq IQ**
>
> The UN Security Council eventually would pass 12 resolutions directed at Iraq. These resolutions demanded that Iraq leave Kuwait (UN Security Council Resolution 660), established a range of economic sanctions to isolate Iraq from world trade (UN Security Council Resolution 661), and finally, authorized that the Coalition could use force to expel Iraq from Kuwait (UN Security Council Resolution 678).

The Bush administration feared that the longer Saddam delayed his withdrawal, the less likely coalition troops could ever be used to expel him from Kuwait. In the end, Saddam could simply hold on to some of the territory, or gain some concessions on the Rumalyah oil field, and be even stronger for his next move (whatever that might be).

Thus the U.S. position: The withdrawal had to be complete and unconditional, in accordance with UN Security Council Resolution 660. Saddam, at this point, was having none of it.

The ground war was set to begin.

# The Ground War

The ground war can be summarized in a quote by Lieutenant General Tom Kelly: "Iraq went from the fourth-largest army in the world to the second-largest army in Iraq in 100 hours."

General Kelly was referring to the fact that the Iraqi army basically surrendered without much of a fight. (In fact, Iraqi soldiers surrendered to TV camera crews when they could not find soldiers to surrender to.) The vaunted Iraqi army capitulated with stunning rapidity.

Command of the coalition forces was divided between the Americans and the Saudi Arabians, with the Americans calling the shots. General Norman Schwarzkopf commanded the Western countries, including the United States, British, and French forces, while Saudi Lieutenant General Khalid ibn Sultan ibn Abd al Aziz Al Saud commanded the 24 non-Western coalition countries, including Saudi Arabia, Syria, Kuwait, and Egypt. The non-Western troops included 20,000 Saudi Arabian troops, 7,000 Kuwaiti troops who had escaped the Iraqi invasion, and 3,000 troops from the other Gulf states.

The joint command structure was another acknowledgment of Arab sensibilities and had helped to keep the Arab states in the coalition. This command structure also recognized Saudi Arabia's status as the nation hosting the Coalition—and footing most of the bill for the staging and conduct of the operations.

## The Sweeping Hook

The ground attack started on February 24, 1991. The Arab troops were divided into two task forces: Joint Forces Command North, consisting of troops from Egypt, Saudi Arabia, Syria, and Kuwait; and Joint Forces Command East, consisting of forces from Saudi Arabia, Kuwait, Bahrain, and Qatar. The North group deployed on Kuwait's western border with Saudi Arabia, and the East group deployed along the Gulf coast below the Kuwaiti border. These troops set up the blocking forces that kept the Iraqi units from moving south when the main attack hit them.

The main attack featured a sweeping hook from the west of Kuwait, spearheaded by U.S. Marines, British, and French forces. These sweeping hooks cut the Iraqi troops off from their communication and supply in Iraq. The 101st Airborne cut the vital Highway 8 connecting Kuwait City with Iraq, effectively isolating a large portion of the Iraqi army.

The Iraqis counterattacked against the 1st Marine Division on the second day, and there were some pitched tank battles with Republican Guard units. In each case, coalition armor prevailed, using superior equipment and tactics against older and more plodding Iraqi tactics. The Iraqi tank troops had learned their craft against the Iranians, who fought in a similar style to the Iraqis. Western military tactics were alien to them, and it showed in the results. One of the largest engagements occurred at a place designated as "73 Easting," and ended up as a route of Iraqi armor.

## The Iraqi Army Collapses

As U.S. and British troops swept across the Iraqi positions, the Joint Forces Command North group broke through Iraqi defenses on the border and pushed into Kuwait. Caught between the U.S. and British troops coming on from the west, and the Saudis,

Kuwaitis, and Egyptians of Command North group coming up from the south, the Iraqi troops fled north or surrendered in place. On the third day, Command East forces drove up the Gulf coast and entered Kuwait City.

The Iraqi forces fleeing Kuwait City were pounded on what became known as the "Highway of Death" by coalition aircraft. The losses were staggering. As they left Kuwait, the Iraqi troops set fire to hundreds of oil wells in Kuwait, in a last vengeful attempt to fulfill one of Saddam's earlier objectives: Drive up the price of oil. With the Kuwaiti production off line, oil prices would have to rise.

Finally, on February 27, 1991, President Bush unilaterally declared a cease-fire, stating that, "Kuwait is liberated. Iraq's army is defeated. Our military objectives have been met." While the military goals of the Coalition were fulfilled, the political goals were not.

Under the smoking skies from burning Kuwaiti oil wells, Coalition and Iraqi military leaders agreed to a cease-fire, and over the next several days agreed to the terms of a lasting cease-fire. Saddam was out of Kuwait, but he was not out of power.

# How Had the Iraqis Done So Poorly?

What happened to the Iraqi army? Why did it surrender so quickly? How was it overcome so decisively?

There were only 148 U.S. troops killed during the fighting, compared to tens of thousands (and some estimates of over 100,000) Iraqi soldiers. These Iraqis were battle-tested veterans of the Iran-Iraq War. Why didn't they put up a better fight?

It was a different kind of war than the Iraqi army was used to. In the Iran-Iraq War, it had become proficient in fighting a grinding, trench-warfare style of campaign. They had proven successful in digging in and staving off Iranian "human wave" attacks. The Iraqi high command prepared for a similar style of fighting in Kuwait. The troops were pushed to forward positions, where they dug in behind a line of fortifications and awaited a coalition frontal assault.

However, the Coalition launched a mobile attack that was designed to cut off the Iraqi troops, encircle them, and then destroy them. The superior speed and mechanization of the coalition forces made the difference almost immediately. The Iraqis were drawn out of their defensive positions and forced to fight on the move. Their tactics and equipment were not designed for this kind of fighting, and they could not match the coalition firepower on the ground.

There was a frontal assault, but by the time it came, the Iraqi troops melted away almost immediately.

---

**Increase Your Iraq IQ**

Why didn't the Iraqi army fight better in face-to-face engagements? A contributing factor was that the allied air campaign had seriously weakened the Iraqi troops on the front line. The five weeks of heavy bombing had taken its toll. The Iraqi troops at the front had received little food, water, or even instructions from their commanders. Many units were effectively isolated from their own military structures. Further, their morale and effectiveness had been severely degraded by the incessant pounding of their positions.

Also, the Iraqi troops were no longer fighting for their homeland, and the foot soldier in the field didn't see the benefit of fighting for Kuwait. The majority of troops were Shiites, and their relationship with the Iraqi Sunni command structure was always distant. As that structure broke down, the Shiite soldiers were more willing to pack it in than their Sunni counterparts. However, even the Sunni Republican Guard units didn't fare well in the fighting—though they didn't surrender in the same numbers as the Shiite units.

---

# By the Numbers

The Iraqi army had about 540,000 troops in Kuwait. Of that number, roughly 100,000 were killed, 300,000 were wounded, and 60,000 were captured. The United States lost 148 troops in combat, 458 were wounded, and 121 were killed in non-combat situations. The Iraqis lost 4,000 tanks and 2,140 artillery pieces. The Coalition lost four tanks and one artillery piece. The Iraqi air force lost 240 aircraft; the Coalition lost 44 aircraft.

# Victory over Saddam (or Was It?)

After President Bush's unilateral declaration of a cease-fire on February 27, the coalition and Iraqi commanders met to hash out the details of the cease-fire on March 3. Iraq's leadership in the negotiations, representing Saddam Hussein, agreed to abide by all of the UN Security Council Resolutions passed against Iraq in relation to the invasion of Kuwait. The following day, coalition prisoners of war were released, and the end game was in play ... or was it?

The Gulf War was over—the military objectives of the Coalition had been achieved. The Iraqi army in Kuwait had been decimated, and its effectiveness as a fighting force was drastically reduced. The coalition negotiators were at the table, setting the terms that would, they hoped, keep Iraq from ever mounting a threat to its neighbors again.

True enough, the Iraqi military had been beaten and was no longer a potent threat as a fighting force. However, its effectiveness as a police force was still very much intact.

In the next chapter, we'll see how Saddam would use that force in the months following his Gulf War defeat to preserve his own grip on power. The Gulf War was over, but the conflict between Saddam Hussein and the West was just beginning.

## The Least You Need to Know

- Operation Desert Shield turned into Operation Desert Storm with the opening of the coalition bombing campaign.

- The bombing campaign was intended to degrade Iraqi military capabilities (which it did well) and effectively destabilize Saddam's grip on power (which it do not do well).

- The coalition troops launched the ground campaign on February 24, 1991. The main attacks went extremely well for the coalition troops, and extremely poorly for the Iraqis.

- The fighting ended 100 hours after it started, with a total Iraqi military defeat.

- Although the Iraqi military had been humbled as a fighting force, it retained its effectiveness as a police force.

# Chapter 21

# The Aftermath: Saddam Survives

## In This Chapter

◆ The Coalition stops short of invasion

◆ A quick settlement

◆ Lingering loopholes

◆ The West waits for Saddam to fall

After 100 hours of ground war, the Iraqi army was fleeing from Kuwait in panicked disorder.

There was no way they could have stopped the coalition forces from driving all the way to Baghdad, or, presumably, from capturing Saddam Hussein. Already, some coalition troops were in Iraq proper and many more were heading that way. Their commanders, however, ordered them to stop.

The Coalition wasn't going to go on to Baghdad. Its mission had been accomplished: Iraq had been expelled from Kuwait. Rather then moving on to Baghdad, the coalition military commanders sat down to negotiate a hastily defined cease-fire with their Iraqi counterparts. As soon as the firing stopped, the chances for the Coalition to resume military operations grew fainter, and the chances for Saddam to survive the overwhelming defeat grew stronger.

With each passing day, Saddam showed how well developed his survival skills had become.

# Mission Accomplished?

Clearly, the Bush administration's stated goal had been met: Kuwait had been liberated and the Iraqi military had been weakened so that it could not be used against other countries.

The unstated goal of the Bush administration, however, was to overthrow Saddam Hussein. The Bush administration had determined by Saddam's invasion of Kuwait that Saddam was a serious threat to stability in the region, and a threat to U.S. interests (including the free flow of reasonably priced oil).

CAUTION

**Oil Spill Ahead**

The likelihood of the Iraqi army invading a neighbor was dramatically reduced after the Gulf War, but the likelihood of Iraq supporting international terrorists was not lessened.

However, as we have seen, this could not be a formal coalition objective, because the Arab states in the region were not willing to fight to overthrow one of their own. At the same time, it was quietly assumed—by both the Bush administration and its coalition allies—that Saddam would fall if his army was defeated.

That, as it turned out, was wishful thinking.

# 20/20 Hindsight

With the door wide open, should coalition forces have invaded Baghdad? Many are inclined to answer that question "Yes" nowadays, which tells you more about the advantages of hindsight than it does about the geopolitical realities facing George H. W. Bush in 1991.

All we can say for sure is that the Coalition and President Bush *didn't* take this step. There appear to be three possible reasons supporting the president's thinking at this time:

1. The Bush administration really did not have a choice, and had to stop.

2. The Bush administration decided it was better to stop and let a militarily weakened Saddam hang onto power.

3.  The Bush administration assumed, like almost everyone else at that time, that the Iraqi people would finish the job the Coalition had started by overthrowing Saddam.

Looking at the first possibility: The American military would have had to enter Baghdad and get Saddam on its own. Such a unilateral move could have almost immediately alienated the Arab allies, and could have reversed all the gains made up to that point. The United States could well have found itself dealing with nine hostile Arab states in the region, instead of just one.

Looking at the second possibility: While this option seems to run against all the rhetoric, it's important to bear in mind that there was (and is) considerable uncertainty regarding the kind of government likely to emerge in Iraq after Saddam Hussein. At the beginning of the Gulf War, Saddam was regarded as a regional threat to U.S. interests, but not necessarily a threat to U.S. domestic security. This view changed considerably at the end of the war, and so the second possibility seems comparatively unlikely.

The most likely reason the Coalition ultimately decided to stop short of Baghdad is a combination of the first possibility and the third one—the assumption that the Iraqi people would finish off Saddam on their own. During the bombing campaign, the Bush administration had tried to oust Saddam indirectly through the strategic bombing of Baghdad, Basra, and other inland Iraqi targets. This bombing was intended both to weaken Iraqi military capabilities and to weaken Saddam's governing capabilities, and perhaps to finish off Saddam himself.

On the last day of the air campaign, the U.S. Air Force pounded a Ba'th headquarters building in the hopes of killing a significant portion of the country's leadership, and possibly even Saddam. Even if the United States couldn't kill Saddam with bombs, its leaders must have hoped that its bombs would end up getting rid of him anyway. If the Iraqi people were made to suffer and see what destruction Saddam had wrought on them, they would rise up and throw him out. Or more likely, a rival clique of army officers would stage yet another coup.

A coup that would oust Saddam and install a more Western-friendly leadership in Iraq was, realistically speaking, about the best that the Bush administration could hope for at the end of the Gulf War.

# Flames in Kuwait

As noted in Chapter 20, the Iraqis had in fact set fire to more than 500 Kuwaiti oil wells and effectively put Kuwaiti oil production off-line for months. The tactic

**Oil Spill Ahead**

Despite predictions that they would last for years, the last oil well fires in Kuwait were extinguished in November 1991. Thanks to the efforts of professional oil well fire fighters from the United States and other oil areas, the fires were out only nine months after the end of hostilities.

resembled the scorched earth policies of the Red Army retreating across Russia in front of the Nazis in World War II, or Sheridan's systematic devastation of the Shenandoah Valley in the Civil War. The environmental impact of 500 flaming oil wells, spewing burning oil across the landscape, was catastrophic. The oil fields were suggestive of what the floor of the pit of Hell would look like, with no sun overhead, searing heat all around, and flames at ones feet.

The Bush administration had also left the door open for a U.S.-led operation to overthrow Saddam at the end of the Gulf War. The National Security Directive 54, Section 10 warns:

> Should Iraq resort to using chemical, biological, or nuclear weapons, be found supporting terrorist acts against U.S. or coalition partners anywhere in the world, *or destroy Kuwait's oil fields*, it shall become an explicit objective of the United States to replace the current leadership of Iraq. [emphasis added]

One of the conditions President Bush pre-defined for overthrowing Saddam (destruction of Kuwaiti oil fields) was certainly met in February 1991. Nonetheless, the Bush administration did not go into Baghdad. Events simply had unfolded too fast, and the need to wrap up the conflict was accelerated by the unforeseen rapidity of the Iraqi military collapse.

# What Bush Didn't Want

No matter how much the Bush administration wanted Saddam out of power, it still wanted Iraq to remain intact. The administration did not want a Shiite-dominated state emerging in Iraq in 1991. The other Arab states, all Sunni-controlled, would not have tolerated a Shiite-controlled state allied to Iran. (Remember that Iran was and still is controlled by a Shiite theocracy.)

**Increase Your Iraq IQ**

"I was convinced, as were all our Arab friends and allies, that Hussein would be overthrown once the war ended."

—George Bush, in *All the Best, George Bush*

The Bush administration also didn't want to see an independent Kurd state. As noted previously, NATO ally Turkey, whose cooperation had been vitally important to the success of Operation Desert Storm, had interests in this regard; the ever-potential antagonist Iran was similarly opposed to an independent Kurdish state on its border. With a collapse of military authority, and a power vacuum at the center, the emergence of a breakaway Kurd state was a real possibility.

Quite possibly, the Bush administration concluded that the best alternative to the dissolution of a defeated Iraq would be a new strongman emerging from the discontented officer corps to replace Saddam.

So it was that the Coalition stopped short of demanding the overthrow of Saddam Hussein, or even of occupying Baghdad. They simply stepped back, waited for Humpty Dumpty to have his great fall, and hoped someone better would come along.

> **Iraq Fact**
>
> The Bush administration wasn't looking to destroy the state of Iraq or carve new independent entities out of it. In fact, National Security Directive 54 stated clearly in Section 9: "The United States recognizes the territorial integrity of Iraq and will not support efforts to change current boundaries."

# Meanwhile, Back at Home ...

As the smoke rose from 500 burning Kuwaiti oil wells, the Kurds in the north and Shiites in the south rose with it. The war ended abruptly, and Saddam was faced with uprisings at home that threatened his supremacy in Iraq. However, these rebellions didn't threaten his power base. In fact, they strengthened it.

Remember that Saddam represented the Sunni minority, and that his power base came from Sunni army officers and ruling elites—not from the Kurds or Shiites. These Sunni elites rallied around Saddam. They appear to have done so in order to preserve their own positions, as much as out of any personal loyalty to him.

# Threat from Within?

A far more potent threat to Saddam would have come from a military coup led by disaffected Sunni generals in his own circle. However, that coup never materialized. Saddam kept tight control over his generals, and they were soon occupied with the battles against the Kurds and Shiites.

The Sunni ruling elite was, as always, completely opposed to Kurdish or Shiite power-sharing, and so the Sunni-run, Shiite-manned army was quickly dispatched to the Kurd areas to battle those insurgents. Meanwhile, the Sunni Republican Guard remnants were sent into Shiite areas to quell the uprisings there. Amid savage reprisals, including helicopter gunship attacks and rumors of biological weapons being used, the rebellions were put down by the end of the year. In fact, the most significant military campaigns against the Kurds were wrapped up before May 1991.

As usual, Saddam moved fast at home to cut off the dissent before it could spread.

**Iraq Fact** _____

Saddam was able to suppress the domestic rebellions that followed the Gulf War for two reasons:

◆ He still had the firepower to do it, and

◆ No one stopped him.

Remember that Saddam began the Gulf War with one of the largest armies in the world. Saddam didn't send all of his troops into Kuwait. He held some back to keep an eye on the Iranians, Syrians, and Turks, and for domestic security. So, even after his armies in Kuwait were smashed, Saddam still had enough troops on hand for domestic control. As for the second reason: Saddam was obviously willing to bet that the Coalition didn't have the political will or unanimity to commit ground troops on behalf of the Kurds or the Shiites. He bet right.

# No-Fly Zones: Too Little, Too Late

In response to Iraqi brutality against the Kurds and, later, the Shiites, the United States, Britain, and France established no-fly zones in the north and south, marking areas where Iraqi airplanes were forbidden to fly. The Northern no-fly zone was established in April 1991; it essentially provided an American air umbrella over the Kurds. Prior to the creation of the northern no-fly zone, however, the Iraqis used helicopter gun ships with terrible effect, and they were able to batter the Kurds into submission.

Saddam was able to do the same to the Shiites in the south prior to the establishment of a southern no-fly zone in August of 1992.

**Desert Diction** _____

The **Northern no-fly zone,** called Operation Provide Comfort, was established to protect the Kurds from Iraqi helicopter gun ships. The no-fly zone area is bounded by the thirty-sixth parallel.

The **Southern no-fly zone** was established to protect the Shiite rebels from Iraqi aircraft. Called Operation Southern Watch, the southern zone was first bounded at the thirty-second parallel (to protect the Shiites in the marsh regions) and later extended to the thirty-third parallel.

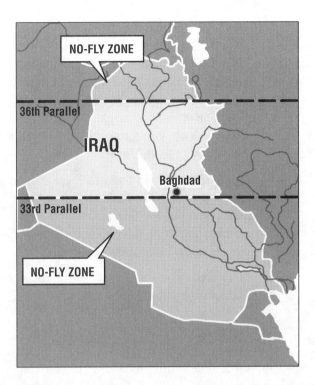

*no-fly zones in Iraq.*

Since the launch of the no-fly zones, the Shiites and Kurds have enjoyed the protection of the U.S. and UK fighter cover, which has stopped the Iraqi aerial assaults on them. However, as we shall see in future chapters the no-fly zones have been as much source of conflict as of protection.

# Hasty Negotiations

It's safe to say that the coalition leaders who negotiated the cease-fire with Iraq did not make the most of the opportunity they were given. Certainly, the battlefield victory did not ensure that the Bush administration's political objectives would be automatically fulfilled.

Why was Saddam so unbowed, despite his battlefield losses? One answer may have to do with the relative brevity of the Gulf War. Saddam's defeat did not have the psychological impact on

 **Oil Spill Ahead**

France withdrew from enforcement activities in December 1996, stating that the no-fly zone's humanitarian mission had been satisfied. The United States and Britain continue to enforce the no-fly zones.

**Oil Spill Ahead**

Prussian military theorist Carl von Clauswitz once wrote: "The ultimate outcome of war is not always to be regarded as final. The defeated state often considers the outcome merely as a transitory evil, for which a remedy may still be found in political conditions at some later date." Saddam probably looked at the Gulf War defeat in much the same way.

him or his people that a longer, protracted struggle (like the Iran-Iraq War) might have had. Furthermore, since the Coalition wasn't coming to get him, Saddam could afford to be as aggressive as he wanted, as long as he stayed in his own yard. The Coalition had shown him that while they would not let him add to Iraq, they were not going to subtract from it, either—or physically remove him from power.

In order to survive, Saddam needed to act as if he had not lost, which is precisely what he did. He set about suppressing opposition at home and fought vigorously at the negotiating table to get whatever he could from the cease-fire agreement.

It worked. The anticipated popular revolt against Saddam never took hold.

## Blowing the Endgame

The speed at which the ground war ended, and the Coalition's lopsided military victory, caught everyone off guard, including the U.S. Central Command. Much time had been spent on planning for the Gulf campaign's beginning and its middle, but little time had been spent on planning for the campaign's end. However, as noted military theorist Carl von Clauswitz has observed, every war has a beginning, a middle, and an end. The "end" is the negotiations that conclude the fighting and secure the political objectives.

The Bush administration was not adequately prepared for the end game. Saddam, on the other hand, seemed more than ready for that part of the contest.

In fact, in April 1991, General Norman Schwarzkopf, commander of the Western coalition forces in the region during the Gulf War (and de-facto commander of all coalition forces in the region), admitted in his report on the battle, "The rapid success of the ground campaign and our subsequent occupation of Iraq were not fully anticipated. Thus, some of the necessary follow-on actions were not ready .... Documents for war termination need to be drafted and coordinated early." And a U.S. Central Command foreign-policy expert was even more explicit when he said, "We never did have a plan to terminate the war."

The Cease-Fire Conditions, as stipulated by UN Security Council Resolution 687 were …

 ◆ Iraq must acknowledge Kuwait sovereignty.

 ◆ Iraq must destroy all of its ballistic missile systems (SCUDs) with a range of more than 150 kilometers.

 ◆ Iraq must repatriate all Kuwaiti and other nationals, and support the International Red Cross and Red Crescent Societies in this area.

 ◆ Iraq must finance a compensation fund to meet its liabilities for damages it inflicted during its occupation of Kuwait.

Nowhere in Resolution 687 is there any requirement that threatens Saddam's domestic grip on power. So as long as Saddam didn't have to negotiate on his own survival, he could accept the cease-fire terms and tend to his business at home. With his own survival covered, he could start over again, building his military, enhancing his prestige, and tightening his grip on power.

## The Least You Need to Know

 ◆ The Bush administration did not overthrow Saddam at the end of the Gulf War because its allies would not have supported it.

 ◆ The Coalition stopped short of intervening to stop Saddam from suppressing Kurd or Shiite rebellions at the end of the Gulf War. The coalition objective was simply to expel Iraq from Kuwait.

 ◆ The coalition military leaders were not prepared to negotiate effectively when the fighting ended.

 ◆ The no-fly zones that were unilaterally set up by the United States, Britain, and France shortly after the war ended, came too late to save Shiite and Kurd rebels from brutal reprisals by Saddam's forces, but they have since protected those groups from Saddam's air attacks.

 ◆ The Coalition underestimated Saddam's grip on power inside Iraq.

# Part 5

# Victory from Defeat

If you haven't figured it out by now, Saddam Hussein is a survivor. He's taken on the world, and although he suffered some startling blows, he managed to cling to power.

Turn the page to find out how Saddam has turned defeat into victory … for now, anyway.

# 22

# Of Sanctions and Inspections

## In This Chapter

- ◆ Iraq's increasingly bold defiance of UN weapons inspectors
- ◆ World opinion turns against economic sanctions
- ◆ Internal repression
- ◆ Rumblings against Kuwait (again)
- ◆ Saddam's definition of success

Throughout the 10 years following the Gulf War, from 1991 to 2001, Saddam was a very busy man. By the end of that decade, Saddam had gone a long way toward wiping away the results of his overwhelming military defeat in the Gulf War.

## A Busy Decade

During the 1990s, Saddam worked steadily on …

- ◆ Shoring up his position at home by portraying himself as the victor in the Gulf War.

- Squirming out from under the weapons inspectors, through defiance and guile.

- Shrugging off the economic sanctions, by waging an effective PR campaign in the United Nations and the world press, and relying on international disinterest.

- Trying to assert his leadership in the Arab world by bullying Kuwait and vilifying Israel and the United States.

We'll look more closely at Saddam's post-war activities in this chapter.

# An Independent Kuwait

One thing appeared certain from the Gulf War experience: Saddam would never, ever invade Kuwait again.

Or would he?

How could he after the disastrous defeat Iraq suffered in 1991? At the end of the Gulf War, Iraqi Foreign Minister Tariq Aziz, representing the government of Iraq, agreed to UN Security Council Resolution 687, which specified that Iraq recognized Kuwait's right to exist as an independent nation. With the dramatic defeat of the Iraqi army, and the presence of U.S. troops in Saudi Arabia and prepositioned equipment in Kuwait, Saddam's ability to bully Kuwait and Saudi Arabia has in fact been significantly decreased.

Nevertheless, Saddam has resorted, from time to time, to threatening Kuwait as a means of attempting to change the price of oil and, just perhaps, to destabilize his smaller neighbor. At the end of the war, the UN declared a demilitarized zone, where Iraqi and Kuwaiti military activities are forbidden. However, in January 1993, just two years after their last move south, the Iraqi military sent its first patrols into the demilitarized border zone. These patrols prompted a series of sharp warnings to Iraq from the United States (led by the Clinton administration), Britain, and France. When Saddam continued to send patrols into the demilitarized zone along the border between Iraq and Kuwait, these three countries responded by bombing military targets in southern Iraq. Saddam pulled back in the wake of the bombing.

Saddam tried to integrate his actions toward Kuwait with the UN inspectors' actions toward Iraq. In other words, Saddam was trying to leverage whatever he could to resist UN weapons inspections. One of the only credible threats he had was that of (re)invading Kuwait. So Saddam continued to "play the Kuwait card"; his belligerence appeared to be a tactic to undercut UN sanctions or inspections. For example, in October 1994, Saddam aimed to lessen the impact and access that UN weapons inspectors and the IAEA (International Atomic Energy Agency) had in Iraq at that time (more on this later). Saddam massed troops on the Kuwaiti border on October 4, 1994. The UN and U.S. reaction was firm and unmistakable, however, and Saddam pulled the troops back by October 16.

Later, in March 2001, Saddam played the same game. In the midst of an argument with the UN over whether Iraq could retain some of its oil revenues to invest in a pipeline across Syria, Saddam's oil minister began to grumble that Kuwait was drawing too much oil from the al-Ratga oilfield that the two countries share. Tariq Aziz demanded—you guessed it—compensation from Kuwait for the oil that had supposedly been pilfered. Kuwait denied the charges and refused compensation. Iraq again made threatening moves toward Kuwait, but pulled back again after being allowed to invest the needed resources in the Syrian pipeline.

Why does Saddam threaten to invade Kuwait every few years? Leverage. Iraq raises the Kuwait threat in order to try to get an adjustment on some other issue, like economic sanctions or weapons inspections. Over time, these kinds of threats have contributed to the complex factors that have helped reduce UN oversight and involvement in Iraq. Saddam uses the threat of force and resistance to UN actions to get some relaxation of the constraints that would otherwise bind his options.

> **Iraq Fact**
>
> The UN Security Council responded to Iraqi troop movements in 1994 with Resolution 949, which condemned the massing of Saddam's forces near Kuwait, demanded their withdrawal away from the Kuwaiti border, and expressly forbade Iraq from massing troops in the southern part of its territory. The resolution also insisted that Iraq cooperate with weapons inspectors.

# New Threats, Different Neighbors

By using the Kuwait card, some extremely effective PR, and growing international indifference, Saddam has steadily managed to work his way out from under some very strict limitations on his military power. Maintaining the second U.S. policy objective—eliminating the potential for Iraq to threaten its neighbors militarily—has become increasingly difficult since 1991.

## Revamping the Iraqi Military Machine

The Coalition had devastated Iraq's conventional military power by the end of the Gulf War, leaving Saddam no choice but to accept the conditions laid down by the Coalition and reinforced by the UN Security Council. Of the 42 Iraqi divisions in place at the start of the Gulf War, 40 were determined to be noncombat ready by the end of the 100-hour war. While Saddam regrouped fairly quickly, the ability of the Iraqi military to mount a credible conventional threat to Kuwait, let alone Iran, Saudi Arabia, or Turkey, was dramatically reduced in the immediate aftermath of the war.

**Desert Diction**

Weapons of mass destruction can kill thousands of people at one time, and, in some cases, wipe out everything in a given area. Generally, biological, chemical, and nuclear weapons are classified as weapons of mass destruction. These weapons tend to be managed by international conventions that prohibit or restrict their use.

After such losses, it would take Saddam a long time to rebuild his conventional arsenal, and reorganize his military. Instead, Saddam began to focus on developing *weapons of mass destruction*, such as biological and chemical weapons, to replace conventional firepower.

It had long been suspected (and is now beyond dispute) that Saddam had used chemical weapons against Iran and also against the Kurds. At the end of the Gulf War, the Bush administration was wary of these weapons and wanted to be sure Saddam could not continue to develop them. The United States was also interested in curtailing Saddam's ability to deliver weapons over longer distances using ballistic missiles.

UN Security Council Resolution 687, which specified the provisions of the cease-fire, included the instruction that Iraq was required to identify and then destroy all ballistic missiles with a range greater then 150 kilometers. This enabled Saddam to retain a missile threat against its neighbor Iran, but kept it from reaching strategic targets in Saudi Arabia or Israel.

Anticipating (correctly) that Saddam would not willingly allow the destruction of these weapons or the missiles that would deliver them, the cease-fire requirements included provisions for UN-managed weapons inspections. Rather than allow the coalition military leaders to establish all the terms of these inspections, the Iraqis negotiated for some limitations on the inspections—limitations that they later leveraged to the hilt.

## President Palaces Sprout Up Throughout Iraq

For example, Saddam's Presidential Palaces were excluded from the otherwise universal access that would be granted to the weapons inspectors. The argument put forth by the Iraqi was that Saddam's personal homes should be off limits, as they were obviously not places where weapons of mass destruction would be stored.

This sounded rational during the negotiating process, and the cease-fire agreement included this exception to the weapons inspectors' access. Almost immediately, however, Iraq decreed tens, and eventually hundreds, of buildings as "Presidential Palaces." Several of these buildings were suspected weapons manufacturing or storage facilities. However, according to the hastily negotiated inspection agreement, the inspection teams were not allowed to search Presidential Palaces. In hindsight, granting this exclusion was a diplomatic fiasco for the Bush (Sr.) administration. The haste of negotiations certainly contributed to the oversight in the inspection agreement.

# The Inspection Two-Step: War by Other Means

Whatever they couldn't legally maneuver around, the Iraqis steadily resisted through simple intransigence. This intransigence grew more and more bold as former coalition partners began to leave the Gulf War alliance and the UN became increasingly disinterested in weapons inspections and more concerned about hardships imposed by economic sanctions (which will be discussed in detail later in this chapter).

Saddam became more and more openly defiant of the weapons inspectors and less and less hesitant about obstructing their ability to carry out their tasks.

Let's start at the beginning of the inspection process, and see how Saddam got away with making a mockery of it, and finally rejected it all together.

## Hostilities Resume

On June 17, 1991, the UN Special Commission (UNSCOM) was created. Its mission was to monitor disarmament in Iraq, along with the International Atomic Energy Agency (IAEA). Just one week later, Iraq defied the *UNSCOM* and IAEA inspectors. Iraqi military personnel opened fire on UNSCOM inspectors who were trying to stop a truck loaded with equipment for use in making nuclear weapons. The equipment was eventually located and destroyed, but Saddam had shown he was going to do his best to undercut the UNSCOM/IAEA inspectors.

**Desert Diction**

The United Nations Special Commission is called **UNSCOM**. Created on June 17, 1991, in the wake of the Gulf War, UNSCOM's mission was to inspect Iraqi weapons facilities, and destroy any weapons of mass destruction and the production facilities to make them, that could be found in Iraq.

## Biological Weapons Found

On August 2, 1991, one year after the Iraqi army invaded Kuwait, UNSCOM inspectors uncovered evidence of a large-scale biological weapons program in Iraq. The inspectors found materials that are used to make biological weapons. Faced with UNSCOM successes, which now included finding his biological weapons, Saddam disallowed UNSCOM access to its own helicopters to carry out their inspections on September 18, 1991.

The United States responded by threatening to shoot anyone who got in the way of the UNSCOM helicopters. Saddam backed down on September 24, 1991, but he had gained a week of time to avoid further weapons discoveries. The United Nations Security Council responded on October 11, 1991, with Resolution 715, which mandated continuous monitoring of Iraqi weapons programs and demanded that Iraq cooperate fully with the UNSCOM and IAEA weapons inspection teams.

## "Yes, We Have Biological Weapons"

By May 1992, UNSCOM inspectors uncovered equipment and weapons hardware to go along with the biological agents that were found in August 1991. Faced with the mounting evidence, Iraq finally admitted that it had been developing biological weapons capability. Saddam insisted, though, that the weapons were purely defensive in nature.

Weapons of mass destruction do just that: destroy massively. It is hard to differentiate a "defensive" weapon of mass destruction from an "offensive" one, but somehow Saddam could make this distinction, as if notions of "offense" or "defense" mattered.

## "Yes, We Have Chemical Weapons"

The UNSCOM inspectors also uncovered stockpiles of chemical weapons in Iraq as well as their production facilities during this time. UNSCOM began destroying the chemical weapons in July 1992. Caught red handed, Saddam admitted that he had chemical weapons and insisted on his right to use them.

Saddam again tested UNSCOM's resolve in January 1993, when Iraq refused to allow UNSCOM to use its own aircraft to move around inside Iraq. (At this time, Saddam also sent his first patrols into the demilitarized zone.) In response to both moves, the United States, United Kingdom, and France launched the air strikes mentioned previously in this chapter. On January 19, 1991, Saddam relented and allowed UNSCOM flights to resume.

# A Dangerous Game of Cat and Mouse

With his biological and chemical weapons systems being sniffed out, Saddam dug in his heels on the delivery systems—his missiles. In June 1993, Saddam rejected an UNSCOM attempt to place surveillance cameras at his missile test sites. Again, there were dire threats from the United Nations, and Saddam backed off by July.

A year or so later, Saddam was up to his old tricks again. On October 6, 1994, he stated that he would not assist UNSCOM, which prompted the UN Security Council to pass yet another resolution—Resolution 949—on October 15, insisting that Saddam allow inspections.

UNSCOM continued to pry into Saddam's weapons programs, and on July 1, 1995, Iraq acknowledged that its defensive biological weapons program was really offensive, but insisted it was not ready for use. It was only after Saddam's own son-in-law, Lt. General Hussein Kamel Hassan al-Majid, who was in charge of the program, defected and told the world that Iraq's various weapons programs were much further along than Saddam had claimed, that Iraq ponied up the details of the program. (Iraq did this rather than face a strengthening of UN economic sanctions, which Saddam was making great progress on getting lifted.)

> **Iraq Fact**
>
> On August 8, 1995, two of Saddam's sons-in-law and their families fled Iraq and ended up in Jordan. The Jordanians granted them asylum. They were Lt. General Hussein Kamel Hassan al-Majid, who was in charge of Iraq's weapons programs, and his brother, Lt. Colonel Saddam Kamel Hassan al-Majid, who was in charge of presidential security. These two men told a great deal about what they knew, which prompted Iraq to come clean on more details of its mass-destruction weapons programs. Amazingly, the brothers returned to Iraq in February 1996, under Saddam's guarantees that he would not harm them. Both Kamel Hassan al-Majid brothers were shot three days after they got back.

Iraq disclosed on August 20, 1995, that it had a stockpile of the deadly nerve agent VX, which is among the most lethal chemical weapon agents known. On top of that cheerful news, Saddam also disclosed that he was on the way to developing crude nuclear weapons, but that the facilities had been destroyed during the Gulf War. Whether true or not, UNSCOM had not confirmed the existence of Iraqi nuclear weapons facilities or weapons themselves.

In May 1996, UNSCOM destroyed Saddam's main biological weapons facility at Al-Hakem.

## The World Sleeps

As 1996 rolled on, the weapons inspectors were becoming increasingly frustrated in their work. It was clear to them that Saddam was hiding more than he was showing. Any information they uncovered, or forced Saddam to disclose, only pointed them toward even more weapons that the inspection teams suspected were beyond their reach. Instead of throwing in the towel, Saddam continued to do his best to thwart the inspectors. He only opened the doors, or the books, when absolutely forced to do so.

Without clear evidence of current weapons capabilities (despite the recent disclosures), Saddam was counting on international indifference to do much of his work for him. He was banking on the fact that the only way the UNSCOM and IAEA inspections could be enforced was through a military strike. As the years rolled on, only the United States and the United Kingdom were willing to make those strikes. And every time the United States or United Kingdom dropped a bomb, they raised murmurs of protest from Arab and Western European countries, who began to see the inspections (and the dire effects of the economic sanctions) as heavy-handed Western bullying. Saddam bet that he could take a hard line without bringing about a major military response.

## The Game Gets Serious

The deadly dance continued, but now Saddam began to lead rather than follow. In March 1996 Saddam openly blocked UNSCOM inspectors from visiting 5 sites for 17 hours. The Security Council voiced its concern, and passed another Resolution (number 1060) on June 12, 1996, but no military response was taken. As Saddam continued to block inspectors during 1997, the UN Security Council passed Resolution 1134 on October 23, 1997, which condemned the actions but did not do much more. Even this mild slap on the back of Saddam's hand only passed 10 to 0, with 5 members abstaining. Saddam was gradually winning the inspections war.

Emboldened by Resolution 1134's soft-pedal approach and lukewarm support, Saddam had the Revolutionary Command Council (the decision-making body in Iraq) declare that Iraq would no longer allow U.S. inspectors or U.S. aircraft to be part of the UNSCOM teams. The Security Council, true to form, condemned the RCC statement with Resolution 1137 on November 12, 1997. This time, the Security Council imposed a travel ban on Iraqi officials in response.

The Russians, looking to get more involved in Iraq's oil industry, brokered a deal that allowed the UNSCOM teams to continue their work in November 1997. However, it quickly became clear that the inspectors were still being blocked from visiting the sites they wanted to see.

During the first few months of 1998, General Secretary Kofi Annan brokered an agreement that would allow UNSCOM inspectors full access, including Presidential Palaces. The agreement, specified in Resolution 1154, did not mandate military response if Iraq did not comply. By May 1998, the travel ban was lifted as Iraq appeared to accept Annan's deal. But, just as things appeared to be calming down, on August 5, 1998, Saddam unilaterally cut off inspection access and stated that inspections would only be resumed when the economic sanctions on Iraq were lifted.

Finally, in the face of this move, the Clinton administration threatened to bomb Iraq. On November 14, Saddam backed down and the attack was called off. Saddam promised complete cooperation. By mid-December, however, he was back to his old tricks and blocking inspectors.

**Desert Diction**

Operation Desert Fox was a coordinated bombing attack on Iraqi weapons targets by U.S. and UK aircraft and missiles. It was launched in response to Saddam Hussein's unilateral refusal to comply with UNSCOM weapons inspections.

This time, the Clinton administration, with British support, launched *Operation Desert Fox*, on December 16, 1998.

However, even with this military action, the tide was shifting at the UN. On December 17, 1998, as Desert Fox was winding down, the Security Council passed Resolution 1248, stating that if Saddam complied with inspections for nine months, economic sanctions could be lifted. The new inspection teams would be called UNMOVIC (UN Monitoring, Verification, and Inspection Commission). UNSCOM was gone.

This was a crucial change of direction. For the first time, economic sanctions and weapons inspections were linked, and Saddam could bargain one limitation on him against the other one. Saddam rejected the offer, and continued to bar the inspections. The standoff continued.

On August 24, 2001, Tariq Aziz insisted that Iraq would not cooperate with UNMOVIC in anyway. After Desert Fox, however, no further military assaults were launched on Iraq for the purpose of gaining Iraqi compliance with weapons inspections.

In 2002, the second Bush administration reiterated the call to open the doors to inspections, but Saddam again refused and said that inspectors would only be allowed in when sanctions were lifted. Saddam reinforced the new Iraqi position: sanctions or inspections, but not both.

Iraqi Vice President Taha Yasin Ramadan made this extraordinary statement February 13, 2002, confirming Saddam's position on inspections: "There is no need for the spies of the inspection teams to return to Iraq since Iraq is free of weapons of mass destruction."

Ripley's would be proud.

# The Sanctions: A Close-Up Look

The economic sanctions that the United Nations imposed on Iraq in August 1990, immediately following Iraq's annexation of Kuwait, were intended to persuade Iraq to withdraw from Kuwait. After the war ended, the sanctions were continued in order to repay Kuwait for economic damages for the war and to limit Saddam's ability to finance the rebuilding of his army or weapons programs.

On paper, the sanctions were intended to cut Iraq off from international trade and only allow imports that were approved by the United Nations. The sanctions started out with the full support of coalition members in 1991, but over the ensuing 10 years, support for the sanctions steadily eroded.

There are three reasons for the waning support for the sanctions: human suffering, greed, and indifference. The sanctions are blamed for the deaths of thousands of Iraqis, mainly children. Also, Iraq has a lot of oil, and trading that oil for products and services means big money for countries like Russia, France, Saudi Arabia, Syria, and Turkey. Finally, many UN members are simply too far removed from the Gulf War to see the need for the sanctions. They view the sanctions as an anachronism whose time has passed.

## The Greed Factor

You'll recall from previous chapters that Iraq makes very little of what it consumes. The only real method for Iraq to get the things it needs (food, medicine, oil equipment, or weapons) is to sell oil and buy them.

By 1995, it was becoming apparent that Iraqi civilians, particularly Kurds and Shiites, were suffering and dying because Iraq was cut off from needed food and medical supplies. The sanctions, aimed at containing Iraqi military might, had actually helped Saddam retain his grip on power in the years immediately following the Gulf War. Why? Well, even though the United States, United Kingdom, and France set up the no-fly zones that effectively limited Saddam's ability to attack the Kurdish and Shiite insurgents militarily, the sanctions gave him the excuse to attack them through denial of food and medicine. Since the sanctions forbade imports of those items, there was none to be had for the Kurds or Shiites.

In 1995, responding to reports that the Iraqi people were suffering terribly under the UN sanctions, the UN Security Council proposed a food-for-oil plan. The plan would be reviewed every 60 days, and the limits could be adjusted as conditions warranted. Under the plan, Iraq would be allowed to sell limited amounts of oil, if the United Nations could oversee how the revenues were allocated inside Iraq, including a guarantee that a portion would be allocated to the Kurds. The Iraqis objected to this last point, and negotiations over the amounts allowed, the types of materials that could be purchased, how much would be allocated to the Kurds, and who would distribute the humanitarian materials, stretched into mid-1996.

Finally, a deal was reached in August of 1996 in which the Iraqis agreed to allocate a portion of the humanitarian aid to the Kurds, with the proviso that the Iraqi government would be responsible for the distribution itself. The United States had objected to this last provision, until it was alone in its objections. Finally, the United States gave in on that point, and the *oil-for-food* deal went forward.

**Desert Diction**

The oil-for-food program allowed Iraq to export a set amount of oil and use the proceeds to buy food, medicine, and other humanitarian items.

After the UN Security Council created the oil-for-food program in 1996, foreign oil companies lined up to invest in Iraqi oil. Over the years, the United Nations gradually increased the allowed export amount, and Iraq's neighbors, including Turkey, Syria, Jordan, and Saudi Arabia, all worked with Iraq to repair oil transmission facilities in their countries.

As these transmission facilities were improved, more oil could be passed through them. More oil meant more transshipment royalties for the host country. Other countries, like Russia, saw opportunities to exert their influence in the region and increase their trade with Iraq by helping to develop Iraqi oil fields.

## Oil and Blood

For Saddam and the Sunnis, the oil-for-food program was a good deal. For the Kurds and Shiites, the program was only partially successful. Remember, Saddam got to allocate the humanitarian items purchased under the oil-for-food program. Thus, the man who openly attacked the Kurds and Shiites in the aftermath of the Gulf War was now responsible for delivering their food and medical supplies. As of this writing, the

One way Saddam tried to keep more oil money, and sidestep UN controls, was by requiring a 50-cents-per-barrel surcharge from anyone moving oil out of Iraq. This surcharge, decreed in December of 2000, was supposed to be paid to a separate account, outside of UN oversight. It is unclear how many shippers pay this fee to Iraq, though the United Nations suspects that some do pay the surcharge.

lion's share of aid stays in the major Sunni cities, like Baghdad. Much less aid makes its way to the Shiite areas in the south, and cities like Basra, or the Kurd areas in the north, and their cities like Kirkuk.

The result of the five years of sanctions after the Gulf War, and the ensuing years of limited oil-for-food trade has been an unmitigated human disaster in the Shiite and Kurd areas in Iraq. Tens if not hundreds of thousands of Iraqi people, most of them children, have died due to poor nutrition and lack of medicine. Even as the United Nations gradually increases the amount of oil Iraq can export each year, most of the aid is not reaching those who need it most. Some is allocated, with UN permission, to oil equipment investments, most is allocated to the Sunnis, and the rest goes to the Kurds and Shiites.

**Oil Spill Ahead** _____

According to the UN Security Council report on the oil-for-food program, in the first half of 2000, Saddam only spent about half of the money ($4.2 billion) Iraq received from the legal exports of oil ($8 billion). The other half has been horded for future use. Of the half that was spent, about 33 percent went to buying food, and only about 2 percent went to buying medicines. Also, it is estimated that Saddam made almost $2 billion in smuggled oil sales during that period, and apparently none of that money was used to by food or medicine. Of the food and medicine that is purchased, most of that remains in Sunni areas. The Shiites and Kurds are denied most of the goods that are purchased. Some food and medicine does make it to the Kurds and Shiites, but at Saddam's pleasure, and nowhere near enough to meet the needs of the people there.

# The Sanctions Become a Fiasco

In the face of this human suffering, the United States maintained that the sanctions were essential to (1) containing Saddam's weapons of mass destruction programs, and (2) countering his conventional military buildup. However, the majority of the world community saw the situation differently. They see the suffering of the Iraqi people as inordinate punishment for the crimes Saddam has committed. Each time the United

States speaks out in favor of keeping the sanctions, and Saddam shows evidence of dying Iraqi children, world opinion shifts further away from the U.S. position, and toward the Iraqi one.

The question that has vexed U.S. administrations since the Gulf War is whether or not Saddam will be stronger if the sanctions are lifted. The consistent U.S. objections suggest that U.S. policy still favors restrictions. However, in 1999, the United States did propose that Iraq be allowed to sell all the oil it wanted, as long as the revenues were used for humanitarian aid only, and as long as a fixed portion went to the Kurds. Saddam, not surprisingly, rejected the proposal.

As it stands, Saddam is achieving his most important objectives without this kind of deal. He is getting some money allocated to rebuilding his oil infrastructure; he is (according to UN experts) smuggling hundreds of million of dollars worth of oil annually; and countries like Turkey and Syria are openly defying the export limits. All the while, Saddam is able to continue to deny adequate humanitarian aid to the Kurds and Shiites, and blame it on the United States.

> **Oil Spill Ahead** _____
>
> The United States intercepted a Russian tanker shipping illegal Iraqi oil in April of 1995, and fined Royal Dutch Shell over $2 million for its role in the smuggling. The Iranians tended to look the other way while Saddam shipped his oil out illegally via the Gulf, which allowed him to move it down the Gulf unmolested. Also, Saddam has shipped oil out of a supposedly closed pipeline through Syria. In January 2002, it was apparent that Syria was exporting a great deal more oil than it had in previous years. Experts suspected that Syria was transshipping Iraqi oil, in defiance of UN sanctions. Turkey announced it was going to import over 80,000 barrels per day of Iraqi oil in 2002. These imports are not covered by the UN oil-for-food program, showing the limits to sanctions enforcement among Iraq's trade partners. Inasmuch as the Bush administration may need to rely on Turkey as a staging area for any future military action against Iraq, the Americans have, thus far, looked the other way.

# Sanctions: How Tough?

Since the initiation of the oil-for-food program in 1996, Iraq has steadily lobbied to sell more and more oil, and also worked to get control of more money from its exports outside of UN control. Saddam has consistently pushed to get more of the oil revenues gained from exports allocated to oil equipment, in order to repair and rebuild oil extracting and transmission facilities. Over time, these limits were raised to the point where the limit was more than the amount Iraq could actually export—due to the poor state of its domestic infrastructure.

It appears that the United States and UK are increasingly unwilling to alienate Arab countries in the region by continually bombing Iraq to force compliance with UN resolutions. In fact, the mounting public outcry over the deadly effect of the economic sanctions probably has more to do with the lack of military action than anything else. Rather than Iraq being isolated, the United States is becoming more isolated due to the apparent mismatch of effect (bombing or dying children) to the cause (Saddam's intransigence over sanctions or inspections).

# American Isolation ... and a Big Question

So, as the years move on, time appears to be on Saddam's side. He has managed to win the peace after losing the war.

Iraq is no longer the isolated pariah it once was. Although not universally embraced, Iraq has gained the sympathy of a broader base of Arab and non-Arab countries that are drawn to Iraq for humanitarian and economic motives. On the other hand, by insisting on defending an increasingly untenable position on the issues of sanctions and inspections, the United States has been increasingly isolated and has been blamed by the international community for the current desperate state of the Iraqi people.

In the aftermath of the September 11 attacks on the United States by the al Qaeda terrorist network, a fundamental question arises. Is Saddam Hussein simply a victim of U.S. bullying? Or is he a part of the international terrorist movement that has transformed Western foreign policy?

## The Least You Need to Know

- Saddam has steadily turned defeat into victory after the Gulf War.

- Iraq has threatened to invade Kuwait even after its 1991 defeat.

- Iraq has managed to block all weapons inspections in its territory.

- Iraq has portrayed the suffering of its people under UN sanctions as the fault of the United States, rather than due to Saddam's allocation methods.

- Saddam has managed to export increasing amounts of oil through legal and illegal means, to the point where the sanctions have lost much of their effectiveness.

# 23

# The Terrorism Question:
# A New Kind of War

## In This Chapter

- ◆ Saddam's use of chemical weapons
- ◆ Saddam's development of anthrax and other biological agents
- ◆ Saddam's use of terror against his own people
- ◆ Is Iraq harboring terrorists?

In the aftermath of September 11, 2001, attacks on the United States by the al Qaeda terrorist network, the United States made going after those terrorists and the regimes that harbor them, a national priority. As President George W. Bush stated in his State of the Union Address to Congress in January 2002:

> States like these [Iraq, Iran, North Korea], and their terrorist allies, constitute an axis of evil, arming to threaten the peace of the world. By seeking weapons of mass destruction, these regimes pose a grave and

growing danger. They could provide these arms to terrorists, giving them the means to match their hatred. They could attack our allies or attempt to blackmail the United States. In any of these cases, the price of indifference would be catastrophic.

**Desert Diction**

Al Qaeda, which means "the Base," is made of Muslim radicals from many nationalities. They are dedicated to getting U.S. troops out of Saudi Arabia, destroying Israel, establishing radical Islamic governments, and removing Westerners from Muslim nations throughout the world. Al Qaeda's model regime was the Taliban in Afghanistan, which practiced radical Muslim theocracy.

**Oil Spill Ahead**

In using "axis of evil" to describe Iraq, Iran, and North Korea, President Bush engendered outrage from the three countries in question, and also the objections and reservations of most Western European countries who had been on the front lines against Nazi Germany (an Axis power during World War II).

In a single day, the animosity of the United States toward Saddam fundamentally increased.

# If It Quacks Like a Duck ...

In the scramble to find the perpetrators of the September 11 attacks, the U.S. administration turned its spotlight on an old nemesis: Saddam Hussein. Given Saddam's public statements against the United States, and the dozen years he has now spent being either enemy number one or enemy number two of the United States, it seems logical that Saddam would be involved in international terrorism. But is he?

Saddam Hussein's Iraq was the only Arab state not to offer condolences to the United States in the aftermath of the September 11 attacks.

Certainly, the Bush administration has made at least a general connection between Saddam Hussein and international terrorism. In his State of the Union Address on January 29, 2002, President Bush included Iraq in an "axis of evil" along with North Korea and Iran, and stated, "The United States of America will not permit the world's most dangerous regimes to threaten us with the world's most destructive weapons."

Why would President Bush put Iraq into this "evil axis" category?

> **Iraq Fact** _____
>
> Excerpts of Open Letter from Saddam Hussein to the United States
>
> "… In addition, we say to the American peoples, what happened on September 11, 2001 should be compared to what their government and their armies are doing in the world.
>
> For example, the international agencies have stated that more than one million and a half Iraqis have died because of the blockade imposed by America and some Western countries. In addition to the tens of thousands who died or are injured in the military action perpetrated by America along with those who allied with it against Iraq.
>
> Hundreds of bridges, churches, mosques, colleges, schools, factories, palaces, hotels, and thousands of private houses were destroyed or damaged by the American and Western bombardment, which is ongoing even today against Iraq … When one million and a half Iraqi human beings die, according to Western documents, from a population of twenty five million, because of the American blockade and aggression, it means that Iraq has lost about one twentieth of its population.
>
> And just as your beautiful skyscrapers were destroyed and caused your grief, beautiful buildings and precious homes crumbled over their owners in Lebanon, Palestine and Iraq by American weapons used by the Zionists … Americans should feel the pain they have inflicted on other peoples of the world, so as when they suffer, they will find the right solution and the right path … Even when the Westerners, and especially Americans insulted the holy sites of Muslim and Arabs by what is almost an occupation of Saudi Arabia in order to launch their evil fires against Baghdad …
>
> Isn't this solidarity, and this in-advance approval by some Western leaders, of a military aggression against an Islamic country, the most flagrant form of the new Crusades, fanaticism. It reminds Arabs and Muslims of the Crusade war launched by the West and NATO against Iraq …"

Let's look at what we know about Saddam and his regime.

## Five Strikes and You're Out

There are five areas where an argument can certainly be made that Saddam qualifies to be called a member of an evil axis:

◆ Saddam has used "the world's most destructive weapons" before, on the Kurds.

◆ Saddam practices terror on his own people in a variety of ways.

**Desert Diction**

A **terrorist** is (according to the most widely accepted definition) someone who intentionally targets civilians to achieve military or political objectives. These groups thrive on creating an atmosphere of fear (or "terror") among the target population.

◆ Saddam has attempted to assassinate former President Bush.

◆ Saddam supports Palestinian bombers, whom many consider terrorists.

◆ Saddam harbors international terrorist groups.

Does the United States have reason to be concerned? The answer is clearly "yes." If a nation *acts* like part of an axis of evil, there's good reason to *consider* it part of an axis of evil.

Let's look at each of these five areas of concern in-depth.

# What ... Me, Mount a Genocidal Campaign Against Civilians?

Saddam has used weapons of mass destruction before, on his long-time nemeses, the Iranians, and later on the Kurds. There is significant evidence, a good deal of it from the United Nations, to support the claim that Saddam used mustard gas during the Iran-Iraq War.

**Oil Spill Ahead**

In March 1984, the war was going badly for Saddam. He had unilaterally offered a cease-fire, only to have the Iranians reject it and press their own offensive into Iraqi territory. In February 1984, the Iranian army seized Manjoon Islands, near Basra. The Manjoon Islands belonged to Iraq, and sat atop a large oil deposit. Saddam was desperate to drive the Iranians back. His conventional weapons had been unable to stop them, so he resorted to chemical weapons to drive the Iranians out. Saddam used mustard gas and killed 1,200 Iranians and wounded 5,000 more. Of course, no estimates were given for casualties among the local Shiite population during the attack or afterward, but if soldiers died in the area, it is safe to assume civilians died, too.

The Iranians claimed (and later were able to prove to the UN and the Red Cross), that Iraq had used chemical weapons on multiple occasions during the Iran-Iraq War. The United States and other countries condemned the Iraqi actions, but did not intervene. Why?

Remember, Iran was the bad guy in the 1980s. The United States had no love for Khomeini in the aftermath of the hostage crisis, and the Sunni Arab states feared the Shiite Persians (Iranians). Saddam's use of mustard gas and other nerve gas weapons was overlooked … perhaps on the assumption that, as long as, Saddam could keep the Iranians in check, there was no real problem. The short-sightedness and moral inadequacies of such a policy have, in recent years, become painfully obvious.

Most of the gas attacks occurred on Iraqi territory, in the Shiite-dominated south. While *mustard gas* does not persist beyond a few days, Shiite civilians no doubt came in contact with the residue. This did not seem to bother Saddam; he used the gas up to 40 times, according to Iranian claims.

**Desert Diction**

**Mustard gas** is 2-chloroethyl sulphide. As manufactured, the chemical agent is an oily liquid that smells like garlic. When distributed as a liquid or as gas, the agent will burn any human tissue it comes into contact with, including skin, eyes, and lungs. The agent works slowly enough to allow it to be ingested fully before it starts to blister and burn. Mustard gas was first introduced in World War I and has been used sporadically since then, including by Italy in Ethiopia in 1936, by Japan in China during World War II, by Egypt during the Yemen civil war in the 1960s, and by the Iraqis during the Iran-Iraq War in the mid and late 1980s.

## Practice Makes Dangerously Perfect

The second mustard gas incident occurred in 1988, toward the end of the Iran-Iraq War. The military situation was much more in Iraq's favor. Iran had suffered setbacks all across the front, and was on the run. Iraq was enjoying tacit support of the United States.

In this environment, with his army increasing in power and confidence each day, Saddam went after the Kurds, who had been waging their perpetual rebellion against Iraq with renewed ferocity while Saddam was preoccupied with the Iranians. The location of the attack was the town of Halabja, a Kurdish city of 80,000 people close to the front lines. Kurdish fighters, called pesh merga, were staging effective assaults on Iraqi troops from Halabja. The pesh merga were a real thorn in Saddam's side, and he was eager to defeat them in anyway he could. With the Iranians on the run, and with the experience of several gas attacks on the Iranians under his belt, Saddam took his revenge.

According to journalist Jeffrey Goldberg, who traveled to the affected areas, the attack began early in the morning as what seemed to be routine shelling accompanied by aerial bombardment. The inhabitants of Halabja went into their basements to wait out the bombardment, as they always did. However, the Iraqi shells contained nerve gas, which settled thick and close to the ground. Those who could, crawled out of their cellars only to find a poisoned atmosphere.

The U.S. State Department estimates that upward of 5,000 Kurds were killed in the attack, although other sources claim many thousands more deaths in that attack and others that may have occurred in the area. Suffice it to say, thousands of Kurds were killed by Iraqi chemical weapons during 1988.

## Making a Science of Killing

During and immediately after the attacks, Iraqi aircraft tested wind direction and speed and filmed the effects. Later, when Iraqi doctors were sent in to collect the corpses, they were debriefed by Iraqi military as to exact locations of the bodies in relation to where the shells had landed. Saddam wasn't just retaliating against the Kurds, he was using them as guinea pigs. He was testing how effective his weapons of mass destruction actually were.

Halabja was not the only place where Saddam attacked the Kurds with chemical weapons. According to Physicians for Human Rights, who had samples tested by the British Ministry of Defence, Iraq attacked the Kurd village of Birjinni on August 25, 1988. Villagers on the scene said that Iraqi planes dropped clusters of munitions on the village, clusters that left the faint smell of garlic in the air. The villagers began to vomit and blister, and four villagers died immediately after the attacks.

**Oil Spill Ahead** _____

Saddam has used chemical weapons on both military and civilian enemies. He has carefully monitored the effects of these weapons—as though he were planning, sometime, to use them again.

There is ample evidence of additional Iraqi attacks, if only from the number of Kurdish refugees fleeing into Turkey who exhibited symptoms of gas attacks and were treated by Western doctors. Saddam was perfecting his craft. From the few hundred casualties per chemical attack against the Iranian army in the mid-1980s, he had become capable of killing thousands of Kurds in the late 1980s.

# Tamping Down Dissent at Home

Saddam has used the facts and rumors associated with his chemical weapons to subdue internal dissent. Journalist Jeffrey Goldberg describes an incident that occurred in 1999 in the Shiite Holy City of Karbala: The Shiites had staged repeated rebellions against Saddam, many of which originated in Karbala. According to an expert cited in the article, Saddam responded by sending a battalion of Iraqi troops wearing biohazard suits to Karbala. They formed a ring around the city, but did nothing.

The effect on the inhabitants was what might be expected: People panicked and went indoors. The agitation died down. Mission accomplished.

# Assassination Alert

Terror comes in many forms. Domestic terror through the use of insidious weapons is one form of terror. Assassination of a nation's leaders for maximum impact on the population is another.

Throughout his career, Saddam made assassination attempts on his enemies as a means of revenge and to spread terror. As noted in a previous chapter, Saddam earned his spurs in the Ba'th Party through two unsuccessful assassination attempts against the prime ministers of the Hashemite monarchy. As a matter of securing his own position, Saddam murdered many around him in a series of purges.

## Target: Former President Bush

Perhaps Saddam's most ambitious attempt at terror-through-assassination came in April 14, 1993, when he tried unsuccessfully to arrange the assassination of former President Bush while Bush was in Kuwait on a goodwill tour.

Three different efforts were foiled by the U.S. intelligence community, operating in concert with Kuwaiti, Egyptian, and other intelligence services. The would-be assassins were plotting to …

- Detonate a remote-controlled car bomb near the Kuwait City airport when Bush arrived.

- Detonate a remote-controlled car bomb when Bush was receiving an honorary degree in Kuwait City.

- Have a suicide bomber wearing explosives detonate himself if he could get close to Bush.

The Kuwaiti police arrested 14 plotters just prior to Bush's arrival and seized the car-bombs. Through testimony of the captured people, including one Wali al-Ghazali who stated that he was the intended suicide bomber, and inspection of the car-bombs, the United States was able to prove that the bombs were like ones the Iraqi intelligence service had used in other places. Experts agree that the evidence points squarely at the Iraqi intelligence service.

The event still staggers the mind. It was as though Saddam was willing to risk anything and everything to remind the American people of the Iraqi leadership's hatred of the United States.

The Clinton administration responded to the attempt by launching a cruise missile attack on Baghdad and other targets inside Iraq. This attack was widely criticized by many former coalition partners and by many people in the United States.

# Domestic Abuses

Not only has Saddam used military force against the Kurds and Shiites in his own country; he has attacked the Shiite way of life, and the very identity of the Kurds.

Many of the Shiites live in the marshlands along the Shatt-al-Arab and the Persian Gulf coast. The Marsh Arabs, as they are called, have lived a unique life in the marshes for centuries. However, this marshy region has also been a hotbed for Shiite rebellions against Saddam's regime.

In the past decade, Saddam has initiated a "land reclamation" program, under which the marshes are steadily being drained, creating an ecological disaster. With their ancestral homelands destroyed, the Marsh Arabs are relocating to crowded slums in north Basra. The result is the loss of a culture and way of life that is over 3,000 years old, and—probably more important to Saddam—the elimination of a haven for people who resist his rule.

The Kurds, meanwhile, were subjected to an "Arabization" program under which they were required to change their legal names from Kurdish to Arabic names in order to receive food rations or get government jobs. Kurd location names were changed to Arabic ones. This tactic has been practiced by dominant cultures over minority ones for centuries. For example, the Polish monarchy forbade the use of the Lithuanian language and writing during their hegemony over Lithuania in the eighteenth century, and the British outlawed the use of Gaelic in Ireland in the late nineteenth century.

Like the Poles and the British, Saddam has not succeeded in wiping out the culture of the people he has attempted to subjugate.

# Support for Global Terrorism

Saddam practices what he preaches, and supports terrorist groups outside of Iraq.

For example, he sends $10,000 to the family of each Palestinian suicide bomber who has killed him- or herself in an attack on Israelis. Saddam also enjoys the affection of *Hamas*, the Palestinian terrorist organization. The Hamas refer to "brotherly Iraq," and in 1993 the Hamas threatened to kill Israelis if the United States attacked Iraq. Like Saddam in the Gulf War, Hamas links the United States to Israel, and by doing so tries to rally the Arabs to their cause and alienate the United States.

**Desert Diction**

**Hamas,** the Arabic word meaning "zeal," is the common name for the Islamic Resistance Movement. Founded in 1987 by Sheik Ahmed Yassin, Hamas is a Palestinian, fundamentalist Muslim organization. The Hamas political wing runs schools, mosques, and clinics, but the militant wing is a terrorist organization that focuses its attacks on Israel.

## Where Does the Money Go?

As we saw in Chapter 22, the Kurds and Shiites are suffering and dying in vast numbers due to shortages of food and medicine. However, Saddam isn't trying to spend all the money he makes from legal oil sales and illegal smuggling on food or medicine.

---

### Increase Your Iraq IQ

The United States buys one million barrels of oil per day (bpd) from Iraq. In fact, Iraq is the fifth largest supplier of oil to the United States. According to the U.S. Department of Energy, the major suppliers of oil to the United States as of this writing are:

- ◆ Saudi Arabia: 1,463,000 barrels per day
- ◆ Mexico: 1,309,000 barrels per day
- ◆ Canada: 1,289,000 barrels per day
- ◆ Venezuela: 1,247,000 barrels per day
- ◆ Iraq: 988,000 barrels per day
- ◆ Nigeria: 513,000 barrels per day

While it may seem odd that the United States would do business with Iraq, the U.S. government has stated that Iraq should be allowed to generate as much revenue as it can from "legal" oil exports (that is, exports within UN sanction limits). Buying Iraqi oil supports that policy.

Some Mideast experts assert that most of the smuggling money goes to building palaces for Saddam or procuring UN-prohibited military items, and that some goes to financing terrorist groups abroad.

The option of cutting off Iraq's oil exports as a form of protest remains open. Saddam unilaterally suspended oil exports on April 7, 2002, in response to a flare-up in the conflict between the Palestinians and the Israelis. By doing this, Saddam hoped to punish the United States for its support of Israel. Most of the oil that Iraq sells under the UN sanctions ends up in the United States, so Saddam was looking for a way to punish the United States at the gas pumps. (A month later, Saddam withdrew the suspension.)

# Iraq as a State Sponsor of Terrorism

The United States lists Iraq as a state sponsor of terrorism. Iraq was on the official State Department list when it was created in 1979. The country was taken off the list in 1982 (remember, the United States was supporting Iraq against the Iranians at that time), but Iraq was put back on, on September 13, 1990, just prior to the outbreak of the Gulf War.

Why does a state sponsor terrorism? The main reason is that state-sponsored terrorists can sometimes enable the state to achieve goals that are not attainable through conventional military or political/diplomatic means. Terrorism is a cheap alternative to conventional warfare, as the terrorists can create physical destruction and popular fear even when the sponsor state is militarily unable to do so. (Consider, in this light, Saddam's orchestration of the April 13, 1993, attempt to assassinate former President Bush.)

**Desert Diction**

**Abu Nidal,** whose real name is Sabri l-Banna, is the leader of the organization that takes his name. The organization, which does not support the Palestinian agreement with Israel, has committed acts of terror outside the Middle East in several countries.

## Safe Harbor for Terrorists

There is mounting evidence that Saddam harbors international terrorist groups. The U.S. Congressional Research Service found that Iraq is sheltering the *Abu Nidal* organization and the Abu Abbas faction of the Palestinian Liberation Front. Saddam also supports Hamas financially, but not necessarily by providing a safe harbor for them.

## Al Qaeda?

The big question after the September 11, 2001, terrorist attacks on the United States is whether Saddam is harboring any elements of al Qaeda, the international terrorist group run by Osama bin Laden and responsible for the attacks. According to Western journalists who have traveled to Iraq since the September 11 attacks, Saddam is hiding dozens of al Qaeda members in the northern reaches of Iraq. In return for the safe haven in Iraq, these al Qaeda members are being used by Saddam to attack Kurd leaders, in an attempt to destabilize the Kurd leadership in the area.

# What Does It All Add Up To?

Saddam has practiced terror domestically and abroad, and he sponsors international terrorist organizations, verbally, physically, and financially. He has made repeated statements condemning the United States, and declaring his dedication to the destruction of Israel.

States sponsor terrorism to undermine their enemies abroad, when their conventional military resources or diplomacy cannot. Weapons of mass destruction, which Saddam possesses, will only increase the impact terrorists can have if they are used as part of an Iraq-sponsored terrorist attack.

Many consider such an attack inevitable.

## The Least You Need to Know

- Saddam has practiced terror on several levels over the decades he has been in power.
- Saddam has used biological and chemical weapons on the Iranian army and the Kurds within Iraq.
- Saddam has attempted assassination for the purpose of creating terror.
- Saddam harbors international terrorist groups inside Iraq and provides financial assistance to other terrorist groups.

# Chapter 24

# On the Horizon: What Happens Next?

## In This Chapter

- ◆ Saddam's potential for harming his neighbors
- ◆ Saddam's potential for harming his own citizens
- ◆ Israel, the United States, and Iraq
- ◆ Saddam's potential for harming the United States
- ◆ How long can Saddam survive?

We've reviewed 8,000 years of history. We've tracked a number of compound errors committed by Western superpowers. We've looked at what happens in closed societies. We've seen graphic evidence of the need of dictators for enemies. We've gotten an overview of some key points in Arab relations with the West. And we're still left with one maddeningly difficult-to-answer question.

What is Saddam really up to?

In this chapter, we look at some of the possible answers to that question—and some of the implications those answers carry for the United States.

# Trouble with the Neighbors?

Is Saddam likely to stir up economic, military, or political trouble again in the region? Let's look at the most important players one by one.

## Iran

Iran is the country that may have the least to fear from Saddam, possessing as it does a large population and capable military. While still the ancient enemy for Iraq, it's not very likely that Saddam will be picking a fight with the Iranians again anytime soon.

The last war against Iran was a disaster for Saddam (regardless of how it was later "spun" to the Iraqi people). He certainly cannot assume U.S. support, tacit or otherwise, of the kind he enjoyed for a time during the Iran-Iraq War. In fact, he should assume the opposite.

## Turkey

Turkey is a member of *NATO*, and NATO policy is that an attack on one NATO member is an attack on all NATO members. In addition, Incirlik Airbase in southern Turkey is a key staging point for U.S. aircraft in any potential military action taken against Iraq. What is more, Turkey is a transshipment center for Iraqi oil and Iraqi imports.

**Desert Diction** _____

The **North Atlantic Treaty Organization (NATO)** was originally created in 1949, as an alliance of European and North American countries. The alliance was created to counter expansion by the Soviet Union into Western Europe. Current NATO members include 19 countries: the United States, Canada, the United Kingdom, Italy, Belgium, the Netherlands, Norway, Denmark, Germany, Turkey, Greece, Czech Republic, Hungary, Spain, Portugal, France, Luxembourg, Iceland, and Poland.

As of this writing, Turkey is even importing Iraqi oil outside of UN economic sanction controls. Continuation of this practice could be Turkey's "fee" for allowing the

United States to use its bases. So, while Iraq may not pose a military threat to Turkey, it could exert growing economic influence through increased oil trade. This influence could serve to drive a wedge between the United States and this vital regional ally.

> **Increase Your Iraq IQ**
>
> Turkey, Iraq, and Iran each share a common problem—a large and restive Kurdish minority. The 25 million Kurds are considered the largest nationality without their own country.

## Syria

Ruled by a rival Ba'th Party branch, Syria has had an on-again, off-again relationship with Saddam. Also possessing a potent military, Syria was part of the Coalition against Saddam during the Gulf War, but since then has gradually warmed to Iraq. Currently, the United Nations believes that Syria is a main smuggling outlet for Iraqi oil, through a supposedly "closed" pipeline. As with Turkey, Iraq could begin to wield increased economic pressure on Syria, although the military option has more weight, inasmuch as Syria is not a member of NATO.

## Jordan

Ruled by a Hashemite monarchy like the one that used to rule in Iraq, Jordan, too, has had an on-again, off-again relationship with Iraq. Remember at one point in the 1960s, Iraq and Jordan formed the Arab Union (as a counterbalance to the Egyptian-led United Arab Republic); later during the Gulf War, Jordan sat conspicuously on the sidelines, and did not join the Coalition.

Jordan would not be much of match for Saddam, but it would not be much of a prize in terms of oil resources, either.

## Saudi Arabia

Saudi Arabia is the only other Arab country, aside from Kuwait, that Saddam attacked during the Gulf War. Saddam launched SCUD missiles at bases inside Saudi Arabia (along with the SCUDs that were launched at Israel).

Saudi Arabia would certainly be a lucrative target for Saddam. Control over Saudi Arabia and Kuwait would give Iraq effective control over a large portion of the world's oil, and would probably mean that the other Gulf oil states (such as Bahrain, Qatar, and the UAE) would be easy prey for Saddam.

**Oil Spill Ahead**

The Saudi government hosts U.S. military units that have become increasingly controversial in recent years.

Preventing Iraqi expansion into Saudi Arabia is currently a major objective of Western policy in the region. However, in recent years, the United States has taken steps to relocate air support facilities into the Gulf states and the British island of Diego Garcia in the Indian Ocean, and out of Saudi Arabia.

## Kuwait

The once and future target?

In 1990, Saddam took a calculated risk that failed. He was confronted with an Arab-Western coalition that held together long enough to drive him out of Kuwait—and almost out of power. However, Saddam has threatened to invade Kuwait on more than one occasion since the end of the Gulf War—with predictable increases in military and diplomatic pressure from the West.

The fundamental difference between 1990 and 2002 is that the Iraqi army is much smaller and weaker in 2002 than it was in 1990. Also, the Kuwaiti state can now resist military pressure more readily, with prepositioned equipment ready for U.S. troops to hook up with in the event of a rise in tensions.

U.S. policy has consistently upheld the defense of Kuwait as a major objective since the Gulf War.

## The Bottom Line

Is Saddam a threat to his neighbors?

Clearly, he *could* be a military threat to Kuwait and Saudi Arabia, if relations between those countries and the United States deteriorated to the point where Saddam felt confident that the United States would not be able to support them. In fact, the same basic principle could be applied to all the Arab states in the region.

> **Oil Spill Ahead**
>
> Don't assume that the "moderate Arab states" are automatic allies for the West. The more hatred and discord the Israeli conflict with the Palestinians produces, the more likely it is that Saddam Hussein will be able to drive a wedge between the United States and its Arab allies.

What could make the Arab Gulf states work in concert *against* the United States in a Middle Eastern war? The same thing that has made the Arab states work in concert in the region numerous times over the last 50 years: Israel.

There is probably no other single element that can unite the Arab states so passionately and so completely as Arab animosity toward Israel. Saddam has, of course, tried to play the Israel card on numerous occasions, in an attempt to rally the Arab states to his causes and to legitimize his claims for leadership within the Arab world.

# More Trouble on the Home Front?

As this book goes to press, the Kurds are less threatened than in anytime during Saddam's reign. The (relatively) impressive degree of autonomy currently enjoyed by the Kurdish minority in their three autonomous regions is substantial, and is currently guaranteed by U.S. and UK airpower.

The Kurds have supermarkets, cell phones, and Internet networks. The horrors of 1991, when 1.5 million Kurds shivered on mountaintop refugee camps, appear to be (at least for the time being) over. The United States insistence that a portion of the Iraqi oil revenues sold under the sanctions go to the Kurds has, despite Saddam's machinations, generated over $4.4 billion into the Kurd territories in Iraq since 1996. As long as the UN oil-for-food program is in place, with the United Nations ensuring that the share of money from the program that is earmarked for the Kurds actually gets to the Kurds, and U.S. and UK fighters patrol overhead, the Kurds will probably continue to enjoy the benefits of the program.

**Iraq Fact**

Are things finally looking up for the Kurds? In a recent article in *The Wall Street Journal*, Kurd Minister of Reconstruction Nasreen Mustafa Sideek said, "It's a golden age. It has never been better for the Kurds in 4,000 years."

The Kurds, who have seen a relative increase in their living standards and overall security, are the least willing to risk all they have gained—unless they could be convinced of getting an even better deal by supporting a U.S.-led attack on Saddam.

## The Shiite Underclass

Since the creation of modern-day Iraq, the Shiite majority in the south has always been on the outside looking in. The Sunni ruling group has always held the power, the money, and —in the decade since the end of the Gulf War—the food and medicine.

Unlike the Kurds, the Shiites in Iraq do not enjoy a specific set-aside under the UN oil-for-food program. The United States did not insist on it, and so Saddam determines how much food, medicine, and infrastructure investment goes to the Shiites. He appears to send just enough to prevent the situation from becoming severe enough to bring about a civil uprising … but not enough to prevent the deaths of thousands of Shiite children and adults.

---

**Increase Your Iraq IQ**

In the year following the Gulf War, the Shiites attempted to rise up against Saddam, with the understanding that the United States would support them. When Saddam came after the Shiites with everything he had left, the United States did not intervene for months. Only later, did the United States, United Kingdom, and France establish a southern no-fly zone to protect the Shiites from continued aggression by Saddam. By then, the rebellion had been crushed.

---

# Trouble Brewing for the United States?

Saddam is clearly a potential threat to the oil-rich Gulf states, and to his own people—but is he a threat to the United States?

On a conventional military level, the Iraqi army poses little threat to U.S. military forces. As Operation Desert Storm demonstrated, Saddam's weakened army is no match for U.S. military equipment, technology, and tactics.

However, Saddam could make up for the lack of conventional power by using weapons of mass destruction or support for terrorist campaigns to level the playing field. In fact, the specter of chemical and biological weapons could act as a significant deterrent to a conventional attack on Iraq. Saddam has demonstrated his willingness to use these weapons, and it is reasonable to assume that, if his back were against the wall and he had an opportunity, he would consider using them against American soldiers or civilians.

The prospect of weapons of mass destruction being used against U.S. troops is a sobering one, but this is a scenario that would only unfold in the event of a land war in Iraq. The possibility of terrorists with links to Iraq using these weapons on U.S. soil, however, is an even more troubling possibility.

## Two Questions

Saddam is known to support international terrorist organizations (see Chapter 23). He harbors some inside his country, and finances others. This leads to two questions about Iraq's leader and international terrorism: *Has he?* and *Will he?*

*Has Saddam financed terrorists who have acted inside the United States or against U.S. interests abroad?*

So far, there is no evidence of that connection.

*Will Saddam send or help send terrorists to wage war on the United States? And if so, would Saddam provide biological, chemical, or other weapons of mass destruction for use during such attacks?*

The relationship between Iraq and the United States over the last 12 years, from the start of the Gulf War through the sanctions and no-fly zones to the present day, is among the most antagonistic of any two states anywhere on earth. Saddam's statements are consistently bellicose and jarringly consistent in their expressed hatred for the United States.

The level of Saddam's bitterness toward the United States and his own desire to go down in history as a great Arab leader, suggests that we should not be surprised if Saddam tries at some point, by some means or other, to reach out and touch Americans at home.

**Oil Spill Ahead**

Saddam may also use his terrorist connections to attack Israel and provoke the wider conflict of which he has clearly been dreaming of for decades.

# What's Next?

As these words are being written, it seems likely that the United States will return to Iraq soon. In fact, there may well be many returns to Iraq by the second Bush administration.

- ◆ It seems likely that the Bush administration will demand a resumption of UNMOVIC (the successor to UNSCOM) weapons inspections, which are currently ceased. Current negotiations between the UN secretary general and the Iraqis are proceeding slowly, but without full and unfettered inspections, it is doubtful that the United States will accept a watered down deal.

- ◆ It also appears probable that the Bush administration will respond more forcefully to Iraqi missile attacks on U.S. warplanes in the no-fly zones in northern and southern Iraq. The increased military pressure will be used to signal U.S. intent in the only way Saddam seems to understand: a show of force.

- ◆ The administration may well try to find a way to work with the Kurdish population in the north—and to a lesser extent, the Shiite majority in the south—to foster a coup within Iraq. In return, the United States will try to promise the

Kurds support for their continued autonomy within a post-Saddam Iraq. However, U.S. promises will fall short of offering full independence for the Kurds. Turkey, the U.S.'s NATO ally, would not abide an independent Kurdistan on its borders, given their own sizable Kurdish minority.

♦ The United States will in all likelihood work with the United Nations to revise the economic sanctions against Iraq into something more sustainable than the current (unsustainable) program. What is envisioned is a package of so-called *smart sanctions*. The fact is that the present sanctions have begun to erode to the point where their control over Iraqi military imports is questionable. There is significant trade outside of the sanctions and a good deal of smuggling, as well. Inspections of materials coming into Iraq are intermittent, and the borders are open to transferring materials, particularly along the Iranian border, where U.S. influence is at its lowest.

**Desert Diction**

Smart sanctions would focus on limiting Iraqi imports of materials that could be used for producing weapons of mass destruction, and limiting imports of conventional weapons.

## Coup or Large-Scale Invasion?

A coup with U.S. military support would be far less costly to the United States in terms of lives lost and equipment used than a military invasion. The strategy of arming in-country opposition, heavy air strikes, and special operations forces was so successful in Afghanistan, with minimal U.S. casualties, that it seems likely the United States will try to employ a similar strategy in Iraq.

Furthermore, an internal coup would not alienate Islamic and Arab allies in the region. Saudi Arabia, Kuwait, Bahrain, and Turkey all have Muslim populations that are increasingly opposed to U.S. military action in Iraq. The current U.S. policy of occasional missile or air strikes on Iraqi targets is unpopular with the populace in these countries that surround Iraq, and it puts those friendly governments in a difficult political position with their own citizens. However, if Saddam is toppled from within, it will not be as easy to blame the United States for his downfall.

**Oil Spill Ahead**

An invasion would probably not have the full support of the Arab states in the region. Unlike the Gulf War, where the Gulf states were equally threatened by Iraqi expansion and control of huge oil supplies, a unilateral U.S. invasion of Iraq without apparent cause would alienate Arab states. Of course, if the United States can catch Saddam in the act, or with the proverbial "smoking gun," then all bets are off.

U.S. government officials estimate that an invasion would require between 169,000 and 250,000 U.S. combat troops, and about 300,000 support troops (about the same number as were deployed during Operation Desert Storm). As of this writing, there are only about 25,000 U.S. troops in the region.

## Would an Internal Takeover Work in Iraq?

Like the Northern Alliance in Afghanistan under the Taliban, the Kurdish rebels in the north control a significant chunk of Iraqi territory. In fact, the Kurds control more territory in Iraq than the Afghan Northern Coalition did in Afghanistan at the start of Operation Enduring Freedom (the military campaign designed to topple the Taliban regime in Afghanistan).

Also like Afghanistan, the Kurd factions often face off against one another, and would need some outside, direct U.S. military action to unite them into action to topple a common enemy. There are about 50,000 Kurds organized into fighting units; however, they are poorly equipped to face off against the Iraqis. They lack tanks, heavy artillery, and aircraft, as well as a sufficient supply of arms and ammunition for a major campaign.

But for all the similarities to Afghanistan, there are some major differences in Iraq. These differences mean the Bush administration cannot necessarily assume a mass uprising against Saddam would be automatic after the United States launched air strikes and helped to coordinate rebel attacks.

Unlike Afghanistan, the United States cannot simply support a pre-existing coalition of opposition groups against the current regime. The Kurds are an ethnic minority in Iraq. The majority of Iraqis are Shiites who have so little in common with the Kurds apart from a wish to see Saddam gone, it is doubtful they would maintain an alliance for any extended period. The Sunnis around Saddam control the army and the government, and they have successfully eliminated most Shiite opposition groups in the past 10 years. They are fiercely loyal to their leader.

The Shiites in the south are less openly ready to fight than the Kurds in the north, and even if they were to fight, they are no more likely to end up in charge of Iraq than the Kurds. The other Arab Gulf states would not tolerate a Shiite-run Iraq, anymore than Turkey or Iran would tolerate an independent Kurdistan.

## How It Might Come Together

A coup to overthrow Saddam might work, provided that the United States and its Western allies managed to …

◆ Rally the Shiite rebels and the Kurd *pesh merga* to fight against Saddam's Revolutionary Guard and units that remain loyal to him.

◆ Assist the Shiite movement in penetrating the Iraqi military and creating a mass desertion from the army, effectively removing Saddam's power base.

If these two objectives are not met, the rebels are likely to be crushed once again.

# The Dream Scenario

What would head the list of events the United States would most like to see happen in Iraq? Probably a Sunni-officer led coup to overthrow Saddam Hussein, supported by the Shiites and Kurds.

The United States would want the post-coup regime to grant more autonomy to the Kurds and ensure more material, food, medicine, and investment to the Shiites. However, the United States would probably settle for simply getting rid of Saddam, assuming that that meant there was (even marginally) more rational and U.S.-friendly leadership in Baghdad. The second Bush administration would doubtless be quite happy to invest reconstruction dollars in a post-Saddam Iraq, much as it is doing in post-Taliban Afghanistan.

# The Nightmare Scenario

A major Iraqi-sponsored strike against U.S. citizens—whether that strike was conventional or terrorist in nature—would give any U.S. administration a reason for retaliatory military action against Iraq.

# Why Is Iraq a Priority?

You might be wondering why the current focus in Washington is on changing leadership in Iraq, rather than the leadership of some other country known to harbor terrorists or possess weapons of mass destruction such as Iran, North Korea, or Libya?

Consider, as a point of reference, the large number of Operation Desert Storm players in the Bush cabinet. This team has already prevailed militarily against one Iraqi "adventure" against U.S. interests, but has watched their work slowly and steadily unravel over the past 10 years. Iraq's role as an adversary is deeply ingrained, and Saddam's animosity toward the United States is a matter of record. The Bush administration, stocked with Desert Storm veterans, sees Iraq (and not without reason) as a major threat, and perhaps *the* major threat, to U.S. interests in the Gulf region—and quite possibly to the U.S. homeland itself.

| Increase Your Iraq IQ |
| --- |
| Like father, like son? |
| Operation Desert Storm Leaders in the current Bush administration include the following: |
| ◆ Dick Cheney WAS: Secretary of Defense; IS: Vice President |
| ◆ Colin Powell WAS: Military Commander; IS: Secretary of State |
| ◆ Condoleeza Rice WAS: Trusted Bush aide; IS: National Security Advisor |

## A Change in Tone

Unlike the Clinton administration, the Bush administration has indicated that the previous U.S. policy of deterring Saddam's nuclear, biological, and chemical weapons capabilities has been replaced by a policy whose objective is *destroying* those capabilities.

The new tone suggests that there is a sense of urgency about Saddam and his capabilities to harm the United States, and that the Bush administration is working on a pre-emptive strategy, rather than waiting for Saddam to make a move.

What has led to this change in tone? Let's review the situation: The UN sanction and inspection programs that were imposed after the Gulf War have failed. Western nations (except the United Kingdom) have ceased direct military operations in Iraq, and the Arab allies have become increasingly impatient with U.S. air strikes that may reduce Iraq's conventional weapons, but do not eliminate their threat. And the United Nations as a whole has stood by while Iraq unilaterally rejected UNSCOM weapons inspections at the end of the Clinton administration. The weapons inspections were interrupted for such an extended period that Saddam has, in all likelihood, won the buffer he needed to complete and hide his weapons work. Unfortunately for U.S. interests, the rest of the Gulf War alliance members, and the United Nations overall, see strong military responses as too strong a punishment for Iraqi noncompliance with the sanctions.

Nonetheless, inspections and destruction of Iraqi nuclear, chemical, and biological weapons facilities remains a key priority of the U.S. diplomatic and intelligence communities. Given the events of September 11, 2001, it is not difficult to understand why the U.S. government is interested in (1) finding out precisely what Saddam is doing, and (2) preventing Iraqi-inspired actions against U.S. interests. The Bush administration will not wait for another building to come down before stepping up the pressure on Iraq.

Now, with the examples of September 11 and the "successful" response in Afghanistan (where the Taliban regime was destroyed and the al Qaeda network seriously damaged), the Bush administration is emboldened to pursue its agenda in Iraq.

Today, Iraq is seen by more and more policymakers as a significant threat to U.S. security—not simply as a thorn in any single president's side.

**Iraq Fact**

Early in 2002, President George W. Bush issued a presidential order directing the U.S. Central Intelligence Agency (CIA) to use "all available tools" to topple Saddam Hussein. These tools included …

- ◆ Support for opposition groups inside and outside of Iraq. The support could be weapons, training, intelligence, and money.
- ◆ Increased covert operations, and more effort to recruit agents from Iraqi dissident groups, inside Iraq.
- ◆ Use of U.S. Special Forces units to kill Saddam.

CIA Director George Tenet is cited as telling President Bush that these tactics, if employed without any other military or economic pressure on Iraq, have only a "10 to 20 percent chance of succeeding," according to the *Washington Post*.

## The Wild Card

One of the biggest potential challenges for the emerging U.S. campaign against Saddam is the state of relations between Israel and its Arab neighbors.

Relations fluctuate from open warfare to uneasy peace. However, in the early part of 2002, the escalating cycle of Palestinian suicide bombers and Israeli reprisals created a sense of crisis that was unusual even in this bloodstained region; the turmoil effectively stopped the Bush administration from moving forward in its campaign against Saddam.

As long as the United States is required to make open shows of support for Israel in a protracted struggle with the Palestinians, the Arab countries will stay away from openly supporting the United States against Iraq. It is not a huge stretch of the imagination to conclude that Saddam and his terrorist proxies know this. Neither is it a huge stretch of the imagination to conclude that these parties have sought to bring about precisely this kind of difficulty for the U.S. government.

> **CAUTION**
>
> ## Oil Spill Ahead
>
> We see that jihad is an "individual duty" prescribed to us as it is prescribed to every faithful and ardent Muslim to liberate, from the accursed and defiled Jews, usurped Palestine from the River to the Sea .... It is the right of every faithful Muslim not only to call into question the elegibility for responsibility, under any title, of anyone who does not believe in this, but also to call into question even the meaning, the level, and the depth of his faith in Islam.
>
> —Saddam Hussein, December 11, 2000, message to the Islamic Summit.

# Survivor

As this book goes to press, the second Bush administration is saddled with the delicate task of supporting its long-time ally (Israel) at the same time it attempts to eliminate a dangerous foe (Saddam). As long as the radical Arab and radical Israeli factions can stir up trouble—which is, let's face it, quite easy to do—the U.S. goal of toppling Saddam by means of a U.S.-Arab coalition seems out of reach.

Which is, one senses, precisely the outcome a certain canny survivor in Baghdad with a troubled family history has gone to great pains to arrange for himself.

How long can Saddam survive? The answer may be no closer than it seemed when the Israelis decided that a "peaceful" nuclear power plant in Iraq spelled trouble; or when the United Nations denounced the invasion of Kuwait; or when George W. Bush labeled Iraq's leadership as part of an "axis of evil." So far, no military, diplomatic, or strategic initiative has yet produced a credible scenario for a post-Saddam Iraq.

The road to Baghdad, it would seem, has many routes, but three that look most likely. It could run through a peaceful West Bank, through the sands of an embattled Saudi Arabia or Kuwait, or through the rubble of a U.S. city.

No matter which way that road runs, it will, in all likelihood, lead to a waiting—and well prepared—Saddam Hussein.

## The Least You Need to Know

- Saddam is a potential threat to his Gulf oil state neighbors.

- Saddam is a strong threat to the Shiites in his own country, and less of a threat to the Kurds (as long as UN money reaches them).

- Saddam isn't much of a military threat to the United States, but his ability to send terrorists armed with weapons of mass destruction to the United States is growing.

- Saddam survives by playing the Israel card to keep the United States and moderate Arab states at odds.

- Both Saddam and the United States are preparing to come at each other, each in their own way.

# A 10,000-Year Timeline for Iraq: 8000 B.C.E. to 2002 C.E.

**8000 B.C.E.** First human settlements in evidence in Jericho.

**5000 B.C.E.** First settlements in evidence in Mesopotamia near modern Jarmo.

**3000–2000 B.C.E.** Sumerians emerge, settle cities of Ur and Uruk in lower Mesopotamian region.

**1900–1600 B.C.E.** Amorite Empire.

**1600–1100 B.C.E.** Hittite Empire.

**1500–1200 B.C.E.** Kassite Empire (in central Mesopotamia).

**1200–612 B.C.E.** Assyrian Empire in Mesopotamia.

**612–539 B.C.E.** Chaldean Empire (also known as New Babylonian Period).

**539–331 B.C.E.** Persian Empire encompasses Mesopotamia.

**331–170 B.C.E.** Greek/Macedonian Empire (led by Alexander the Great) encompasses Mesopotamia.

**170 B.C.E.–224 C.E.**    Parthian Empire in Mesopotamia.

**224–637 C.E.**    Sassanid Empire includes Mesopotamia.

**638–1100**    Arab Empire and Golden Age of Baghdad.

**661**    The Shiite Schism. When Ali ibn Abi Talib, Mohammad's cousin, son-in-law, and last of a group known as the Rightly Guided Caliphs, was assassinated, and a non-family member was made caliph. Debates regarding succession lead to the development of Shiism, a sect of Islam that recognizes Mohammad's descendants through Ali as the only legitimate heads of the Islamic community.

**770–945**    Abassid Empire.

**945–1045**    Buwhayid Empire.

**1045–1258**    Seljuk Empire.

**1155–1258**    Local strongmen rule various territories in Mesopotamia.

**1258–1355**    Period of Mongol invasions. Baghdad plundered.

**1355–1400**    The Jalayirids rule Mesopotamia.

**1401–1405**    Tamerlane invades Mesopotamia. Baghdad plundered again.

**1500–1722**    Savafid Empire in Mesopotamia.

**1534–1918**    Ottoman Empire. Three vilayets: Mosul, Baghdad, and Basra are formed, which will later become modern Iraq, are established during this period.

**1900**    British become interested in Mesopotamia, first as land-link to India, and later as source of oil.

**1912**    Turkish Petroleum Company (TPC) formed.

**1914**    Anglo-Persian Oil Company (British owned) takes 50 percent stake in TPC; World War I begins. British invade Mesopotamia to safeguard their Turkish Petroleum Company holdings.

**1918**    World War I ends. Iraq established as a "Class A" Mandate, under British protection.

**1921**    Faisal I is set up as King of Iraq, though British influence remains strong.

**1928**    Gulf Oil Company joins TPC, the first U.S. oil company to enter Iraqi oil fields.

**1929**    TPC changes name to Iraqi Petroleum Company (IPC).

**1932**    Mosul Oil Company formed to manage northern IPC concessions.

**1932 (October 13)**   Iraq admitted into League of Nations as an independent nation.

**1938**   Basra Oil Company formed to manage southern IPC concessions.

**1941**   Britain again invades Iraq, establishes pro-British government in Baghdad.

**1948–49**   Israel War of Independence; Iraq participates in attacks on Israel and is one of the most belligerent adversaries in the Arab coalition confronting Israel.

**1954**   The Eisenhower administration agrees to provide military aid to Iraq, to help defend their oil interests in Iraq. Marks the transfer of influence from the British to the Americans.

**1955**   Baghdad Pact formed, as bulwark against Soviet expansionism. Iraq is a founding member.

**1958 (May 12)**   Arab Union formed between Iraq and Jordan.

**1958 (July 14)**   Iraqi General Abdul Karim Kassem leads a coup d'état that overthrows the Hashemite monarchy.

**1960 (July)**   Iraq threatens to invade Kuwait. British respond by sending troops. Invasion never happens.

**1963 (February 8)**   Ba'th coup overthrows Republican government, but is overthrown itself within six months.

**1963 (November 18)**   Abdul Salam Arif leads officer coup that overthrows brief, bloody Ba'th regime.

**1966**   Republican government repeals 99.5 percent of original IPC concession, Mosul Oil nationalized.

**1967**   Six-Day War. The economic chaos in Iraq as a result of reduced oil exports during the fighting contributes to Ba'th coup in July 1968.

**1968 (July 17)**   Ba'th Revolution that finally establishes Ba'th control over Iraq.

**1972**   Ba'th government repeals remaining IPC concessions.

**1973**   Ba'th government nationalizes Basra Petroleum Company.

**1973 (October 6–October 23)**   Yom Kippur War. War eventually leads to Egyptian-Israeli détente and re-assertion of Iraq leadership in pan-Arab affairs.

**1979 (July 16)**   Saddam Hussein becomes President of Iraq, taking over for Hassan al-Bakr. He stages a public purge of Bakr supporters, to consolidate his own grip on power.

**1980 (September 23)** Iran–Iraq War begins.

**1981 (June 8)** Israel bombs Iraqi nuclear reactor at Osirek.

**1982 (June 10)** War-weary Iraq announces a cease-fire, but Iran ignores the offer.

**1982 (July 13)** Iranian troops make first push into Iraqi territory.

**1983 (July 20)** Iranian troops attack northern Iraq.

**1984 (February)** Iraq uses mustard gas on Iranian troops in central Iraq around the Majnoon Islands.

**1984 (March)** "Tanker War" (Iran and Iraq attack each other's Gulf oil shipments) starts.

**1985 (May)** "Battle of the Cities" phase of Iran-Iraq War begins. Both sides launch bombing and missile raids on each other's cities.

**1986 (August 2)** Saddam Hussein proposes peace in open letter to the Ayatollah. The offer is rejected.

**1987 (May 17)** Iraq mistakenly hits the USS *Stark* with a missile. Thirty-seven U.S. sailors die. Saddam apologizes for the attack.

**1988 (March 16)** Saddam Hussein attacks Kurds around Halabja with chemical weapons. More than 5,000 Kurds are killed.

**1988 (April)** Iraq begins to make progress in the war, Iran slowly retreats from Iraqi territory.

**1988 (August 20)** Iran-Iraq War ends in cease fire, as a stand-off.

**1990 (July 18)** Iraq accuses Kuwait of "stealing" Iraqi oil. Saddam threatens dire consequences. Kuwait denies the charges.

**1990 (August 2)** Iraq invades Kuwait.

**1990 (August 6)** Operation Desert Shield, the military build up in Saudi Arabia by an Arab-Western coalition, begins.

**1990 (November 29)** The UN Security Council passes Resolution 678, authorizing use of force to "expel" Iraq from Kuwait.

**1991 (January 17)** Operation Desert Storm begins with coalition bombing that continues for the next five weeks.

**1991 (January 22)** Iraq launches SCUD missiles on Israel and Saudi Arabia in attempt to draw Israel into the war and split the U.S.-Arab Coalition.

**1991 (February 24)**    Ground phase of Desert Storm begins.

**1991 (February 26)**    Ground phase of Desert Storm ends.

**1991–1992**    Iraqi army attacks Kurds, 1.5 million Kurds flee to Turkey.

**1991 (July 25)**    Northern no-fly zone established.

**1992 (April 2)**    Southern no-fly zone established.

**1993 (April 14)**    Hussein attempts to assassinate former President Bush while Bush is visiting Kuwait. Clinton administration responds by launching cruise missile attack on Iraqi intelligence center in Baghdad.

**1994 (October)**    Iraq moves troops toward Kuwait. U.S. and UK bombing forces bomb the Iraqis to stop them short of invading again.

**1995 (August 8)**    Two of Saddam's sons-in-law and their families flee Iraq and end up in Jordan. They are Lt. General Hussein Kamel Hassan al-Majid, who was in charge of Iraq's weapons programs, and his brother, Lt. Colonel Saddam Kamel Hassan al-Majid, who was in charge of presidential security. The information they disclose prompts Iraq to offer more details on its mass-destruction weapons programs. The brothers return to Iraq in February 1996, under Saddam's guarantees that he will not harm them. They are shot three days after they return.

**1998 (August 5)**    Saddam Hussein unilaterally evicts UNSCOM weapons inspectors. As of this writing, inspectors are still not allowed back into Iraq.

**1998 (December 18)**    In response to Saddam Hussein's unilateral refusal to comply with UNSCOM weapons inspections, the United States and UK launch Operation Desert Fox. The campaign is a coordinated bombing attack on Iraqi weapons targets by U.S. and UK aircraft and missiles.

**2001 (September 11)**    Terrorist attack on World Trade Center and the Pentagon. Saddam is the only Arab leader not to express condolences for the attack.

**2002 (January 29)**    President Bush lists Iraq as a member of the "Axis of Evil" that includes Iraq, Iran, and North Korea. The inference is that these countries foster state terrorism.

**2002 (April 23)**    Iraq suspends oil deliveries in protest of escalated violence between Palestinians and Israelis. Suspension lifted one month later.

# Yours Truly, Saddam Hussein: Speeches and Letters

As you'll find out when you read the following excerpts from his speeches and letters, Saddam has a lot of say, and most of it isn't very nice—at least when it comes to addressing the United States. These are derived from websites, but the content is generally considered as being Saddam's actual words, or letters he directed to be written.

## Iraqi Military Power

"Our military capabilities are now bigger," Saddam announced confidently in late August. "Conditions in Iraq have this year become better than previous years, economically and in our capacity to face up to challenges and confront the Americans."

—Article published October 17, 2001. Source: www.newsmax. com/archives/articles/2001/10/16/132.shtml

# Why the Planes Came

But, when any member of this family of mankind oppresses, exploits, unjustly wages wars on them, or lies and deceives others, he would be acting like a devil in the form of man …

But do you know that your administration has, one way or the other, deprived the people of Iraq from food and medicine? Do you know the meaning of the death of one million and a half human beings, in addition to those who are killed by bombs and missiles? Maybe, you and the majority of the peoples of America, do not know that American bombardment, and death harvest caused by fighter jets, and missiles, are ongoing in Iraq for the last eleven years, and have not stopped until the moment of writing this letter? Do you know why you don't know?! Because the media in your country, which is controlled by Zionism, do not want you to know. And because your administration, which says that it is necessary for the peoples of the world to know, does not want you to know. You should ask your administration, why doesn't it speak to you about facts? Why doesn't it present you any information except its devilish fancies? As for me, I can tell you why Zionism doesn't want you to know the harm inflicted on the people of Iraq. The Zionist and the American administration believe that it is necessary that Iraqis die …

So, the Arabs and Muslims did not cross the Atlantic, as invaders or aggressors. They did not colonize America. It is America that brought them all kinds of sufferings …

Maybe you don't know that many of the members of our leadership were victims of terrorism and terrorist. Some of them escaped death, by the will of God, after being injured or missed by the terrorists, in addition to the pain inflected to our people. Do you know brother, that your administration's reaction to that, was one of encouraging it and rejoicing? Do you know that your administration has been encouraging terrorism against us for the past eleven years, calling to overthrow us by force, allocating special funds to do so, and boasting about not fearing God, as it publicly announces that on TV screens, because Iraq does not have the same destructive force and armament of America?

Wishing that you will have the opportunity to see the fact as they are, and not as your administration present them,

Yours truly,

Saddam Hussein

—Excerpts from e-mail sent to U.S. computer engineer Christopher Love, October 18, 2001. (Love had sent an e-mail to Saddam asking for his explanation as to why the September 11 attacks on the United States occurred.)

## Saddam on Personal Hygiene

It's preferable to bathe twice a day, but at least once a day. And when the male bathes once a day, the female should bathe twice a day. The reason is that the female is more delicate and the smell of a woman is more noticeable than the male ... If a woman can't afford to brush her teeth with toothpaste and a toothbrush, she should use her finger.

—Quote attributed to Saddam Hussein. Source: more.abcnews.go.com/sections/ primetime/2020/primetime_010222_saddam_feature.html, February. 22

## God Backs a Winner

Whoever has God on his side never gets defeated.

—Statement by Saddam Hussein. Source: www.cnn.com/SPECIALS/ 1998/iraq/saddam.profile/

## Message to the Iraqi Army

Once again, the hopeless cowardly Americans were back to repeat their cowardly act hiding behind a technological advance that God, most gracious, wanted it to be their curse and cause for shame.

We have come to expect you—and your people and the Arab nation are calling upon you—to resist them and teach them a new lesson full of meanings their weak and empty souls do not know.

—September 3, 1996. Source: www.cnn.com/WORLD/9609/03/saddam.transcript/

## Saddam's Views on Israel and Palestine

Therefore, we see that jihad is an "Individual Duty" prescribed to us as it is pre-scribed to every faithful and ardent Muslim to liberate, from the accursed and defiled Jews, usurped Palestine from the River to the Sea, together with its Crown, al-Quds, the third of the central sanctuaries of Muslims, besides Mecca and the Shrine of Allah's Messenger, Mohammed b. Abdullah (Allah's blessing and peace be upon him). It is the right of every faithful Muslim not only to call into question the eligibility for responsibility, under any title, of anyone who does not believe in this, but also, to call into question even the meaning, the level and the depth of his faith in Islam.

—Excerpt from Saddam Hussein's Message to Islamic Summit, Doha, November 12, 2000.

## On the Palestinians

Destiny makes it incumbent on [the Palestinian] people to assume their share of honour and virtue and makes them an example before God, his peoples and history, in line with the weight of their ability and faith and action, when facing difficult circumstances and a hard test, in terms of their success in overcoming difficult paths with rates and degrees that please God and the people.

—April 8, 2002. Source: news.bbc.co.uk/hi/english/world/monitoring/ media_reports/ newsid_1917000/1917361.stm

I address you this time in the name of the leadership and people of Iraq directly. It is a brotherly call addressed to you after the flood has reached its climax and after the destruction, terror, murder and sacrilege practiced by the aggressive, terrorist and criminal Zionist entity, together with its tyrannical ally, the US, have come to a head against our brothers and our faithful struggling people in plundered Palestine. If evil achieves its objectives there, Allah forbid, its gluttony for more will increase and it will afflict our people and other parts of our wide homeland too, in addition to the suffering that has been and is still being inflicted upon the people of Palestine.

—Excerpt from Saddam Hussein's "A Call to Brother Arabs: Regimes, Governments and People," December 15, 2001. Source: www.uruklink.net/ iraq/e2001/ ecall.htm

## Survival Means Victory

Dear brothers,

Similar conditions have put our nation in a difficult dilemma in past times, our glorious nation had always proved to be equal to the challenge, and faced it in the name of God, and proved itself and gained victory over those who wanted to humiliate it, usurp its right in life in general, or its right to chose its way and aims that do not harm the principles of humanity at large, and its right to recover its rights from usurpers, so as to lead a free and decent life, after making due sacrifices by a unified and organized action that leads the nation to achieve certain aims on the basic of the good intentions and collective will of joint action.

—Excerpt from Saddam Hussein's address to Arab leaders, April 22, 2000. Source: www.uruklink.net/iraq/e2002/espee22402.htm

## Oil as a Weapon

Whereas the enemies of the nation and humanity do not understand but a practical language, and the reactions that undermine their interests and affect them in a way that exasperates their evil indications and hostility to the Arab nation including the Palestinian people.

—Excerpt from Saddam Hussein's decision to stop oil exports in protest of conflict between Israel and Palestinians, April 8, 2002. Source: www.uruklink.net/iraq/e2002/eoil.htm

## Loser or Winner

Today is a day in the Grand Battle, the immortal Mother of all Battles. It is a glorious and a splendid day on the part of the self-respecting people of Iraq and their history, and it is the beginning of the great shame for those who ignited its fire on the other part.

—Excerpt from Saddam Hussein's address on the eleventh anniversary of the "Mother of All Battles," the Persian Gulf War. (Note that Saddam considers the Mother of All Battles a victory). Source: www.uruklink.net/iraq/e2002/e17j-02.htm

## You Guys Are the Best ... Really

Whenever an occasion makes it necessary that I speak about the Iraqis or about the army, whose attributes I have summed up in this and in other speeches, I feel embarrassed. It is not because I cannot say or write what should be said or written about them, but because I fear that I may not recall all that they deserve to be recalled about them and, thus, give them only part of their due in the light of what my soul likes to say about them and what does justice to their history. I am afraid that some narrow-minded people may interpret what I say as merely panegyric of a state which the speaker is part of.

—Excerpt from "The 81$^{st}$ Anniversary of the Establishment of the Valiant Army of Iraq on January 6, 1921," January 6, 2002. Source: www.uruklink.net/iraq/e2002/e6jan2002.htm

## Saddam on Good Citizenship

Brothers and brother President, leaders of the people of Palestine, do not look for victory outside yourselves and outside the circle of your people. What is outside yourselves, Palestinians, is of little manly qualities under the official titles and their related nomenclatures. It is covered by misleading darkness on the whole. So, like the avant-guarde amongst you, be a lamp to guide and be a beacon to whatever pleases Allah and pleases the honest people in Palestine and your Arab brothers and people all over the world. Be like your brothers and sisters in Iraq, where leadership and people have become one and where official titles are no more than an additional honorable commitment towards good citizenship and towards serving the people and uplifting the voice of right and the nation. Be on your full guard against anything that divides you, because if you are divided, Allah forbid, you will loose the foundation of your strength.

—Excerpt from "Saddam Hussein's Address on the 13th Anniversary of the Great Victory Day" (the end of the war against Iran), August 8, 2001. Source: www.uruklink.net/iraq/e2001/e8aug-01.htm

## Iraq Is the Representative of the Arab World

Let me point out the gist of what I want to say: being the living essence and the authentic representatives of the Arab nation, did the Iraqis choose their role, or is it destiny that chose their role for them, after having shown their preparedness and their fervor and mindfulness?

—Excerpt from speech by Saddam Hussein, January 17, 2001. Source: www.uruklink.net/iraq/e2001/e17july-01.htm

## Vote for Me

In all cases, let the one whom you choose as a leader to your assembly, has qualities higher than you or like the best of you in his sword, mind. He should regard defeat as a disgrace, he should not be from those who confuse between black and white or equate, according to his criteria, between honest and dishonest.

—Excerpt from Saddam Hussein's speech to the Iraqi National Assembly regarding his election as president. Source: www.uruklink.net/iraq/e2001/econ_5_17.htm

## On the Persian Gulf War

At that time, on a day like this day ten years ago, Evil and all those who made Satan their protector lined up in one place, facing those who represented the will to defend right against falsehood and who had Allah as their Protector. They chose the sublime meanings and jihad, with hearts humble in prayer to Allah, glorified be His name, as their path towards His good pleasure, to win His forgiveness, pardon and satisfaction through faithful obedience.

Do you know, brothers, who deserved the latter description? I do not think that you do not know him who identified his name through the quality of his action on the path of jihad and virtue and the path of every human meaning, which is sought by all those who seek it to achieve even a part of it.

—Excerpt from speech by Saddam Hussein, January 17, 2001. Source: www. uruklink.net/iraq/e2001/e17j-01.htm

## Give Us a Chance

If the Iraqis have their historical chance, they are capable of creating an army, undefeatable and powerful, by right, to break down falsehood and defeat it always.

—Excerpt from Saddam Hussein's "Address on the 80th Anniversary of the Establishment of Iraqi Army," January 6, 2001. Source: www.uruklink.net/iraq/ e2001/e6jan2001.htm

## May Evil Befall Them ...

Is it not shame and disgrace on those who harbour shame and disgrace that the planes of the aggressors take off from their land and territorial waters to bomb the citadel of the Arabs and the cradle of Abraham (peace be upon him) and to destroy the property of the Iraqis and kill them all ... women, men and children? Is there any other way than this to describe treachery and disgrace?

May evil befall them, for evil indeed are the deeds they do!

It is they who have sold out their souls and have appointed (the occupying foreigner) to rule over everything that is dear and precious in the values and wealth of their people. Whatever they find saleable they have sold to the United States and Zionism, thus becoming mere agents getting commissions deducted from the wealth of their own people and getting ignoble authority chairs to sit on.

Glorious Iraqi men and glorious Iraqi women,

You have become the yardstick of values, potency and highmindedness. You have become the guides on a path that discerning eyes cannot miss.

—Excerpt from Saddam Hussein's "Address On the 12th anniversary of the Great Victory Day, 8-8-1988" August 8, 2000. (The Great Victory Day, also called the "Day of Days," marks the end of the Iran-Iraq War in 1988.) Source: www. uruklink.net/iraq/e2000/e8aug-00.htm

# What Did You Do Before Me?

Before the July Revolution, the condition in Iraq can be described as follows: It was a wasteland that had no agriculture to be taken into account and no livestock to be proud of although it had much water. Is it possible that life and land suffer from thirst while water exists?

The Iraqis knew that they had the potential, but they did not know how to muster up that potential. Their rulers did not take the responsibility on the basis of that potential.

The leader and the guide who was able to put that potential on its right course had not yet emerged from amongst them. Even when some had discovered that potential, they did not know how to deal with it. Nor did they direct it where it should be directed so as to enable it to evolve into an effective act that could make life pulsate and fill hearts with happiness.

—Excerpt from Speech of the President, July 17, 2000. (July 17 is the officially recognized date of the Ba'th Revolution that took power in Iraq.) Source: www.uruklink.net/iraq/e2000/e17j-00.htm

# Really, It's Going to Get Better ...

You are now the nearest to Him and ranking highest in His love. Your chance of winning His satisfaction, glorified be His name, is greater than that of any other people, that is because you have sacrificed so much for your high principles out of love for your people, your homeland and your nation. Pioneering your sacrifice, to guide it through to the sure arrival and to throw bright light to embody forth its significance, colour and shape, is the blood of our dutiful martyrs—our beloved, the beloved of the people, the homeland and the nation, or rather, the beloved of every truthful and loyal believer.

You have sacrificed so much, and I have never doubted, not even for a moment, that you love God and that God loves you even more for your nearness to Him has been proportional to the degree of your faith in Him and your love for Him and your sacrifice to win His satisfaction with you.

Now, you love your nation even more, and your nation loves you and appreciates your role even more. You love Iraq—you love its earth, sky, water and air. Keep up your love in order to reach your target, for you are definitely reaching it. By God's permission, happiness after suffering is at hand, at hand, at hand.

—Excerpt from Saddam Hussein's "Address on the Ninth Anniversary of the Grand Battle 'Mother of All Battles' January 16–17, 1991," January 17, 2000. Source: www.uruklink.net/iraq/e2000/esp17-00.htm

# You're OK, I'm OK ...

The virtuous example we are talking about—the example set, in the name of God, by our army—was not set under favorable circumstances. It did create this ideal characteristic and its underlying significance all by itself and for itself. It wrenched it away from the claws of predators to whom many, many heads, on this Earth of God, have bowed. Some of these heads are honest but powerless and some are dishonest and ignoble. So, too, from among those who are counted in the list of Arab rulers and holders of titles of responsibility, are some who have weakened and some who have abased themselves through treachery.

—Excerpt from Saddam Hussein's "Address on Army Day of the Year 2000: The 79th Anniversary of the Establishment of the Valiant Iraqi Army on January 6, 1921," January 6, 2000. Source: www.uruklink.net/iraq/e2000/e6jan2000.htm

# The Winner Writes the History

Despite all reiterative calls, before and after the encounter, for deliberation and detachment from the motives and spots of evil and despite all appeals for peace released by Iraq from the highest and various levels, the slogans, drums and guns of aggression and war had persisted beside the slogans of hopeless, greedy ambitions which were all defeated. The slogans of invasion and its premeditated and pre-planned intents were also frustrated. Right had triumphed over falsehood; it was a victory for the sublime morals of humanity at large, including those Iranian peoples that believe in an anti-aggression course of policy.

—Excerpt from "Speech of the President" on August 8, 1999, on the anniversary of the end of the Iran-Iraq War. (Saddam claims the war was started by Iran, when in fact Iraq started it, and that the bloody stalemate at the end was an Iraqi victory.) Source: www.uruklink.net/iraq/e1999/esp88.htm

# Iraq as the Bulwark Against Israeli and U.S. Aggression

On the basis of these principles, your great people, the vanguard of your Nation, the proud, faithful, and capable people of Iraq, is resisting, as it has so far, all attempts of the thwarted Zionism and the despot of this age: the successive U.S. administrations which have employed the economic, technological and scientific potentialities directly on behalf of Zionism, known for its hatred and vengeance upon the Arabs, the Muslims in general, and indeed the whole humanity by means of the U.S. Zionized Jewish administrations.

—Excerpt from "Speech of the President," on July 17, 1999. Source: www.uruk-link.net/iraq/e1999/e17j.htm

# Saddam on Being Arab

An Arab should realize that his belonging to the Arab nation is a great honor because this sense of belonging confirms his and her roots. This sense of belonging is not a defect but an ability; an effective and deep capability. It is not a burden.

—Excerpt from speech delivered by Saddam Hussein on the benefits of Arab Unity and its positive implications, September 24, 1997. Source: www.iraqi-mission.org/Church.htm

# Love Is Contagious

Peace be upon every student, intellectual, soldier, farmer, worker, women and men, youths and children. Peace be upon you and for, and upon the people of Iraq, both men and glorious women, the comrades of Saddam Hussein in the leadership, your brother and the son of your people and Nation: Saddam Hussein who is infected with the disease of your love: the disease without which any official in his nation will be sick. It is the disease with which some Arab officials have charged Saddam Hussein when they said that he is infected with the disease of the Arab masses, thinking that this is a defect in Saddam Hussein, but it is a fact, brothers, and it is an honor for us to be infected with the disease of loving the sons of our Nations in the streets, cities, villages, factories, poor districts and countryside. We were sincerely hoping that this disease would infect those Arab officials instead of the disease of loving Zionism and America, submission to them, implementing their orders and responding to their schemes at the expense of the Arab's security and their highest issues and interests. Had this disease, which is health and honor, infected some Arab rulers, the Nation would not have been subjected to what it had suffered from Zionism, America and their supporters.

—Excerpt from "Address of His Excellency President Saddam Hussein on the Eighth Anniversary of the Thirty-Nation Aggression Against Iraq 16–17 January 1991, in the Name of God, the Compassionate, the Merciful." (The "Thirty-nation aggression" is Saddam's term for the Coalition that was assembled to expel Iraq from Kuwait in 1991.) Source: www.uruklink.net/iraq/e1999/jan17_1_e.htm

# Diseases, Again

At any time power finds itself free from force in Iran, Iran will be the victor. And at any time Iraq abandons power in pursuit of the brute force only, God forbid, its loss will be heavy.

Judging from this yardstick, we see that some Arabs have been infected with a new and serious disease. This disease does not fall within the terms of the illusion of force, but it falls within the illusion of weakness. Thus, they have begun to look for force rather than for power to cure their fatal sense of weakness and their hope-dispersing illusions. They have felt fatigued and frustrated when faced with tables of quantities and figures on their part and on the part of their enemies, while comparing force with force.

—Excerpt from Hussein's "Address on the 10th Anniversary of the Day of Days, 8 August 1988," August 8, 1998. Source: www.uruklink.net/iraq/e1998/e_vict 1.htm

## Don't Think That the Sanctions Are Going to Work

If the enemies of Iraq imagine that they are able to deceive a people mobilized with all the factors of national zeal and the experiences of life it has experienced, burned with the fire of its enemies, motivated by the factors of defending life in the midst of its great principles and the immortal legacy of our nation, towards those who wanted and are still trying to assassinate them, a people that made tens of thousands of generous sacrifices of valuable lives every short period of time as a result of the shortage of food and medicine and due to the use of force, we say to them, in the name of the great people of Iraq, that they are wrong and it is better for them to re-read the ancient history and this glorious history carefully in order to derive the lessons that distant us and them from the abyss of their evils and their souls inciting them to evil.

—Excerpt from "Speech of His Excellency President Saddam Hussein on the Thirtieth Anniversary of 17–30 July 1968 Revolution," July 17, 1998. Source: www.uruklink.net/iraq/e1998/ejly17.htm

## The Winners Were Losers

Today is January 17 when, seven years ago at 2:30 early morning, the devil implicated America and others who were also involved (in the aggression) after their feet went astray from the true path of God. It was the day when 28 armies led by the American tyranny acting on behalf of more than 30 states that had allied themselves for aggression, unleashed the shells of malice, hatred, evil and whim at Baghdad, the city of virtue, great history, glory, and of distinctive mark in attitude, and characteristics in the entire Arab Nation of glory and virtue. It was God who chose for the entire Arab Nation and Iraq roles and messages in appreciation of the characteristics of Iraq to which it is the capital. It is a role to serve tortured humanity throughout ages against despots of successive eras and the ruthless devils on their way to hell.

—Excerpt from Saddam Hussein's "Address on the 7th Anniversary of Mother of All Battles," January 17, 1998. Source: www.uruklink.net/iraq/e1998/e_spch3.htm

## "An Extraordinary Event"—Saddam on September 11, 2001

"In the name of God, Most Gracious, Most merciful."

Once again, we would like to comment on what happened in America on September 11, 2001, and its consequences.

The comments we made on the next day of the event represent the essence of our position regarding this event and other events.

But the aftermath of what happened in America, in the West in particular and in the world in general, makes it important for every leader to understand the meaning of responsibility toward his people, his nation, and humanity in general to follow up the development of the situation.

To understand the meaning of what is going on, and hence to elaborate his country's and people's position so as not to restrict oneself to only following the event.

When the event took place Arab rulers and the rulers of countries whose religion of their people is Islam, rushed to condemn the event. The Westerners rushed within hours to make statements and adopt resolutions, some of which are dangerous ones, in solidarity with America and against terrorism.

Even before being sure, western governments decided to join their forces to the America even if that meant declaring war on the party that will be proved to have been involved in what happened.

It is only normal to say that by the explanation of the present situation, as it has been said or by comparison to the action previously taken by America against specific countries.

It could be enough for some of the executors of the operation to have come from a country named by America or said to have instigated the operation, for the American military retaliation on what they call an aggression.

We don't know if they would do the same thing whether any of the planners and executors of the operation were found, to have lived or held the nationality of a Western country or whether the intention and the designs are already made against an Islamic party.

It is most probable from the beating of media war drums that America and some Western governments are targeting a party who won't be but Muslim.

The event that took place in America is an extraordinary event. It is not a simple one.

According to figures announced by official American sources or by what has been spread by the media, the number of victims is great.

Nobody has any doubts, or denies that America and the West have the capabilities to mobilize force and use it, to inflict destruction on others on the basis of simple doubts or even whimsically.

And can send their American missiles and the NATO fighters to where ever they want to destroy and harm whomever America decides to harm in a fit of anger, by greed, or by being pushed by Zionism. Many countries of the world have suffered from America's technological might, and many peoples do recognise that America had killed thousands or even millions of human beings in their countries.

The event that took place in America was an extraordinary one. It is not a simple event.

It is the first time that someone crosses to America to unleash the fire of his anger inside it, as indicated by what was said by the media, on the hypothesis that the executors of this act came from abroad.

Since this event is unprecedented, is it wise to deal with it by precedent methods that can be used by whoever has the technical and scientific capacities of America and the West!? If the target and the aim is one or more Islamic countries, as it has been said by the media and the intelligence services of some Western countries, this would only fall in the same direction that America and the West have always taken by targeting their fire on wherever they want to experiment a new weapon on.

We ask again: America's targeting the fire of its weapons on specific targets, and harming it or destroying it with the support of Western governments and of a fabricated story would it solve the problem? Would this bring security to America and the world? Or isn't the use by America and some Western governments of their fire against others in the world including, or in the forefront of whom the Arabs and the Muslims, is one of the most important reasons of the lack of stability in the world at the present time?

Isn't the evil inflicted on America in the act of September 11, 2001, and nothing else is a result of this and other acts?

This is the main question and this is what the American administration along with the Western governments or the Western public opinion should answer in the first place with serenity and responsibility, without emotional reaction and without the use of the same old methods that America used against the world.

On September 12, 2001, we said that no one crossed the Atlantic to America carrying weapons before this event, except the Westerners who established the United States of America. America is the one who crossed the Atlantic carrying arms of destruction and death against the world.

Here we want to ask a question: wasn't the use of American weapons, including the nuclear weapon against Japan, enough before September 11, 2001, for America to prepare to use it in a heavier and a stronger way?

Or isn't using it in an irresponsible way, and without justification as does any oppressive force in the world, is what made America the most hated country in the world, starting from the Third World, to the Medium World and passing to the civilized world, as is the world divided by the West and America?

The national security of America and the security of the world could be attained if the American leaders and those who beat the drums for them among the rulers of the present time in the West or outside the West become rational.

If America disengages itself from its evil alliance with Zionism, which has been scheming to exploit the world and plunge it in blood and darkness, by using America and some Western countries.

What the American peoples need mostly is someone who tells them the truth, courageously and honestly as it is.

They don't need fanfares and cheerleaders, if they want to take a lesson from the event so as to reach a real awakening, in spite of the enormity of the event that hit America.

But the world, including the rulers of America, should say all this to the American peoples, so as to have the courage to tell the truth and act according to what is right and not what to is wrong and unjust, to undertake their responsibilities in fairness and justice, and by recourse to reason, passion, according to the spirit of chance and capability.

In addition, we say to the American peoples, what happened on September 11, 2001 should be compared to what their government and their armies are doing in the world.

For example, the international agencies have stated that more than one million and a half Iraqis have died because of the blockade imposed by America and some Western countries.

In addition to the tens of thousands who died or are injured in the military action perpetrated by America along with those who allied with it against Iraq.

Hundreds of bridges, churches, mosques, colleges, schools, factories, palaces, hotels, and thousands of private houses were destroyed or damaged by the American and Western bombardment, which is ongoing even today against Iraq.

If you replay the images of the footage taken by the Western media itself of this destruction, you will see that they are not different from the images of the two buildings hit by the Boeing airplanes, if not more atrocious, especially when they are mixed with the remains of men, women, and children.

There is, however, one difference, namely that those who direct their missiles and bombs to the targets, whether Americans or from another Western country, are mostly targeting by remote controls, that is why they do so as if they were playing an amusing game.

As for those who acted on September 11, 2001, they did it from a close range, and with, I imagine, giving their lives willingly, with an irrevocable determination.

For this reason also, the Americans, and the world with them, should understand the argument that made those people give their lives in sacrifice, and what they sacrificed themselves for, in that way.

When one million and a half Iraqi human beings die, according to Western documents, from a population of twenty five million, because of the American blockade and aggression, it means that Iraq has lost about one twentieth of its population.

And just as your beautiful skyscrapers were destroyed and caused your grief, beautiful buildings and precious homes crumbled over their owners in Lebanon, Palestine and Iraq by American weapons used by the Zionists.

In only one place, which was a civilian shelter, which is the Ameriyah Shelter, more than four hundred human beings, children, young and old men and women, died in Iraq by American bombs.

In the same day, the 11th of September, one of their aggressive military airplanes was shot down over Iraq.

As for what is going on in Palestine, if Zionist let you see on your TVs the bodies of children, women and men who are daily killed by American weapons, and with American backing to the Zionist entity, the pain you are feeling would be appeased.

Americans should feel the pain they have inflicted on other peoples of the world, so as when they suffer, they will find the right solution and the right path. All that has been inflicted on the Arabs and Muslims by America and the West didn't push Muslims to become racists and harass the Westerners who walk in the streets of Baghdad, Damascus, Tunis, Cairo and other Arab capitals. Even when the Westerners, and especially Americans insulted the holy sites of Muslim and Arabs by what is almost an occupation of Saudi Arabia in order to launch their evil fires against Baghdad.

And when the American carriers roam the Arab Gulf, and their fighters daily roam the sky to throw tons of bombs and missiles over Iraq, so that about two hundred thousand tons of bombs have been used against Iraq, in addition to using depleted uranium!!

All these are facts that are very well known not only to Arabs and Muslims, but to the whole world also. But because of only one incident that happened in America in one day, and upon unconfirmed accusations so far, Arabs and Muslims, including some who hold the American citizenship, are being harassed openly and publicly in America and some Western countries. Some Western countries are preparing themselves to participate in an American military action, against an Islamic country as the indications point out. In this case, who is being fanatic?

Isn't this solidarity, and this in-advance approval by some Western leaders, of a military aggression against an Islamic country, the most flagrant form of the new Crusades, fanaticism? It reminds Arabs and Muslims of those Crusade wars launched by the West and NATO against Iraq.

Finally, if you, rulers respect and cherish the blood of your peoples, why do you find it easy to shed the blood of others including the blood of Arabs and Muslims? If you respect your values, why don't you respect the values of Arabs and Muslims?

America needs wisdom, not power. It has used power, along with the West, to its extreme extent, only to find out later that it doesn't achieve what they wanted. Will the rulers of America try wisdom just for once so that their people can live in security and stability?

In the name of God, Most Gracious, Most merciful.

Invite all to the way of thy Lord with the wisdom and beautiful preaching, and argue with them in ways that are best and most gracious, for the lord knoweth best who have strayed from His path and who receive guidance.

—"Open letter from Saddam Hussein to the American peoples and the western peoples and their governments" regarding September 11, 2001. Source: www. uruklink.net/iraq/e2001/emss15.htm

# Glossary

**Abbasids**   Named for Abo Abbas, the early leader of the group that founded an empire in 770 C.E. that included Mesopotamia.

**Akkadians**   Invaders of Mesopotamia around 2340 B.C.E. The Akkadians were a Semitic people and spoke a language that is related to Hebrew and Arabic. They founded a capital city at Akkad, later called Babylon.

**Amorites**   Invaders of Mesopotamia around 1900 to 1600 B.C.E. The Amorite capital is known as Old Babylon, and the Amorite Empire is known as the Old Babylon period.

**Arab**   A linguistic group of 256 million that many experts believe originated in the Hijaz region in what is now Saudi Arabia. The Arabs have spread across northern Africa and the Middle East. The Iraqis (except the Kurds) are Arabs.

**Arab League**   Formally called the League of Arab States, includes Egypt, Jordan, Lebanon, Saudi Arabia, Syria, Yemen, and Iraq. The Arab League was formed with British encouragement, as a bulwark against Soviet expansion into the Middle East. The League exists to this day, but its mission now focuses more on issues that affect the collective Arab states

**Arab Union**   Short-lived combination of Iraq and Jordan, founded in 1958. Established as a counter to the Nasser-dominated UAR.

**Assyrians**   Invaders who established an empire in Mesopotamia from 1200 to 612 B.C.E. The Assyrian capital was a new city, called Nineveh.

The last great Assyrian king, Ashurbanipal, assembled a huge library of Sumerian writings at Nineveh. The Assyrians were a highly militaristic society. They developed a number of innovative weapons, and their technological advancements include the development of latitude and longitude, 360-degree partition of the circle, medical science, iron swords, body armor, and the battering ram. Modern Assyrians remain a sizable minority in northwestern Iraq.

**Ayatollah Ruhollah Khomeini** (1900–1989)   A supreme religious leader of the Twelver Shiite, and leader of Iran from 1979 to his death in 1989. The last decade of his life was filled with turmoil, notably the hostage crisis at the former U.S. Embassy in Tehran and the Iran-Iraq War.

**Babylon**   Ancient city that emerged from the ancient Akkadian capital of Akkad. Babylon was the central city for the Chaldeans during the "New Babylonian Period."

**Baghdad**   Capital city of Iraq. As heart of the Arab Empire, it was second only to Constantinople in terms of size and grandeur in 1000 C.E.

**Hassan al-Bakr** (1914–1982)   President of Iraq from 1968 to 1979. Relative of Saddam Hussein.

**Basra**   City in southern Iraq, heart of Shiite territory. Chief city of Ottoman vilayet of the same name.

**Ba'th**   The Arab Ba'th Socialist Resurrection Party. Formed by two Syrian university students, Michel Aflaq and Salah ad-Din al-Bitar, and formally founded on April 7, 1947. The Ba'th Party tenets include adherence to socialism (including state ownership of the key segments of the economy), political freedom (an inclusive process), and pan-Arab unity. Ba'th parties are in power in Syria and Iraq.

**Buwayhids**   A powerful military clan that originated in Shiite Iran, they ruled Mesopotamia from 945 to 1045 C.E.

**Caliph**   Spiritual leader of Islam.

**Chaldeans**   Ruled Mesopotamia after the Assyrians, from 612 to 539 B.C.E. Their period of rule is dominated by Nebuchadnezzar II.

**Cuneiform**   Wedge style writing, originally created by pressing a reed end into wet clay. "Cuneiform" is the Latin word for " wedge-writing." The writing form first emerged around 3600 B.C.E. Cuneiform was at first a pictographic language (like Chinese), where the symbols represented things, but it gradually evolved into an alphabet style language, with syllabic "letters" that formed "words." Because the cuneiform was written on clay, lots of tablets have survived and they are invaluable to showing us daily life in Mesopotamia.

***Epic of Gilgamesh***   A collection of legends of the ancient Sumerian king, Gilgamesh. Around 2600 B.C.E., Gilgamesh was king of Uruk (known as Erech in the Hebrew Scriptures). *The Epic of Gilgamesh* offers a number of stories recounting his exploits as king, his friendship with Enkidu, a wild man, and their adventures together. They are in actuality both elements of the same humanity, and their stories reflect not just man's struggles against outside evils, but also man's struggle to master himself

**Euphrates**   One of two main rivers in ancient Mesopotamia (now modern Iraq, eastern Turkey and northern Syria).

**al-Faw**   A peninsula on the Iraqi Persian Gulf coast, where the offshore oil terminals are located. Scene of heavy fighting during Iran-Iraq War.

**Golden Age of Baghdad**   The period from 638 to 1100 C.E., when Baghdad flourished as a center of learning, commerce, and philosophy, at the heart of the Arab world.

**Hammurabi Code**   Early compilation of law based on *lex talonica*, a principle that establishes the role of state as agent of revenge for wrong-doing, instead of individuals.

**Hashemites**   The Hashemite kings came from a prominent Saudi Arabian family. Iraq was ruled by a member of the Hashemite family of Husayn ibn Ali, sharif of Mecca, who claimed descent from the family of the Prophet Muhammad. The British placed Faisal, who was a member of this family, as the King of Iraq.

**Hittites**   Invaders who ruled Mesopotamia from 1900 to 1100 B.C.E . The Hittites were responsible for spreading Sumerian culture through trade and hegemony.

**Iran**   Now the Islamic Republic of Iran, it borders Iraq to the east. Iran's population is mostly Persian, with Kurd and Arab minorities. The majority of Iranians are Shiite Muslims (the only Shiite-dominated Muslim country in the world). Persian Iran is the ancient enemy of Arab Iraq.

**Iraq**   Republic of Iraq *(Al Jumhuriyah al Iraqiyah)*. Country created in 1923, by a European convention, from the Ottoman vilayets of Mosul, Baghdad, and Basra. The Iraqi people are mostly Arabs, with a Kurd minority.

**Islam**   Religion founded by the Prophet Muhammad. "Islam" translates as "submission." "Muslim" translates as "one who submits." The emphasis in Islam is on submission to the will of a single God. The "five pillars" of this great and enduring religious tradition are: (1) Confession of faith in God and in his prophet Muhammad ("There is no God but God; Muhammad is the Prophet of God"); (2) Ritual worship; (3) Almsgiving; (4) Fasting; (5) Pilgrimage.

**Israel War of Independence**   1948–1949. Egypt, Transjordan, Iraq, Palestine, and Syria waged war against the new state of Israel; the Arab states eventually negotiated separate armistices after military attacks failed. Iraq was particularly aggressive in this war.

**Jalayirids**   The Jalayirids ruled Mesopotamia from 1355 until about 1400 C.E.

**Jarmo**   The area where the first indications of human settlement are found in Iraq, including pottery and domesticated animals.

**Jericho**   The city located in modern Israel where the first indications of urban life are found, dating back to 8000 B.C.E.

**Kassites**   Invaders who established a competing empire with the Hittites, in central Mesopotamia, from 1500 to 1200 B.C.E.

**Al-Khawarizmi**   Abu Ja'far Muhammed ibn Musa al-Khawarizmi was the leading Arab mathematician of the Golden Age who lived in Baghdad. Al-Khawarizmi developed some of the key concepts of what would eventually be known as algebra, and he presented the new concept of the zero to the West.

**Khuzestan**   region in Iran, bordering Iraq, that has Arab population instead of Persian (that dominates elsewhere in Iran).

**Kirkuk**   City in northern Iraq, in Kurd region

**Kurds**   Nationality of 25 million people. The Kurds are not Arab, Turkic, or Persian, yet their traditional homelands are located in Iraq, Turkey, and Iran. The Kurds have waged an ongoing rebellion for autonomy in these three countries, with limited success. Saddam Hussein has waged extensive military campaigns against the Kurds in Iraq, including gas attacks in 1988. After the Persian Gulf War, under the protection of a U.S. and UK maintained no-fly zone, the Kurds enjoy relative autonomy and prosperity in northern Iraq. The prospects for an independent Kurdistan are minimal, given the adamant refusal of Turkey and Iran (and Iraq) to grant independence to their Kurdish minorities.

**Kuwait**   Kingdom on southern border of Iraq. Occupied by Iraq in 1990. Kuwait was founded on June 19, 1961. There are less than one million ethnic Kuwaitis living in Kuwait. Kuwait is one of the richest oil producing nations in the world. The country is ruled by Shaykh Jabir al Ahmad.

**Lawrence of Arabia**   Thomas Edward Lawrence (1888–1935), a British Military Intelligence Service officer stationed in Cairo at the start of World War I. Lawrence cultivated a strong bond with Prince Faisal (later King Faisal of Iraq). During the war, Lawrence organized and fought alongside these Arab allies against the Ottoman armies in the region. He died in a motorcycle accident in England in 1935.

**Mamluks**   Slave-warriors and palace guards. Under the Buwayhids, they were officers and even administrators in the Baghdad bureaucracy.

**Mandate**   League of Nations term for status of Iraq immediately following World War I. Mandates were "administered" by a Western power. Iraq was a "Class A" Mandate (meaning it was intended to gain independence) under British protection from 1918 to 1923.

**Mesopotamia**   The Greek term meaning "the land between the rivers" includes the area between the Tigris and Euphrates Rivers. This region stretches from the Persian Gulf through modern Iraq, into the northwest portion of modern Syria. With abundant water, fertile land, and an agreeable climate, early civilizations emerged here.

**Mohammed**   The founder of Islam. Mohammed was born in Mecca (in present-day Saudia Arabia) around the year 570. He is believed to have experienced the first of a series of intense religious visions around the year 610 in a cave near Mecca. The Qur'an, Islam's central religious text, is held to record that encounter and the later revelations of Mohammed, and is regarded as the final and authoritative word of Allah (God). After over a decade of preaching, Mohammed had been unsuccessful in converting Mecca to the new faith; in 622 he and his followers moved to Yathrib (later known as Medina, the "City of the Prophet"). Mohammed continued to encounter resistance in spreading the new doctrine, but his followers eventually mounted a military and religious campaign that succeeded in unifying Arabia behind a single faith. Mohammed is regarded by Muslims as Allah's final prophet, and Islam is seen as the fulfillment of all previous human religious experiences. Mohammed's birthplace, Mecca, is now regarded as the great Holy City of Islam, and is the destination of annual pilgrimages by millions of Muslims.

**Mongols**   Invaders from the Asian steppes, originated from the area that is now Mongolia. Led by Hulegu Khan, the grandson of Ghengis Khan, the Mongol horde took Baghdad in 1258 and plundered the riches of the city.

**Mosul**   City in northern Iraq, oil processing center, and central city of Mosul vilayet during Ottoman times.

**Mother of All Battles**   Saddam Hussein's name for the 100-hour ground war during Operation Desert Storm. Saddam portrays the battle as an Iraqi victory.

**Muslim**   An adherent of the global religion known as Islam, which traces its origin to the prophet Mohammed (570?–632).

**Gamal abdel Nasser**   First independent Arab leader of Egypt, he competed with Iraqi leaders for leadership of Arab world during the 1950s.

**No-fly zones**   The United States, Britain, and France unilaterally established two no-fly zones in Iraq. The Northern no-fly zone, called Operation Provide Comfort, was established in April 1991 to protect the Kurds. The no-fly zone area is bounded by the thirty-sixth parallel. The Southern no-fly zone was established in August 1992 to protect the Shiite rebels. Called Operation Southern Watch, the southern zone was first bounded at the thirty-second parallel (to protect the Shiites in the marsh regions) and later extended to the thirty-third parallel.

**OPEC**   Organization of Petroleum Exporting Countries. These oil-rich countries control a significant portion of the world's oil. Iraq is a member of OPEC.

**Operation Desert Shield**   Military build-up of Arab-Western coalition troops in Saudi Arabia in 1990 and early 1991.

**Operation Desert Storm**   Military operations that started on January 16, 1991, with a bombing campaign, followed by a ground invasion on February 23 and 24, 1991. The ground war lasted 100 hours and resulted in a spectacularly one-sided military victory for the Coalition.

**Ottomans**   Turkic people who established an empire that first emerged in Anatolia in 1301, conquered Constantinople (now Istanbul) in 1453, and the Arab lands (including what is now Iraq) from 1516 to 1517. The empire became known as the "Sick Man of Europe" in the decades leading up to World War I. The Ottoman Empire formally ceased to exist in 1918.

**Pan-Arabism**   The international Arab movement, dedicated to the creation of a unified Arab state and promoting Arab interests.

**Parthians**   Invaders from Persia, who consolidated their grip on Mesopotamia from to 170 B.C.E. to 224 C.E.

**Persians**   Ethnic group that settled in what is now Iran. The Persians were rivals for control of Mesopotamia with the Greeks, and later the Arabs.

**Portsmouth Treaty**   Signed in 1948, the treaty defined the relationship between Iraq and Britain in a way that was completely in Britain's favor. The agreement required Iraq and Britain to reach agreement on all matters pertaining to Iraqi defense. The treaty severely compromised Iraqi sovereignty, and outraged Iraqi nationalists.

**Republican Guard**   Iraqi troops, recruited from the Sunni ruling elites who are personally loyal to Saddam Hussein. The Republican Guard is considered the elite fighting force in the Iraqi army.

**Revolutionary Command Council**   Otherwise called the RCC, the council is the real decision making authority in Iraq . The RCC consists of 8 to 10 members, and is directed by a chairman, currently Saddam Hussein. The chairman of the RCC is also the president of Iraq, the supreme commander of the military, and general secretary of the Ba'th Party, and the prime minister. The Revolutionary Command Council was formed after the July 30, 1968, coup, when the Ba'th Party finally assumed complete control over the country.

**Saddam Hussein** (1937–   )   Ba'thist leader of Iraq from 1979 to present. Saddam is President of Iraq, Chairman of the Revolution Command Council, Commander in Chief of the Army, and (apparently) a descendent of Mohammed.

**Safavids**   Turkman and Kurd invaders of Mesopotamia who took control around 1508 C.E.

**Sanctions**   UN-imposed set of restrictions on imports into Iraq. The sanctions were intended to limit Iraq's ability to re-arm, and develop weapons of mass destruction. The shortages of food and medicine caused by the sanctions has resulted in the deaths of thousands of Iraqi civilians, and become a PR nightmare of the United States. The United States is pushing to redefine the broad sanctions to a more narrow, more strictly enforced "smart sanctions" that will focus only on military items, but allow unlimited imports of foods, medicine and humanitarian supplies.

**Sassanids**   Invaders who ruled Mesopotamia from 224 to 637 C.E. The Sassanians resisted Roman and later Byzantine attacks on their territories.

**Saudi Arabia**   Oil-rich kingdom bordering Iraq to the south. The Saudi ruling family is considered the protector and custodian of Medina and Mecca, the holiest sites in Islam. The formal title of the current Saudi King is: "Fahd bin Abd al-Aziz Al Saud, Custodian of the Two Holy Mosques, King of the Kingdom of Saudi Arabia."

**SCUD**   Soviet-made, medium-range ballistic missiles that Saddam Hussein launched at Israel and Saudi Arabia during the Persian Gulf War.

**Seljuks**   Turkman invaders who ruled Mesopotamia from 1045 to 1258 C.E. At its height, the area that was to become Iraq experienced a minor renaissance. Infrastructure was rebuilt, and science and cultural institutions were refounded in the major Arab cities.

**Shatt-al-Arab**   Waterway created by the confluence of the rivers Tigris and Euphrates, it flows to the Persian Gulf.

**Shiite (also called Shia)**   Only significant surviving Muslim sect other than the Sunni. Less than 5 percent of all Muslims worldwide, the Shiite make up 60 percent of Iraq's population and almost all of Iran's population.

**Sultan**   A ruler in the Ottoman Empire. The Sultans assumed political authority over their territories, unlike the Abassid caliphs who claimed both religious and secular authority.

**Sumerians**   Founders of urban centers in the lower Mesopotamia area around 3000 B.C.E.

**Sunni**   The vast majority (97 percent) of Muslims worldwide. In Iraq, the Sunni are the minority (32 percent) compared to Shiite.

**Tamerlane**   Timur "the Lame" Central Asian atabeg, whose army plundered Baghdad in 1400 C.E.

**Terrorism**   The practice of waging war on civilian populations by nonmilitary forces.

**Tigris**   One of two main rivers in Mesopotamia (now modern Iraq).

**Tikriti**   Saddam Hussein's tribal group, centered around the town of Tikrit, in central Iraq.

**Turkey**   A Muslim country, bordering Iraq on the north. A member of NATO, Turkey is a critical U.S. ally in the region. The people of Turkey are Muslim, but they are not Arab (they are Turkic). Like Iraq and Iran, the Turks also have a Kurd minority within their borders. Turkey emerged at the end of World War I from the ruins of the Ottoman Empire.

**UAR**   The United Arab Republic, established by Egypt and Syria in 1958.

**UNMOVIC**   The United Nations Monitoring, Verification, and Inspection Commission that was created as replacement to UNSCOM. The Iraqis have refused to allow UNMOVIC inspectors into the country.

**UNSCOM**   The United Nations Special Commission on Inspections, created at the end of the Persian Gulf War, to identify and destroy Iraqi weapons of mass destruction.

**Ur**   Ancient city in Mesopotamia, and center of early empire in the region.

**Uruk**   Also called Erech, an ancient city in Mesopotamia, and home to Gilgamesh.

**Vilayet**   Province in the Ottoman Empire. Modern-day Iraq was pieced together from three Ottoman vilayets (Mosul, Baghdad, and Basra).

**Weapons of Mass Destruction**   Chemical, biological, and nuclear weapons. These weapons are capable of destroying enormous numbers of people and vast areas, hence the name. Saddam Hussein has used weapons of mass destruction on the Iranian army during the Iran-Iraq War, and on the Kurds in 1988.

**Yom Kippur War**    On October 6, 1973, the Jewish holy day of Yom Kippur, the Arab states around Israel attacked. Initial Arab gains were reversed by Israeli counter-attacks. U.S. and Soviet diplomacy, along with a rapidly deteriorating military situation for the Arabs, forced a cease-fire on October 23, 1973. Egypt and Israel signed a peace treaty in November, but Syria and Iraq kept fighting until 1974.

**Ziggurats**    Temples that the Sumerians and their successors built throughout Mesopotamian city-states, to honor various deities. The ziggurat temple was a tower. Like Medieval cathedrals, ziggurats were as much a symbol of the power and prestige of the city that built it, as they were an affirmation of faith.

**Zoroastrianism**    Religion that originated in Persia. Zoroastrians see the world as an epic struggle between the forces of good and evil.

# Magazines, Websites, and Books

## Magazines

Several popular magazines regularly feature articles on Iraq, and the Middle East in general, and are excellent sources for keeping up with ongoing developments.

Bowden, Mark. "Tales of the Tyrant." *The Atlantic Monthly*, May 2002.

Curry, Andrew. "The First Holy War" *U.S. News & World Report*. April 8, 2002.

Freedman, Alix, and Steve Strecklow. "How Iraq Reaps Illegal Oil Profits." *The Wall Street Journal*. May 2, 2002.

Goldberg, Jeffrey. "The Great Terror." *The New Yorker*. March 25, 2002.

Hanson, Victor Davis. "East vs. West: Our War Didn't Begin on September 11 … It Began 3,000 Years Ago." *American Heritage*, March, 2002.

Kaplan, R. D. "Iraqi Indigestion." *New Republic*. October 8, 1990.

Pope, Hugh. "Prosperity's Price: Iraqi Kurds, Flush with Aid, Lose Desire to Take on Hussein." *The Wall Street Journal*. February 12, 2002.

Rose, David. "Iraq's Arsenal of Terror." *Vanity Fair*. May 2002.

"Special Report: Inside Saddam's World." *Time*. May 13, 2002.

Sudetic, Chuck. "The Betrayal of Basra." *Utne Reader*. March–April 2002.

# Websites

Many websites offer information and opinions on Iraq, Saddam Hussein, and the ongoing sanctions. I encourage you to review all web resources, but please be mindful of the source and political motivations of the website creators. The following sites provide a variety of views of Iraq:

### Encyclopedia Reference to Iraq

encarta.msn.com
Microsoft(™)'s Encarta(™)encyclopedia website

### Governmental Sites on Iraq

www.un.org
United Nations' website, with specific sections on UNSCOM and the sanctions applied to Iraq.

www.loc.gov
The Library of Congress website, with links to Congressional Research Service reports.

www.state.gov/www/global/terrorism/index.html
Website of the State Department Office of the Coordinator for Counter-Terrorism.

www.energy.gov
Website of the U.S. Department of Energy, with information on OPEC, Iraqi oil and U.S.-Iraq oil trade.

### Iraq-Sympathetic Information

www.iraq.org
Website of group advocating the lifting of UN Sanctions on Iraq, includes links to the Permanent Mission of Iraq at the United Nations, and lists of official Iraqi government announcements.

www.iraqinews.com
Website of the Iraqi State News Agency.

www.iacenter.org
Website of the International Action Center.

**Western Views of Iraq**

www.countrywatch.com
CountryWatch monitors geo-political developments around the world.

www.hrw.org
Website for Human Rights Watch. This group monitors human rights around the world.

www.iraqwatch.org
Website maintained by the Wisconsin Project that monitors Iraq's weapons of mass destruction programs.

www.foreignpolicy2000.org/home/home.cfm
Website of the Council on Foreign Relations, a think-tank that focuses on a variety of issues affecting U.S. foreign policy.

www.kurdistan.org
Website of the American-Kurdish Information Network, promoting Kurdish causes in the United States.

# Books

Arendt, Hannah. *The Origins of Totalitarianism*. New York: Harcourt Brace Javanovich, 1973.

Bush, George. *All the Best, George Bush*. New York: Scribner, 1999.

Economist Intelligence Unit. *Iraq: Country Report*. London: The Economist Newspaper, 1988.

*Encyclopedia Britannica*. Chicago: Britannica, 1996.

*The Epic of Gilgamesh: An English Translation*. N. K. Sanders, translator. New York: Penguin, 1987.

The General Establishment for Travel and Tourism Services. *Iraq: A Tourist Guide*. Baghdad: State Organization for Tourism, 1982.

Ghareeb, Edmund. *The Kurdish Question in Iraq*. Syracuse: Syracuse University Press, 1981

Helms, Christine Moss. *Iraq: Eastern Flank of the Arab World*. Washington, DC: Brookings Institution, 1991.

Hodgson, Marshall. *The Venture of Islam*. Chicago: University of Chicago Press, 1974.

*The Holy Bible*. King James Version. Camden, NJ: Thomas Nelson, 1972.

Lukitz, Liora. *Iraq: The Search for National Identity*. London: Frank Cass & Co, 1995.

Kramer, Samuel Noah. *History Begins at Sumer*. New York: Doubleday & Company, 1969.

Mallowan, M.E.L. *Early Mesopotamia and Iran*. New York: McGraw-Hill, 1985.

Marr, Phebe. *The Modern History of Iraq*. Boulder, Colorado: Westview Press, 1985.

Orwell, George. *Animal Farm*. New York: Harcourt Brace Jovanovich, 1949.

U.S. Central Intelligence Agency. *World Fact Book*. Washington, DC: USGPO, 2000

# Index

# N